They are, of course, simply words and ideas.

The Creation of Me, Them and Us

Heather Marsh

First edition

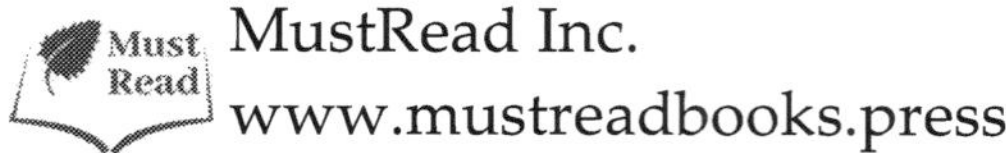
MustRead Inc.
www.mustreadbooks.press

Layout and editing by Rafael Torres

ISBN: 978-1-989783-01-6

Table of Contents

Note to reader

The single greatest tool for making moral people commit atrocities is group affiliation. The single greatest tool for promoting global human rights and equality is to end group affiliation.

This book is an expansion of the thought above, written in *Binding Chaos* in 2013. In 2013, so many things seemed simple and self-evident. In 2020, the goal seems as clear as ever, but the road seems much longer and many things have to be examined in detail that were glossed over a decade ago. Like our journey, this book is more complicated than the book written almost a decade ago. It will take longer to read and longer still to debate, but like Spain's 15-M movement used to say, *we are moving slowly because we are travelling a long way.*

When our quest for justice falls apart we, like Inigo Montoya, need to go back to the beginning. This book is the beginning. It is part of a series that will cover the structure of our institutions, but before we can discuss our institutions, we need to discuss who we are. This series begins by examining the nature of self, life, will, reality and power. The rest of the series looks at the societal institutions which have grown up around nations, economy, law, governance, architecture and technology. These books are all a further examination of the problems identified in *Binding Chaos* in 2013.

By the time we reach the end of this series, we will hopefully be back on the road to building a better world, armed with a better understanding of where and how we were derailed. I hope it is some help to each of you on your own paths.

H.

The Binding Chaos series

A look at the world - *Binding Chaos*
Self – *The Creation of Me, Them and Us*
Life - *Abstracting Divinity*
Reality – *Shaping Reality*
Will – *Free Will and Seductive Coercion*
Power - *Great Men, Commoners, Witches and Wretches*
Nation – *The Fourth Age of Nations*
Economy – *The Approval Economy*
Law – *Law and Chaos*
Governance - *Autonomy Diversity Society*
Architecture – *Rethinking the Moats and Mountains*
Technology - *Code Will Rule*

The creation of self

The heart has its own order; the intellect has its own, which is by principle and demonstration. The heart has another. We do not prove that we ought to be loved by enumerating in order the causes of love; that would be ridiculous. -Blaise Pascal, *Pensées* 1670.

There was once a clear distinction in English writing between the soul, which held life, the mind, which held consciousness and the heart, which was the home of social interactions. This was already a very simplistic view compared to the vocabulary richness found in most other languages, but it was then reduced even further. The three distinctions were largely erased by a Cartesian focus on individual consciousness and a mechanist biological outlook. This lack of a clear distinction between self, life and consciousness has crippled our understanding of humanity and social structures.

A self is not consciousness and a self is not life. A self is the unique positioning of an individual relative to society. Self is a wholly social creation.

The fact that there is no self without society has been demonstrated repeatedly in cases of extreme child neglect.

The interactive self of extremely isolated children is fully unformed. This is evidenced by pediatric catatonia and other developmental delays and regression which occur as a result of severe infant neglect. These children have life. They have consciousness. But they have no self.

Psychologists have consistently agreed that each person must undergo a process of identity formation upon birth, and they interpreted this formation as separation and individuation. They almost universally saw this process as a traumatic and singular event in a person's life and focused almost all attention on the separation from a lifegiver-self and the subsequent formation of an autonomous individual self.

While many early psychologists recognized that the self would never be complete or unchanging, they yet saw it as a singular whole. From this position, they saw challenges arising as this theoretical, autonomous self sought to re-establish parasitic relationships, sought to defend their newly-formed boundaries, and sought to come to terms with the overwhelming stress of a constant existential threat posed by the unavoidable eventual dissolution of this autonomous and isolated self. The field of psychology has been less than successful at explaining human behaviour. It has been far less successful at establishing a normative ideal for human development.

Psychologists and philosophers created a world where anxiety, fear and struggle are the norm, where happiness and peace are impossible to attain or available only to the most adept after long torment, and where existence is, above all, futile. In this world, people must constantly struggle with and repress what is supposedly their true nature for an end that is, at best, an abstract morality. Any outside assistance is impossible as all interpersonal interactions are also a continual existential struggle. Every outside person can only be the subject or the subjugated in this world, and all love is simply object desire. Existence here has no joy, no connection and no purpose. The happy ending is death.

After over a century of disastrous influence, psychiatry today is largely operating with no underlying theory. The field treats symptoms with drugs or attempts behaviour modification with no further attempts to understand human avarice, hostility and ultimate existential failure. Neuroscience may ask *how*, but academia has largely given up asking *why*. The hottest topics and the most fascinating findings in neuroscience and modern psychology are completely ignored in our daily lives as they are still falling into a framework of institutions and social sciences created on myths from past centuries. Psychology has left humanity with the saddest of all creation myths and the means to mask their pain through drugs and normalized exploitation of others. Perhaps we could try again.

The idea of an autonomous, impermeable, individual self provides a framework through which all modern thought has developed. Even the experience of teachings of ancient rites from the Vedas or similar traditions are regularly misinterpreted as emptying the mind and relaxing when they are clearly meant to fill the body with an external force. The aversion, even taboo, against any challenge to the inviolable individual, with the fully aligned individual body, life and consciousness, prevents even such an elementary understanding in a realm far removed from western science. Politically, the autonomous individual has been carried so far as to make all individuals equal under the law, as though wills were universally free and equal, and in the construction of an economic system which holds a newborn baby to be an economic unit as responsible for their own survival as any adult.

In less individualist countries, primarily those in Asia, society is anthropomorphized to godlike status and referred to on a daily basis, but with very little examination of the nature of this beast which requires the sacrifice of so many individual wills. The source of the will and authority of this society is as poorly examined as it is in places which view society as a collection of autonomous individuals. In individualist regions, society is unrecognized even while it is worshipped as the equally anthropomorphized economy.

Autonomy is freedom from interactions involving power, which results from unequal, coercive force. In order to have autonomy, it is necessary to identify the sources and causes of power, the nature of the freedom the healthy, autonomous self seeks, and the path to acquiring that freedom. These are the questions addressed in this book and the others in this series.

It is impossible to understand governance, organization, economy, information technology, or any other institutional structure without a proper understanding of self, life and consciousness. Most theorists have hopelessly intermingled the three concepts into one indistinguishable unit, usually referred to as *the individual*. Both ancient belief and (finally) modern science show that the three are clearly separate. Western science separates an individual from society as resolution to a territorial dispute between psychology and sociology and places them in eternal conflict. It would be far more useful to view society as a wider form of self.

Some people believe, not only that there is a separation between science and philosophy, but that science does not need philosophy. Philosophy provides both the ideas scientists use to interpret their answers and the ideas they use to formulate their questions. Science is the study of How. Without the parallel study of Why, not only are the details revealed by science open to misinterpretation, we also risk never asking the right questions. Without a clear philosophy, science is accumulating facts and leaving their language and frameworks of interpretation to the unexamined ideology of industrialists and politicians.

The purpose of this book is not to present new evidence or summarize the latest scientific findings. Instead, this is an attempt to provide a new framework to hold the abundant evidence which has already been gathered, both within the various branches of sciences and academia and in our daily lives and history. The evidence all around us is, and has been, forced into theories which cannot hold it and used to produce conclusions which are increasingly detrimental to our personal and social well-being. This is a new structure within which to organize our thoughts. If everything fits, nothing is left poking out and there are no gaping empty spaces, then this framework can lead us to new areas of necessary research and new conclusions which can be drawn from that research.

The scope of the research in this series necessarily results in a *jack of all trades, master of none* level of analysis, and it clearly needs more detailed understanding in each area it touches. Nevertheless, it will hopefully stimulate some thinking in this area, and if this particular framework proves to be not quite a good fit, it may yet inspire someone else to restructure the evidence in a more useful manner. There is no Truth; there are just more or less useful frameworks, and we are in urgent need of a more useful one.

Finding integrity

A self is not something static, tied up in a pretty parcel and handed to the child, finished and complete. A self is always becoming. - Madeleine L'Engle, *A Circle of Quiet*

To form an autonomous self, one must establish boundaries for the personal being. This entails defining what is internal, what is external and the relationships between both. This is not, as most philosophers and psychologists envision it to be, a binary exercise but rather a layered one.

The self is consistently presented, in both psychology and philosophy, as an individual and a complete object, or subject, residing within, and inseparable from, the body. To examine the nature of a self, we must first escape the idea of one self per body or one body per self. We have multiple selves within one system in the human body. The human body is a host for an immeasurable amount of lives, from human to bacterial, all of whom influence the body's health and behaviour and often have very contrary goals and opposing interactions. Just as the self does not stop at the body, neither is it necessarily omnipotent or able to wield exclusive control within the body. Modern institutions choose to view all influences on a person as human, but it is very apparent during illnesses that other forces sometimes overpower human impulses. As one example, yeast, cancer cells and other bodily occupants can cause cravings for sugar (including alcohol) even while that substance is killing the human body. There are many other examples of such influence found in parasites, viruses and bacteria.

Just as a body is not restricted to one self, a self is not restricted to one body. Self begins when a woman gives birth to a child. The ability of one life to affect another, or the changes wrought in one individual by interaction with another, are fully demonstrated during pregnancy and birth. A mother's bodily autonomy, free will and physiology are thoroughly disrupted by what will become a separate life form. Hormonal changes in the mother can create an overwhelming urge to nurture and protect a strange and separate human or an overwhelming urge to kill the helpless infant. With lactation, mood-altering hormones can stay with the mother for years. The act of giving birth leaves lifelong physical effects. There is evidence that cells from the fetus cross over and remain in the mother's body, possibly influencing her physiology for years and transferring cells to younger siblings.[1] There are indications that the fetus may receive DNA from not just their father but also previous men their mother received sperm from.[2] The DNA effects of traumatic experience or environmental stressors in one life may be passed through generations to other lives.[3]

The physical reality of an autonomous individual created by parasiting off another person and receiving input from many more, not just before birth but for years after, is the root of the self. Life is not an individual achievement, but a continuum passed from one generation to the next, through a vast number of life forms. A self is already a vast collection of interactions when it is first formed.

A fetus is not a separate self from a woman while they share the same body and experiences any more than the enteric nervous system creating 'gut instinct'[4] constitutes a separate self from that in the mind. When an infant is born, the establishment of a protective membrane is an urgent existential necessity. However, an infant cannot define a membrane around simply their bodily host, as that is in no way autonomous, and they would immediately feel overwhelming existential threat. This has been resolved in psychology by the theory of narcissistic delusion in the infant which must later be overcome.

There is a much simpler explanation in the process the infant uses to define their self. The infant defines a light personal membrane, and casts another bubble around themselves and a lifegiver, a further membrane outside a circle of caregivers and yet further around a nation. A self is not a clearly defined entity delimited by a body, but a concentric circle of membranes with various thicknesses. This requires no delusion and does not waste development in creating structures which must later result in a struggle to tear down.

Our physical host is not our self. The self is not a subject and it does not interact with outside self-objects. Our memories do not contain static objects. They contain events and emotional responses, or interactions, and it is from these interactions that our self, internal and external, is formed. A self is a web of interactions in a constant state of flux and entirely subjective to the perspective of the onlooker or the person who experiences an interaction with that self. There is no self-concept that is not reflected externally. Self-concept is memories of experiences and imagination of possible experiences, all of which involve interaction or external reflection. Even an apparently fully objectified self is an image of external reflection of that object. Even self-perception changes depending on environment and interactions. A person who is perfectly confident and self-content can change their self-image abruptly in an uncomfortable situation or after a demoralizing interaction. This has been shown in studies of traumatic events which change the self's perception of past events.[5]

Societies can not be understood by understanding the individuals within the society, as though society was an inert mass and individuals simply atoms with static, objectively measurable attributes. The unified and holistic self sought by most psychologists is not possible. The self is not one thing as there are many circles of self and each circle is made up of relationships. Each relationship is different and none is static, as a relationship is an accumulation of interactions viewed from continually changing perspectives. Self is not something that occurs in one mind. Self is the result of a multitude of perspectives reflected back onto the individual. There can be no autonomy without society as there is no self without society. Personal autonomy can only be achieved through the health of the interactions which create the individual self. A healthy interaction is one which does not take place through an involuntary transaction of unequal force. Autonomy is not a state of power, it is a state free from power.

As an infant grows into adulthood, one or more of their self-membranes will thicken and others will thin or dissolve. If the personal membrane becomes strong enough, the individual will develop personal integrity, which will provide the strength to be able to venture out of their inner circles and establish connections with other individuals and social circles.

In understanding personal dignity and integrity, it helps to consider what the northwest First Nations people of western Canada called *face skin* or in Asia was referred to simply as *face* or in Arabic as *face water*. Slightly related terms adopted into English are *thin-skinned* or *thick skinned*. There are significant cultural differences between such terms as face and honour, most notably the difference between communal vs hierarchical approval. Feudal system honours were from those above and such English terms tend to relate to a hierarchical perception of honour. In northwest coastal nations of North America, face was an integral part of the person, not just an outside perception. This is possibly more closely aligned with *lian* or Confucius' concept of *ren*. The Chinese concept of *lian* is closely related to personal integrity while *mianzi* is closer to pride. Politeness, dignity, ethics and norms are all about preserving the personal dignity of the self and others but the vast diversity of terms and meanings shows clearly how variable the formation of self is in different societies. They also show clearly the different sources of personal integrity depending on social structure.

Personal integrity, dignity and autonomy are only possible with a healthy membrane of self-esteem and balanced interactions surrounding a person or social grouping. It is impossible to create a strong autonomous membrane without bodily autonomy, a situation common to many people in subjugated positions. The personal membrane of a person who has had no control over their body is going to be very different from the personal membrane of an emperor who was placed out of physical contact with other people since childhood. The difference between rape and other forms of assault is this increased violation of the personal membrane and the destruction of bodily autonomy or personal dignity. Such violations may result in long term damage to the self. People today talk of *boundaries* and sometimes even *personal bubbles* to protect themselves from what are referred to in some circles as *psychic predators*. All of these terms refer (in slightly differing ways) to a personal membrane which holds self-esteem, dignity, integrity, honour and respect from others or from oneself. Here, we will simply use the term *personal membrane*.

It is through this membrane that all of our interactions with the outside world occur and contribute to the health or damage of that membrane. All social relationships and societies are based on the nature and strength of these membranes and our relationships with space, time and reality are as well. This membrane is the medium through which relationships with others are established or deflected and this membrane holds an individual in a surrounding and nourishing atmosphere of dignity and esteem. This atmosphere is also referred to in many cultures. In English it is usually referred to, inadequately, by its effects on well being, as *mental health* or *self-esteem*.

Self esteem is widely recognized as being distinct from self concept or self image. A person may clearly understand their own exceptional achievements and still derive no value from them in terms of self-esteem. This is because the self esteem many would obtain from such achievements is being diverted. Self esteem is the euphoria we receive from positive interactions and that euphoria can be intercepted if interactions are subject to external control. In a balanced interaction, that euphoria adds to the atmosphere of dignity and self-esteem in the personal membrane, which we will refer to simply as *euphoria*. Damage to a personal membrane or depletion of its euphoric content is an existential threat to the individual inside. An ideal state of personal autonomy is the possession of a healthy membrane and the network of relationships and interactions required to maintain its euphoric health. Integrity is obtained through maintenance of a wide network of euphoric conduits and balanced interactions. A person with integrity has the strength to be trusted even during times of stress or when under duress.

Most people recognize the existence of a *mask*, real or figurative, which one wears for those outside oneself or outside a closed social group, especially when one's personal membrane is insufficient protection. In animism, it is very common for channelers of divinity to wear masks in order to host a different spirit, and it is also common in theatre, where masked players channel shared euphoria. When a mask is a substitute in daily life for one's own personal membrane this is, in effect, a hardened membrane. Such a membrane creates an *endoself*. They can receive euphoria from others but are unable or unwilling to participate in balanced interactions. They can only exist through predatory transactions with others as they are unable to access primary sources of euphoria themselves. Much of psychiatry and most of the institutional structures in place today aim to develop an endoself with its appearance of autonomy and self-sufficency.

If self is simply a cluster of interactions, optimal development of self must be marked by continual expansion, not by stages of development as postulated by psychologists such as Lacan and Freud. A person does not pass through a caregiver stage. There is never a point in development when a healthy person will not receive euphoria from giving or receiving voluntary caregiving. Neither will there be a time when it is not beneficial to explore the unconscious of the lifegiver-self or when euphoria cannot be obtained by discovery or creation or contact with a loved nation or through spirituality. A healthy self retains all past development intact and continues expansion for their entire lives. This outward expansion, facilitated through interactions to establish euphoric conduits, will be referred to here as *exosocial expansion* and the healthy self which continues such expansion will be referred to as an *exoself*.

An unhealthy self is one that becomes blocked at a certain point in development by the creation of an *endosocial membrane*. An endsosocial membrane results in the formation of an *endoself* or *endogroup*. All violations of personal integrity or dignity are committed in order to weaken the strength of the exoself until it can be sublated into an endogroup or used as prey for an endoself.

It is not possible for any living being to be purely an exoself or an endoself. They would no longer be living if either extreme were attained. Like most human conditions, these terms refer to a tendency, not an absolute category. Neither is any endoself tendency a permanent, unchangeable state. An endoself tendency is a response to environmental (including bodily) conditions, and it can be changed by a change in those conditions.

There are four elements of a healthy self: a *personal membrane, euphoria, euphoric conduits* and a drive to *exosocial expansion*. The obstacles to creating this self are *endosocial membranes*.

In addition to personal relationships, there are other types of relationship possible, such as that of a person to their own creations and ideas. People can be very bonded, to the point where they do not need personal relationships with others, to either the act of creation or development of ideas. The creative passion seems to be, in some circumstances, an effective substitute for interpersonal passion. A person deeply involved in a creative project can avoid becoming endosocial by pouring energy and attention into euphoric sources embodied in a project instead of a person. This is seen in many mystics and prisoners throughout history who do not or cannot establish personal relationships but maintain euphoric conduits through connection to ideas that are commonly presented as *bigger than them* or *bigger than all of us* or simply *divine*. While social acceptance or rejection of one's creation or ideology may cause pain, it is possible for someone who is deeply bonded to ignore all outside opinion, even when it involves extreme coercion or a threat of personal harm. This may be partly why unusual opinions have often been deemed an existential threat to an endogroup. If creation and discovery allow autonomy of an individual it would weaken their loyalty to the endogroup.

Spirituality can take the place of other people or living beings in providing the validation and reflection people require in order to create their own individual selves but this is effective only insofar as the person has already reached a certain stage of development. Spirituality can assist those with damaged membranes and replace drugs or other harmful behaviour as shown by the work of Toni Wolff and Carl Jung and confirmed through Alcoholics Anonymous. Spirituality has been used to help people through trauma or times of great challenge throughout history. It can fortify a personal membrane in times of great stress.

Self-expansion can be viewed in circles of increasing diversity and scale. When it is born, the self has already been affected by every hormonal reaction during pregnancy, all history carried in the DNA of the sperm and egg, traces from earlier children and sexual partners, parasites and other body host co-occupiers, and environmental pollutants and stressors. A person is born into a lifegiver-self and immediately begins establishing a caregiver-self. From about two years of age until twelve, they will hopefully develop a nation-self. After adolescence, a hormonal imperative urges further expansion into a wider nation, discovery and creation self. Eventually, if they have persevered, they will arrive at a divine-self which will neither desire regression, nor fear death.

At this point, the self has lost the earlier protective membranes and expanded, through exosocial interactions, far beyond the confines of the body, and faces no existential threat from bodily mortality. An exosocial person can feel empathic pain, but not be debilitated by it, as it is not an existential crisis. They are supported by networks, not any one membrane, and their personal membrane is nearly replaced through many connections. The endoself idealized by psychology cannot be immortal, but exosocial interactions can. There are, however, a lot of roadblocks along the way, which is probably why fear of death is overwhelming today when it was reportedly almost non-existent in many earlier cultures.

In all the above circles, an endoself will attempt to participate through object possession instead of experience. Instead of discovery, they will obtain credentials and post experiences on social media. Instead of creation, they will acquire ownership. Instead of spirituality, an endoself will look for a ready-made religion to provide answers and their participation will be performative, not experiential. In all aspects of life, they expect their growth to be served to them as objects to possess. In all aspects of life, they are destined to boredom and frustration, a true hell on earth.

The health and happiness of a person does not depend on how diverse or extended the interactions they establish are. Many people are very happy with interactions only with their own land and community. Many others devote all of their interactions into discovery or creative outlets. There does not appear to be any inherent value of one over the others, as long as each person has the freedom to choose their interactions and those choices do not cause guilt or conflict with endogroup roles or membership.

Being exosocial does not mean a person has travelled the world or experienced many things. As long as a person is open, curious, empathic and able to access the joy around them, they are exosocial. Many exosocial people have never left their village and many extremely endosocial people travel constantly and seek out new experiences as proof of their status, not because of any genuine openness or curiosity. An intense focus on one area of life, such as commonly occurs during pregnancy and early childhood caregiving, or intense periods of discovery and creation, is not an unhealthy development path if no endosocial membrane is formed. All exosocial conduits established are equally beneficial.

Jean Piaget and most other child development experts recognized a time when children begin to develop a sense of separation and the ability to understand outside perspectives. These researchers attribute such development to a greater understanding in the child, not a changed experience. Perhaps the child became aware of endosocial boundaries, or perhaps they had none before. Perhaps their earlier self, which is a structure of empathic conduits built through interactions, had no endosocial boundaries to wider empathy. Perhaps they gained a cognitive ability, perhaps they lost an empathic ability or perhaps the cognitive development eclipsed the empathic. The conflation of life, consciousness and self and the individuation of all has limited such questions.

Karen Horney, along with most researchers since, believed that empathy was imagination,[6] a word which no one has ever provided anything but a circular definition for. We do not imagine the feelings of a loved one in distress. We feel their distress. Sometimes we feel their distress before we know of it. Sometimes we feel an emotion empathically which we have never experienced directly. Empathy is the ability to experience the feelings of another. This happens to those who share empathic conduits or a self-membrane. People commonly speak of *electricity* or *connection* with another but there is no clear, common English term to describe the connection, and neuroscience is debating the methods by which empathy operates, so here we will use *empathic conduits* and *euphoric conduits* as terms which represent a black box of unknown methods of transfer.

Empathy from mother to child, such as the fear transference easily observed in mammals, is a result of one lifegiver-self. The same empathy can later be felt in a caregiver-self or nation-self. If fear and emotional pain can be induced in an external body, then the self that can induce these responses does not stop at its own body and is not fully internal. Through interactions and layered self-membranes, our self includes others. The extreme pain and loss of self experienced by most parents suffering the death of a child is evidence enough of this.

A sleeping baby knows if their mother is in the room or bed, as they know the location of their self. They will wake up if she leaves, not because they are a narcissistic tyrant who wishes to cannibalize the mother's bad breast, as psychoanalyst Melanie Klein would have it, but because they are still a part of their lifegiver-self and have established insufficient new ties to a wider caregiver-self. Likewise, the mother may wake when the baby wakes, even if the baby has not moved. If the baby is forced to dissolve the membrane around their lifegiver-self before they are ready, they may experience a panic which will lead to both social regression and a strengthening of the membrane. Regression is evident on the part of a child who responds to the birth of a sibling or a traumatic event with a wish to return to their former role in the lifegiver or caregiver self. Such regression is experienced through every circle of expanded self as a reaction to trauma. The later groups are no different.

Membership in different social groups and subsequent change in the individual is recognized in many cultures by name changes, most notably in China up until recently. These name changes can correspond either to different life stages or different social groups and also imply social distance and one-way vs two-way respect. In most countries, until the last few decades, it was common to call people by their titular and surnames unless they were familiar or inferior to the speaker. This change in custom has accompanied a change in relationships which are now marked by instant familiarity and egalitarianism, a sign of both widespread endoselves and weakening endogroups.

Founding psychologists bypassed clear evidence of an expanded self throughout all history and culture with an airy assertion that they were all now enlightened and there was no need to compare enlightened men with any of their predecessors. The modern man was an individual, who thought, therefore he was. As sociologist Emile Durkheim stated in his preface to *Suicide,*[7] *"if no reality exists outside of individual consciousness,* [sociology] *wholly lacks any material of its own."* and all study of human behaviour is the domain of psychology. Since, as Durkheim points out,*"societies cannot exist if there are only individuals"* and societies clearly do exist, with their own group behaviours and characters, a group reality must also exist. Even while defending sociology's existence, however, Durkheim quickly states *"we of course do not at all intend to hypostasize the collective conscience. We do not recognize any more substantial a soul in society than in the individual."* He has no such squeamishness in referring to the individual soul or consciousness as incontestable fact that requires no explanation or qualification and there is no attempt to differentiate either *soul* or *consciousness* from self. While he later discusses a collective consciousness, in *The Division of Labour in Society,* this is strictly in terms of cultural mores or knowledge.

The work of Toni Wolff and Carl Jung in exploring connections between what they termed the individual and collective unconscious also maintain the individual unconscious as a whole. Marie-Louise von Franz and Emma Jung recognized a collective consciousness but neither conceived a self outside the bounds of the individual. They too were careful to maintain the supposed integrity of the individual self in exploring the group consciousness. Marianne and Max Weber are among the few writers in sociology or psychology to recognize a self composed of several people, but they depicted it only as a historical, magical or legal curiosity.

It has been a long time since the findings of psychology, or neuroscience, have had any correlation to the individualizing nature of psychology, much less psychiatry. A large amount of studies have been conducted which inform participants that they have a certain status or power and observe the effects of that status or power on the subject's perspective and behaviour.[8] [9] [10] These studies make clear, not only that many aspects of perspective and behaviour are modified by power and status, but that people are capable of taking multiple perspectives across multiple different relationships, or interactions. These studies show that attempting to diagnose an autonomous individual instead of interactions is an attempt to create static categories from a constantly mutating situation. Due to the interactional and external nature of the self, the idealized self image that psychologists examined can also be external or part of a shared group.

It is not individuals which need examination and diagnosis. It is social structure and the nature of social interactions. These are responsible for self formation and these cannot be cured by pathologizing individuals. With regards to the self, all is not psychology, all is sociology. It is clearly evident that psychologists realize this, since a large part of supposed psychological studies are now actually researching sociology or neuroscience. Still, their findings are interpreted and solutions implemented by institutions set up on the basis of the mythical autonomous, individual self. Worse, the nature of the diagnosing authoritative institutions as part of a group self remains unexamined.

empathic conduits	*The means by which emotion can be shared or jointly experienced between two sources.*
euphoric conduits	*A path or method allowing the transfer of euphoria from one primary source to another.*
personal membrane	*A strong and permeable inner circle of self which controls intimacy and permits the establishment of euphoric and empathic conduits.*
euphoria	*Joy which contributes to well-being and self-esteem. May be acquired through euphoric conduits to primary euphoric sources.*
exosocial expansion	*Uninhibited expansion of self through continual establishment of euphoric conduits through relationships, discovery, creation, spirituality, etc.*
endosocial membrane	*A membrane which blocks empathic and euphoric conduits and thereby creates endoselves and endogroups.*
endoself	*Predator who can only exist, or prefers to exist, through acquisition of secondary euphoria.*
endogroup	*A group of affiliated people who use inclusion and shunning to define their society and are bound by an endosocial membrane. An endogroup may be temporally unlimited to allow ownership of property, identity, achievements and victimhood from generations past.*

The law of uninhibited expansion: When an exosocial person is unable to form euphoric conduits at any level of expansion, they are uninhibited from forming them at a further level of expansion and experience an increased drive to do so.

Something larger

If an educational act is to be efficacious, it will be only that one which tends to help toward the complete unfolding of life. To be thus helpful it is necessary rigorously to avoid the arrest of spontaneous movements and the imposition of arbitrary tasks. - Maria Montessori, *The Montessori Method* 1912

The concept of identity, which asserts the concept of equality, is easy to render ridiculous and has been both struggled with and ignored but never resolved. As Bertrand Russell pointed out, *"two terms plainly are not identical, and one term cannot be, for what is it identical with?"*[11] If terms are not one, they must be separate and cannot share an identity. If they are not separate, they must be one. Nevertheless, despite pointing out that the concept is *"terribly ambiguous, and great care is necessary,"* Russell and the rest of the world have soldiered on, putting out continual fires of paradox and contradiction but refusing to let go of an obviously useless and easily falsifiable concept.

The answer to the riddle posed by identity groups is that they are one entity and their identity is that of their ideal. There can be no shared identity among people, as each person is unique. When many people become bonded into one self, as an endogroup, an artificial person is created as an ideal. This endogroup ideal, or *endo-ideal* becomes the group. Its identity is adopted by every member of the group and the individuals also become the endogroup. The group identity subsumes the self for all except the endo-ideal, creating a special subset of reality which here we will call an *endoreality*. As seen from the outset, the very creation of an endogroup requires a suspension of belief in universally recognized reality.

Group selves explains why groups feel they can act as individuals and vice versa. An endogroup acts as an individual self. It therefore needs only one mind to lead it, or the ideology of one mind. Those that become the *endo-ideal* are forever entitled to the service of others and ownership of the group. Those that become the *reflectors* are forever assigned to the service of others and the duty to reflect. Those that are cast as the *negative image* are condemned to carry all guilt and undergo all penance.

The endogroup is an emergency measure undertaken by a group of people in order to withstand some dire existential threat facing the group. It is a condition of crisis. It is not normative development. An endogroup changes the nature of the individuals inside of it by assigning them roles. The sometimes incomprehensible behaviour of those within an endogroup is because they are not fully formed while they are in an endogroup role. No one in an endogroup is a fully formed individual person functioning in a way that is rational to anyone in universal reality.

Threat to an individual or group self requires increased solidarity and increased power to the group leader. The endogroup membrane acts as a sort of Emergency Powers Act in increasing power to the leader and removing autonomy from the other members to create a totalitarian group structure. This ability to create endogroups has a definite advantage in being able to meet existential threat to the group. In this structure, all power of the group that is not needed to keep them barely alive is transferred to the endo-ideal. This produces both energy and euphoria in the endo-ideal and removes fear, risk assessment and the ability to assess reality except as reflected by the group. The endo-ideal becomes addicted to the secondary euphoria and this, combined with the inability to properly assess risk or exist without reflection, coerces them to stay and defend the rest of the group. Their reflectors and negative image are also coerced to stay as their perspective is solely that of the endo-ideal and their mandate is to protect the endo-ideal.

Endogroups are created from two primary causes. The first cause was a fear response. The second cause, brought about in all probability by those who wished to retain their temporary powers, is a guilt response. Endogroups use a symbiotic relationship between fear and anger to create dependency bonds between people as a method of group defence. Rage inhibits fear and causes a lack of judgment in risk-taking, a blinded assessment of reality, and an inability to empathize. These are all possibly very useful traits in a temporarily empowered defender of a group of people facing existential threat. They are not great traits with which to run the world indefinitely, however. This power structure, which has become institutionalized, has put people with no empathy, no risk assessment and extremely poor understanding of the world in charge of our governance and our knowledge with predictably disastrous results.

While endogroups have a built-in motivation for their continuance, as the addiction to power and the duty to support the endo-ideal create the centripetal force for the power ponzi schemes seen today, there is also a marked egalitarian tendency found in most earlier societies and studied in children. This egalitarian impulse provides a strong centrifugal counter force when no immediate threat is present. Since institutional structures were created to enforce the power transfer and suppress egalitarian force, endogroups have grown and been absorbed into ever-larger transcendental endogroups.

From the family head of the caregiver-self to the chief or state leader of the nation-self to the scientific or media department heads of the discovery-self, the CEOs of the creation-self and church leaders of the divinity-self, the endo-ideals increase in power at each level of endogroup transcendence. This is not true for an exoself. All types of exosocial interactions are equal with regards to the euphoric reward they bring. The sequence of endogroup expansion gives larger endogroups, hence more power, at each circle of expansion. Each endogroup is sublated to the endogroup which transcends it. While exosocial development does not occur in stages, transcendental endogroups have demarcated expansion into stages of endogroup advancement, each sublated to the higher.

Where there is an imbalance and endosocialism, there will be hierarchy. This is seen in child to adult, progeny to parents, ignorance to knowledge, apprentice to master, family to state and every other inequality when it is forced into an endogroup structure. While the structure of power is unchanged at every level, authoritative endogroups have been designated at higher and higher levels. The strengthening of one endogroup involves the weakening of another. In hierarchical society, the attachments made in each endogroup are part of a stage to be left behind when the transcendental endogroup is entered. Mothers are abandoned for caregivers, families are abandoned for school, school is abandoned for work, and work is abandoned for the wait for death. Additionally, each level is at the service of the next. The lifegiver must raise a child to meet with approval of caregivers who mould the child for education which forms them to specifications set by industry which devalues them until they are suitable product for 'care' facilities.

History and legends are full of examples of parents or children being forced to prove their allegiance to a nation-self by destroying bonds to a caregiver-self. Murder and other betrayal of family members have been demanded by militias, industrialists, states and churches. Countless historical events attest to the requirement to prove allegiance at each new level. Rulers ordered to choose between son and nation, devout followers ordered to sacrifice a child, children in filial cultures ordered to turn in their parents, new gang members ordered to commit atrocities against their communities and employees forced to destroy their own communities are all proving their successful transcendence to a higher authoritative endogroup.

Transcendence which requires such great sacrifice and devotion is coerced by a diversion of the exosocial drive. If the only expansion possible is upward, people will fight for the one window out of their current restrictions in an endless dream of freedom.

There are six components to every endogroup:

- An identity which enables exclusive membership.
- An idealized source of collective reality, residing in a person or ideology.
- An existential threat from external forces.
- An exceptional myth justifying unequal entitlement.
- A negative image, made up of people identified as opposite the ideal.
- Reflectors which may exist separately from the negative image in groups of more than two.

As the self is made up of a set of constantly changing and diverse interactions, it is interactions that need to be examined for a power dynamic, not the person. One person is capable of occupying many different roles and belonging to both extreme endogroups and exosocial networks at the same time. Even in interactions between the same two people, the power dynamic may change drastically depending on the surrounding circumstances, people or subject matter. People that are perfectly exosocial in a casual environment may suddenly demand the endo-ideal position in an area they feel they ought to dominate in or when they are surrounded by a different social milieu. People that have an abundance of interactions in which they are the negative image may persecute their own negative image at the first opportunity that arises, or participate in a rolling tyranny such as filiality. It is impossible to judge a self as an unchanging object with any consistency. It is only possible to look at roles and unbalanced force in interactions.

Without knowing whether the child was raised in an endo-ideal, a reflector or a negative image role, studies which purport to describe child development are of very limited value. Without knowing a person's dominant and authoritative endogroups and the roles they play in each, as well as any conflict between the two, behavioural studies are of very limited value. The unwillingness to accept that people who share social groups may have very different behaviour to others depending on the status they assign to them is a key factor in the invisibility of atrocities against those cast as the negative image. This is a result of the myth of the individual self, with static, objectively measurable attributes, instead of the constantly mutating and variable interactional self.

A couple may be a particularly intense endosocial bond, especially if that is a caregiver-child bond or a romantic couple, as there are no reflectors, simply an all good endo-ideal and an all-bad negative image. In either case, a power imbalance that sees one person as the endo-ideal and the other as the negative image can be particularly damaging as the flow of euphoria is not supplemented or adulterated by other relationships. The need to avoid being cast as the negative image sometimes leads to extreme vilification of those outside the endogroup as an alternate negative image.

A healthy couple relationship includes outside bonds to rely on. A sign of healthy interactions is when each partner feels both pride and gratitude towards the other and interactions are both voluntary and reciprocal, not forced and not unidirectional. If pride is replaced by shame and gratitude by entitlement or bitterness, that is a sign that a couple bond has become a power struggle within an endogroup. In such cases, the endogroup itself often becomes more important to the couple than the people within it. People will express that they want to preserve their marriage, family or friendship rather than a wish to continue interactions with the specific person.

Falling in love is a terrifying and euphoria-releasing event in which the person in love opens their personal membrane and allows another to enter, forming a bonded couple. If the beloved does not reciprocate, the first person either becomes a reflector or negative image in a couple endogroup or, if rejected, they will feel the extreme pain of unrequited love and be left with a damaged self membrane. If they are accepted, they will feel instead the intense euphoria of acceptance into an exclusive endogroup. Their self membrane expands to receive another and they exist to reflect the other. *"You complete me,"* is an expression of this phenomenon.

A lesser version of the same euphoria and risk is felt by those who attempt to join other exclusive endogroups. Joining such endosocial groups, or couples, brings both identity and membrane security as well as ongoing replenishment of euphoria. The pain of breakup is greater in a more bonded couple or group as the damage to their own membrane is greater the more it is merged with another and the less outside attachments they have to rely on. The common phrases describing couples, such as *two are joined as one* or wider endogroups such as *the family unit* make clear that this depiction of the merging of many into one is a common perception.

The creation of endogroups has, throughout history, been a formalized and sacred affair and one which involved wider society as witnesses and validators. The most enduring of such formal contracts are marriage rites and the most modern is the legal creation of corporations and employment contracts, both of which are usually regarded in third age nations as mere legal bureaucracy. In *Economy and Society*, Weber explains how they once meant much more: *"contracts were originally either straightforward magical acts or at least acts having a magical significance. ... By means of such a contract a person was to become somebody's child, father, wife, brother, master, slave, kin, comrade-in-arms, protector, client, follower, vassal, subject, friend, or, quite generally, comrade ... The contract rather meant that the person would "become" something different in quality (or status) from the quality he possessed before. ... Each party must thus make a new "soul" enter his body. At a rather late stage the symbolism required the mixing and imbibing of blood or spittle or the creation of a new soul by some animistic process or by some other magical rite.*[12]

Weber's description of fraternization contracts describe the rituals by which people became bonded to another. These contracts usually depicted the union as inviolable, at least for a specified time, and declared which part of the union was to subordinate itself to the other part. The endo-ideal remains intact and maintains its integrity, but the reflector or negative image must give up their own self and replace their self with that of another (the endo-ideals may be an abstracted idea or entity). These rituals were bonded with magic, quite often involving both spells and circle dances. This was in order both to make the bond unbreakable and to sublate the individual selves and create, not just a physical master and slave unit, but also a psychic or spiritual one. These creations were once recognized as creating a new divine form, outside and transcending the individual.

Group membranes are often apparent in traditional punishments. Local councils in rural India are regularly shocking international news with their refracted punishments, such as allowing a man to rape another man's sister as retribution for the second man's offense.[13] Traditional punishments in many regions of the world included the enslavement of children for a father's debt, retribution by a group if one member was wronged or punishment of a group if one member committed an offence. Peace negotiations around the world nearly always demanded such group retribution. Punishment of the negative image of the group redeems both the group and the endo-ideal of the group. Punishment in third age societies is still by group but now that group is the state. If the endo-ideal acquires debt, the endogroup pays. The endo-ideal decides crimes and punishments and assigns guilt to the negative image.

Weber describes the depiction of groups as one social entity, implicated in group guilt and compensated for group victimization.[14] *"X; a member of Group Y, has committed against me, A, or my fellow group member, B, a wrong of the type of C. and for this reason he and his comrades owe expiation to us, the fellow members of A. (In Arabic legal parlance one does not say' "the blood of A has been shed," but "OUR blood has been shed.")"*

Endogroups may seem an archaism, as such mergers are not recognized in third age nations, but they still exist unrecognized. They are apparent in the allocation of credit in endogroups and they are apparent in the strange pronoun usage of endo-ideals. They are apparent when those outside the endo-ideal are commonly accused of 'ego' for any attempt to gain status or recognition for their own work. Ego is a Freudian term for self, one which the same magic rituals have denied to the negative image and reflectors for millennia along with ownership and credit. Ego is often used as a negative term implying insubordination by those constrained to solely reflect the endo-ideal. Under laws of coverture and similar, marriage was recognized as producing one legal person out of two as recently as a few decades ago, and sometimes still today, especially under those laws derived from the Napoleonic Code. These rights of the endo-ideal are also apparent in the rights of hereditary ownership of people now accorded to states. The group self is still fully recognizable in corporations which absolve the individuals creating the corporations from liability for their actions and credit them for the labour of those in employee bondage.

Magical bonds never created collectives that collaborated using consensus. They always create single entities that are ruled by one mind or group of minds. All others are subsumed to the endo-ideal and the credit for their ideas and labour, as well as complete control over their actions, thoughts and time, were given to the endo-ideal. The rituals created a bond which allowed one mind to use multiple bodies according to their will, exactly as schools, corporations and governments still do today and still perform magical rituals through the use of signatures on what are still called binding agreements. The law is, and was always, an institution to protect the magical rites of subordination, presided over by a god, a man-god, or an abstracted state-god.

States and corporations are both involuntary endogroups for the vast majority of the people they are granted ownership rights to. Their rights of ownership are established through hereditary ownership or magical rites claiming acceptance through participation. As a girl or woman was once held to have accepted sublation through standing in a circle during a marriage dance, people are held to have accepted sublation to a state through voting ballots or to a corporation through employment contracts and currency tokens. Many of these organizations are themselves personified as abstracted endo-ideals, although their human forms are merely cloaked behind the abstractions. Groups such as churches and states are credited with cultural identities, autonomy and the right to exist. This is more real personhood than is assigned to women, children, non-citizens and the other reflectors and negative image of many societies.

The joining of selves is evident in the allocation of pride and shame. *I'm so proud of you*, or conversely, *I'm so ashamed of you* are sentiments that do not make sense unless the speaker is addressing a part of their extended self. The embarrassment over a child, parent or spouse who acts in a way that the subject would not is a well-recognized phenomenon, as is embarrassment of other groups, even including sports teams. People often say they join groups to find meaning or to be part of something bigger and they mean those expressions literally. If others are not joined to us in one self, how would it be possible to worry about their well-being, to feel their pain and to feel existential pain of our own, to the point of contemplating or committing our own suicide, upon their death?

The fact that the self has undergone a change is measurable in the fact that it is not the same after the loss of a bonded relationship. The well-being of the self is harmed even where the environmental conditions remain the same. When a mother leaves, a bonded infant cries as though they have lost an essential part of themselves because they have created an endogroup of themselves and their mother. Later, that group may expand to include other caregivers to create an expanded endogroup which they will miss almost as sharply. Power determines the individual's place in this relationship. Although a mother may be so strongly bonded that she also will experience extreme distress on separation, that is not necessarily the case. Likewise, an employee may experience a crisis, including grief and dissociation, upon retirement, and student suicides upon graduation are a regular occurrence, but neither the corporation nor the school are effected by the loss of employees or students.

This inequality is due to the sublation of self for everyone outside the endo-ideal which causes dissociation and a need for rediscovery of another self when the dominant one casts them out or is lost. The purpose of institutional restrictions and coercion at every level of endogroup is to create this level of sublation. These crises of endo-ideal or endogroup loss often lead to regression to the last real or imagined circle of self. Failure at the level of the creation-self will lead a person back to the caregiver self in an attempt to redo social circles such as marriage. Failure at the discovery-self may lead to xenophobia in an attempt to recreate the nation-self.

Transcendence provides an artificially wider view that can temporarily appear to be a different structure. State or church education creates a citizen of a state or church endogroup and an authority external to the family which initially appears wider, and even different, from the earlier power structures. Higher education does not in itself make a person more tolerant, particularly when accomplished within endogroups. It is often depicted as doing so, in studies conducted by those with higher education, but those studies invariably define intolerant as being aligned with national bigotries. Those with a higher education often simply enter a transcendental endogroup that is not as concerned with national endogroup negative images. They are not at all tolerant of their own negative image, those outside academia or those with less education due to a lack of interest or ability in academic subjects. They are seldom tolerant of non-professionals or those with low or no income either. They are not even tolerant of their own caregiver group if that group is now part of their academic negative image.

The markings of an endogroup are an endosocial membrane, an endo-ideal which defines reality and embodies virtue, and reflectors whose job is reflection and validation of the endo-ideal. All credit is attributed to the endo-ideal and all blame is deflected to the negative image. It is the reflectors' job to shun anyone who offends the endo-ideal and anyone outside of the endogroup. People have very different status based on their proximity to or membership in the endo-ideal and that status is reflected in social and legal power and approval. Those in the negative image are stripped of personal dignity and there is an attempt to destroy their personal membranes or personal integrity in group reputation, relationships and self esteem. There are usually secrets kept for the endo-ideal and no privacy for the negative image.

As the number of people in an endogroup grows, the structure evolves. In an endosocial pair there is an endo-ideal and there is a reflector who is also the negative image. If there are multiple people they may compete for or even alternate which occupies the role of obedient reflector and which is cast as the negative image. The constant threat of role reversal is one way the endo-ideal can torment the rest of the group and create enmity and competition between them. If there is only one person outside the endo-ideal, they will be in a daily struggle to maintain their reflector status and they will live an unpredictable and bipolar life alternating between the two.

Reality and ideology are defined by the endo-ideal and questioning of endoreality is not tolerated. Those outside the endogroup are depicted as enemies, but the only people the endo-ideal may seek out as equals are endo-ideals of other groups. This phenomenon is the basis of global politics. Politicians who require armed protection from those that states define as *their people* dine and socialize happily with other politicians, just as the heads of corporations who are afraid to face their own employees without security are at home dining with those they depict as *their rivals*.

Negative images are subject to near constant violation of what pre-schools today refer to as *personal bubbles*. From the government-mandated sexual assault of U.S. and U.K. airport 'security', to stop and frisk customs of state police, to regular groping of women and children, the denial of bodily autonomy is a feature of all endogroups towards its negative image.

Extreme endogroups are maintained by extreme shunning and inclusion. The endo-ideal is upheld through deliberate and frequently lethal shunning of the negative image. State affiliation is maintained through hard borders, militaries and prisons. Cruelty and, at best, an unconcern for the well being of those outside an endogroup is a feature, not a bug. Endogroups are created in hostile environments in which outsiders are perceived as an existential threat. Civil wars create endogroups even when the roots of the conflict did not align at all with the subsequent divide. Violence breeds violence because violence strengthens the membranes of endogroups with external existential threat.

As Hannah Arendt reported in *Eichmann in Jerusalem: A Report on the Banality of Evil, "The trouble with* [Nazi war criminal] *Eichmann was precisely that so many were like him, and that the many were neither perverted nor sadistic, that they were, and still are, terribly and terrifyingly normal. From the viewpoint of our legal institutions and of our moral standards of judgment, this normality was much more terrifying than all the atrocities put together."* There is nothing more normal than endogroup atrocities to outgroups. Indeed, enabling atrocities to outgroups is probably the primary purpose of our ability to form endogroups. The acquiescence with 'state security', no matter how brutal, is partly a reflection of the wish to strengthen endogroup membranes. (The other part is dread of being cast as the negative image as conflict within an endogroup is limited to the self-policing rivalry between the obedient reflectors and the negative image.) War creates extremism and endogroups, while peace allows groups to start to dissipate and the membranes to become permeable.

If the endogroup has undergone some trauma which left it with a damaged membrane those within will experience a greater exosocial drive, especially if they have an outlet that helps them develop it. This is one reason the greatest opportunity for implementing human rights agreements and education is following a great and widespread social pain. Exosocial behaviours are often observed during times of natural disaster or sudden crisis when the usual endogroup authorities have been forced to relax their grip. At an individual level, this increased drive is so well established it has its own term, *posttraumatic growth*.

Vulnerable individuals with no personal membranes are attracted to, and easily exploited by, endogroups. Stripping the dignity and power, or personal membrane, of all group members outside the endo-ideal is common as a means to strengthen the group membrane. This is seen in totalitarian states, religious and other cults and abusive relationships of all kinds. These members will then put themselves at risk to attack a perceived group enemy as shown by anyone defending their group in battle or voting for, or otherwise enabling, an extreme nationalist when they are themselves a vulnerable negative image. Their defence of the endogroup which persecutes them is a result of their lack of any other protective membrane.

Hazing rituals lower individual self-esteem to increase the desirability of the endogroup. If a person does not have a healthy personal membrane or if they are unable to access euphoria through their own conduits, they will seek a larger self to complete them. Both Weber, in *Economy and Society*[15], and Cohn, in *Pursuit of the Millenium*[16], documented the fact that women had everywhere shown a particular susceptibility to religious endogroups. Fear is used to strengthen a group membrane. People with no recent negative experience to cause xenophobia are usually excited to have company. Strangers bring the prospect of new food, ideas, stories, music, romantic prospects and friends. This is not the case in endogroups, however. Babies will cry at the sight of a face which is not imprinted as part of their tribe if they are raised in a closed group. Those who feel at risk of being completely shunned will bully those weaker to increase the barrier between them and those outside and increase their role and value as reflector.

Most, or all, ideological cults operate as endogroups. It is also a familiar pattern in institutions like states, corporations or organized religion and it is a pattern repeated in patriarchal or extremely filial family groups. Corporations attempt to produce exceptional myths through mission statements and indoctrination into accepted endoreality through training. The fired and retired were once considered outcast and suffered all the harm produced by extreme shunning. In a less obvious manner, this is also the structure of closed classes such as science and academia and media. Here too, outsiders and critics are shunned and depicted as inferior, endoreality is defined by the endo-ideal, and those outside, students, sources or research subjects, are objects made to reflect the reality and superior status of the endo-ideal. Global institutions are designed for only one type of sociability. They are universally endosocial, never exosocial.

When an endogroup meets an exosocial group, the endogroup has everything to lose. A wall with a public park or wild habitat outside will encourage those trapped behind the wall to escape. A wall with enemies without will encourage those inside to stay inside and fortify the walls. This is why the best defence of the endogroup is to push in any way possible for the exosocial group to build walls and borders. This is why the enemies of the European Union do everything in their power to encourage the strengthening of Fortress Europe, to push for walls, hard borders, controls, persecution and differentiation. This is why the stronger the European Union becomes, the more vulnerable it is to the growth of nationalist movements within and enemies without. Its true strength is in its weakness, in the permeability and flexibility of its outer membrane and the strength of the personal membranes of those people (not endogroups) within.

Outgroups are always perceived as an existential threat and despised by endogroups. Facts do not change perception. Even when people discover a person convicted of a crime was innocent, they do not necessarily change their opinion of them. As is often pointed out regarding France's

Dreyfuss Affair, the effect of accusation is sometimes permanent even if the accusation is disproved. This is because the intensifying of endogroup solidarity was permanent and the new facts do not affect the new endoreality. Within an endogroup, the negative image is despised due to the laws of endoreality which assign them all guilt and shame for the group. Those without the endogroup (outgroups) are both despised and feared, as a result of an endosocial membrane and the exceptional myth.

Not caring for others to the same degree as yourself is the sign of an endosocial membrane and the measure of the difference depicts the strength of the membrane. In some, the care for others is greater than care for themselves. These are the reflectors and negative images in endogroups. In others, the care for their individual self is greater and they become the endo-ideal or an endoself. The reflectors will justify to themselves and others why they really don't need as much attention and care as they lavish on those in the endo-ideal and those in the endo-ideal will demand more with similar justifications.

These allegiances are relatively easy to measure, both in neuroscience and observation. A simple chart asking which column(s) would the subject choose to die to save the lives of which rows is enough for boundaries to emerge. A less dramatic example would ask who they would share chocolate or money with. Any social grouping can have their relative membranes assessed by daily observation. Discussions in which the answers to these questions become evident are heard every day. They are a particular staple of political discussions as the purpose of politics is to create and enforce endogroups

	You	A member	Many members	An outsider	Many outsiders
You					
Another member					
A group of members					
The leader or ideology					
An outsider					
A group of outsiders					
An outside leader or ideology					

People who accept a job to die to save the life of a state leader, those that greet the news of terrorist attacks with concern for the reputation of the terrorist's endogroup, not the victims, and those that limit their interest in human rights to any social group, are saying with their actions that some lives matter to them more than others and they are willing to sacrifice one group for another. Frequently, they are saying that lives outside their endogroups do not matter to them at all, even when this is covered with rationalizing language. This can be seen in the willingness to buy from corporations which exploit and murder outsiders or willingness to vote for politicians and policies that do the same or an unwillingness to fight these threats to others with the same urgency they would for their endogroups.

Lifegivers have an involuntary pact to sacrifice their lives for an infant but it is not necessarily what many would choose. This is evidenced by the different choices they make when options are available and the fact that infants in many societies throughout history are killed or abandoned when they are too much for the mother or social group to look after. Caregivers often make surprising choices of allegiance. The police officer in the United States who chose to put pictures of his children on his shooting targets was ensuring that he strengthened his police endogroup over his family.[17] There are many cases when caregivers will believe or defend the reputation of a paedosadist, especially one in a position of authority, over the safety of their child.

There are perhaps a surprising amount of people who value their own lives less than that of complete strangers. These people, who would answer Yes to the entire first column, show up in jobs from volunteer fire fighters to gang members to mercenary soldiers. The people who enter these situations voluntarily with no initial social attachment may have a thinner personal membrane relative to any endogroups. They may fill those roles due to societal expectations and economic pressures, but there are still many who choose these roles voluntarily. Another possibility is that they are endoselves, and obtain euphoria through adrenalin or cruelty, or they are endo-ideals, incapable of realistic risk assessment. Lastly, they may be a negative image seeking self-punishment.

The world is lately becoming far more holosocial because of all the relationships established by travel and social media. Only very exosocial people have a perspective unfiltered through endoreality. Exosocial individuals must have enough of a personal membrane for independent thought and self esteem sufficient to stand in opposition to groups, but not so thick it will cause them to value themselves above others. These attributes are becoming more common but so are the attributes of an endoself. Both are developing due to the weakening of lower endogroups under a transcendental mono-empire.

All endogroups are harmful. They focus on their own perceived victimization by outsiders and their own superiority and they dehumanize or degrade others. They practice solidarity for their endogroup first or feel empathy for their endogroup first which causes them to degrade their ability to establish outside connections. The endo-ideal or their negative image will increasingly feel an existential threat to themselves from the continued existence of the other which may eventually result in civil war or genocide and produces everyday hostility. Endogroups clearly define the endo-ideal, reflectors and negative image and assign credit and guilt according to the laws of endoreality, ignoring universal fact. Any critique of the group or any person or idea associated with the endo-ideal is forbidden.

Despite all the potential for harm above, the worst part of endogroups is that they necessitate increasingly unbalanced transactions which produces great social repercussions. An exosocial relationship is open and balanced. It is marked by admiration, respect and gratitude in reciprocity for benefit received. Opportunities for expansion are met by an exoself with excitement. To those trapped in an endogroup, opportunities for expansion cause disloyalty guilt with associated anxiety or boredom and punitive repercussions. As opposed to the excitement generated by an exosocial network with myriad one-hop relationship possibilities, an endogroup is focused on the relationship with the endo-ideal and the policing and persecution of other members. An exosocial network produces excitement. An endogroup, sooner or later, produces dread.

Endogroups are held together by very strong bonds created by all roles in the group. Anyone who is contemptuous of a person who stays in an abusive relationship should ask themselves why they allow their state to govern their daily lives or their school or employer to control their creation and discovery. The binding process of an endogroup is the same at every level.

endo-ideal	*The idealized self of an endogroup, embodying all virtue, ownership, victimhood and credit.*
reflector	*An endogroup role which causes a person to adopt the perspective of an external endo-ideal and uphold the laws of endoreality. Seen as obedient and selfless and so avoids the guilt and shame assignment of the negative image.*
negative image	*An endogroup role which causes a person to adopt the perspective of an external endo-ideal and uphold the laws of endoreality. Seen as the inverse of the endo-ideal. Embodies all vice, guilt and shame assignment within the endogroup.*
endoreality	*A reality which exists only within an endogroup and is created to uphold the laws of endoreality. Endoreality is filled with magical words which impart no meaning but serve to cast people as the negative image or endo-ideal. Endoreality is relative and has no meaning outside the perspective of the endo-ideal or endoself. Endoreality can change at the whim of an endo-ideal.*
transcendence	*The sublation of smaller endogroups into a higher authoritative endogroup.*
sublation	*The process by which an individual self or an endogroup is merged into a larger endogroup and identifies more strongly with the larger group's endo-ideal than with their earlier self.*

The law of endoreality: All virtue, ownership, credit and victimhood are assigned to the endo-ideal and all vice, guilt and punishment are assigned to the negative image, by all committed members of the endogroup.

The law of the last circle: When an endogroup collapses with no transcendental endogroup incorporating it, the committed people within it will revert to their last real or imagined endogroup loyalties.

The law of authority: Authoritative endogroups are those with the institutional power to enforce their endoreality. Anyone opposing authoritative endoreality is declared criminal or insane as they define reality and law.

The law of power: Power is a result of actions of unequal force. The structure of power is created by endogroups allowing only involuntary interactions of unequal force.

The law of inhibited expansion: Endogroups are formed and strengthened by intercepting and removing all external euphoric conduits in order to redirect all euphoric interactions to the endo-ideal.

The law of transcendence: With no egalitarian counter force, endogroups will be continually sublated to larger, transcendental endogroups, At each level of transcendence, endogroups become larger and endo-ideals more powerful. Each level of transcendence is at the service of the higher group.

The law of diverted exosocial expansion: As all exosocial expansion in an endogroup is diverted into a force towards transcendence, this creates a voracious centripetal force driving a ponzi scheme of power.

The exceptional myth

The greatest evil perpetrated is the evil committed by nobodies, that is, by human beings who refuse to be persons. Hannah Arendt *Some Questions of Moral Philosophy*

Where there is an endogroup, people will create an identity for it, based on anything or nothing. The identity is a magical word and its effect is unrelated to its meaning. A word in universal reality is a symbol used to convey a very specific, universal and unchanging meaning. A word has a definition and is intended to aid communication. In endoreality, a word is a purely magical symbol with no coherent or consistent meaning. Often, words in endoreality have membership lists instead of definitions. Any definitions that do exist are mutable, relative and assigned by the endo-ideal. These magical words are used to identify the endo-ideal and cast out the negative image. Words used as endo-identities serve to set the group off as exceptional and create difference where none exists. This is the sole purpose of any endo-identity.

No endo-identity has a coherent, consistent, factual meaning that can stand up in universal reality for the reasons pointed out by Bertrand Russell in the last chapter. All endo-identities can be changed at the whim of the endo-ideal. People will form endogroups around words that do not apply to the group in question, or words with no meaning, as seen in many societies and cults and neo-identities. There is no need for any common belief, history or experience within the group. The exceptional myth, endo-ideal, negative image and reflectors will appear anywhere the endogroup forms. There is plenty of evidence throughout history of people intensely bonding to groups they had just learned of and the nature of their subsequent organization and development is universal.

An endo-identity is essential in creating an endogroup. Without a unique identifier, it is impossible to describe the group, and since an endogroup is an abstract construct, it must be described in order to exist. The creation of an endo-identity is usually done under the influence of great euphoria and extreme reactions can be expected against anyone challenging this creation.

Often, the endo-identity casts as wide a circle as possible in order to appropriate as much exceptional credit and victimhood as possible under its umbrella. Anyone refusing the endo-identity at this point is vilified as considering themselves exceptional and lacking solidarity, or worse. Second, often significantly later, a special identity is created within the first group to represent the endo-ideal. The endo-ideal are the only people permitted this special status. Reflectors are permitted no identity of their own. Any reflector who pushes for an identity will find that their identity makes them the negative image as any non-ideal identity is always its negative image.

Frequently, a convenient endo-identity is already provided and widely recognized by other endo-ideals due to its use in history or in currently portraying a group of people as the negative image. The only criteria is that the identity is not currently owned by an endo-ideal, so it is available for colonization by a migratory endo-ideal. The new endogroup does not have to have anything to do with the group of people originally assigned to the identity and they may be both physically and temporally as well as culturally and economically far removed from the original people. The endo-ideals most certainly have little in common with the originals of a negative image identity as a negative image cannot be an endo-ideal and almost never transforms into one.

For this reason, leaders of negative image groups are almost always people who grew up in a different place and time. This was seen in the wealthy, noble leaders of revolution and anarchy in the past and it is seen in the wealthy, urban thought leaders of today. Since the endo-ideal has the exclusive right to define, the educated and aggressive urban returnees who define their birth or ancestral homes as endogroups also define themselves as the endo-ideal. They represent their claimed groups to the outside world and to the group itself. Academia has been a great boost to this pattern as graduates are taught to view themselves as superior and in exclusive possession of the only endoreality for their group. Migratory endo-ideals are the 21st century Habsburgs who create empires and kingdoms wherever they alight.

Where the migratory endo-ideal is not present, the negative image nearly always fails to attain endogroup status and remains marginalized because a negative image cannot define endoreality. In addition, where the negative image wants liberation from their status as the negative image, the endo-ideal wants recognition and reflection of the same status. Not only do the endo-ideal not want the liberation of the negative image, the prospect of their persecution ending is an existential threat to the endo-ideal. The freedom of an endo-ideal and a negative image are in opposition to each other, no matter how much an endo-ideal claims otherwise. The liberation of the negative image will not occur under an endo-ideal who seeks their subordination. The exosocial expansion of the negative image will be blocked by the endo-ideal seeks to entrap them into an endogroup. The tragedy of endogroups is that the negative image or reflector cannot lead and the endo-ideal will not have goals which benefit anyone else.

At times, a new endo-identity is invented. The only difference in this process is the lack of a ready made population of pre-sublated negative image and reflectors and exceptional myth. Besides an identity, every endogroup must have an exceptional myth. The purpose of the exceptional myth is to uphold and justify the laws of endoreality, which assign all ownership, virtue, credit and victimhood to the endo-ideal and all vice, guilt and punishment to the negative image.

The purpose of the endo-ideal is to establish a unique identity and the personification of an endogroup, in order that a multitude can be represented by one or a few. The purpose of the exceptional myth is to establish a basis for the persecution of people outside the endo-ideal. The exceptional myth includes both victimhood and superiority, as either can be used as a justification for dehumanization of the negative image and those outside the endogroup.

It is the exceptional myth which creates an endogroup from groups that were once a negative image, and it is the exceptional myth which justifies exceptional treatment within the group. Exceptional myths encourage both unjustified glorification of the group and its endo-ideal and unjustified demonization of the negative images as well as other endogroups and their endo-ideals. If the superiority or victimhood of the endo-ideal is ever questioned, or there are any attempts to assign guilt to the endo-ideal, it is the exceptional myth that forestalls any such challenge. The exceptional myth creates the narrative to cast any opponent as the negative image.

Like the endo-identity itself, the exceptional myth is a purely magical creation. The only consistent fact about either the endo-identity or the exceptional myth is that they are defined solely by the endo-ideal. The details of the myth do not matter any more than the meaning of the endo-identity. It is seldom that two members of an endogroup will relate at all similar versions of the myth when asked, if they have any understanding of the myth at all. Usually, the only aspect of the myth that anyone is confident about is that it is true, and they are confident of that to a degree only ever felt in endoreality. They seldom ask each other or refer to details of the myth, and the details are constantly in flux and only open to interpretation by the endo-ideal. Science, history and observation are invoked when convenient and rejected when inconvenient, often at the same time. Even where the details are clearly written down, the language or interpretation is continually changed. The purpose of the myth is its function, not its meaning and its function is to establish the endo-ideal as the sole source of reality.

The five primary types of exceptional myths address *creation, leaders, superiority, persecution* and *destiny*. If the endo-ideal is presented as exceptional through group superiority or leaders, then the legends of their brilliance and achievements casts anyone who questions them as stupid and crazy and all of their actions as necessary and good. If it is their destiny or creation that makes them exceptional, any opposition is doomed to failure and is also evil as it attempts to forestall a great destiny or divine creation. If exceptionalism is achieved through victimhood, then every action is justified as defence and any criticism is presented as evidence that the opponent is allied with the real or imagined enemies of the endo-ideal. Most endogroups use a combination of these factors in their myth. They are presented as exceptionally wise and wonderful until the evidence is overwhelming that they are not, and then they are presented as exceptionally justified by virtue of their victimhood or their destiny. If all of these fail, they are presented as the lesser evil against their real or imagined enemies.

Credit and victimhood appropriation often focuses on historical figures, born long before the endogroup was formed, or people with true negative image status. The purpose in both cases is to remove the possibility of the victims of this appropriation denying association with a group they have never heard of or have no connection to. How many countries now claim Nikolai Tesla as their own? According to the rules of endoreality, all victimhood and credit can travel through time and space and transfer from one body to another. Men who appropriate the experience of their single mothers to add to their own exceptionalism are no more reasonable in universal reality than anyone claiming the experience of a cat because their family lived with one when they were a child. This is perfectly reasonable behaviour in endoreality, however, and it is a phenomenon that scales to every size of endogroup.

An interesting aspect of victimhood as an exceptional myth is that trauma may create DNA changes in animals, possibly including humans, thus there is a possibility that the behavioural changes that create social structures can be a part of a temporally infinite (or at least extended) filial self. The victimhood itself still requires endoreality magic in order to traverse time and space, however.

Exceptional myth is also created by propaganda dedicated to the purpose. The devotion of millennia of volumes of writing attempting to create an industrialist exceptional myth which would separate humanity from other animals or life itself was an attempt to cast all of nature as the negative image to be conquered. The industrial-scientific myth employs all five of the above types of myth including revered founders who are credited with the discovery of all knowledge, and the only holders of the one path of progress, or the destiny of all humanity. They also regularly appropriate victimhood where they were perpetrators, such as claiming to be victims of the Catholic Inquisition which they orchestrated against women and indigenous people and claiming to be victims of climate change deniers, despite providing all the apologia and technology required by industrialists to persecute and murder land and community caregivers. The same patterns can be found in every endogroup exceptional myth from an abusive family to a cult or a state.

Books such as *The Sovereign Individual* or *Atlas Shrugged* offer both exceptionalism and victimhood to those at the top of a trade economy pyramid scheme, or billionaire endo-idealism. The myth of the *meritocracy* or the *self-made billionaire* are transparent fantasy, but they are upheld in endoreality for the exceptionalist justification they offer. The exceptional myth can never be applied to anyone outside the endo-ideal even if they meet all the criteria. Hence, U.S. billionaires rail at Chinese businessmen who use their own rules of capitalism to take their billions. Charles Darwin was celebrated for the 'greater good' argument he offered in favour of the victimization of those weaker but he carefully excluded women from 'natural' selection as he said allowing women choice over mating partners would *"divert the orderly process of evolution"* and *"unchecked female militancy threatened to produce a perturbance of the races."*[18] The so-called 'father of anarchy', Pierre-Joseph Proudhon demanded liberation of all men but also demanded those men have the right to murder any woman for insubordination to tyranny.[19]

Even such idealists as Confucius and Plato both agreed that rules to govern all humanity were not meant to apply to exceptional men, or those men the group myth deemed exceptional. More recently, the United States helped to draft international war crimes and human rights law and enforce those laws on every other country but instantly claimed exceptional exemption to those laws for themselves. Following in the U.S. footsteps, every later endo-ideal claims the same right of exemption and now claim to follow international norms instead of international law.

The same inconsistencies are found in every endogroup because every endogroup follows only one set of laws. Those are the laws of endoreality which assign all ownership, virtue, credit and victimhood to the endo-ideal and all vice, guilt and punishment to the negative image.

The exceptional myth manifests in unequal principles. Any demand for benefit to the group is denied to those outside and any persecution outside is justified within the group, based purely on exceptionalism. This same exceptionalism is implemented legally by defining certain groups of humanity by identity categories such as *citizens, authorities* or *terrorists* and judging the same actions as criminal or not based on these groupings.

The exceptional myth also manifests in unequal goals. Anyone who attempts to include an experience or goal outside of the laws of endoreality is accused of selfishness and a lack of solidarity or assured that their needs are really the same as the endo-ideal and the advancement of the endo-ideal will also advance their subgroup. As Silvia Federici wrote, regarding the struggle to get women's unpaid work recognized in movements against worker oppression, *"We are seen as nagging bitches, not workers in struggle."*[20] This is because the supposed struggle for workers' rights was an exceptional myth. The real issue at stake was not a struggle for workers' rights but for endogroup dominance. The so-called workers' struggle was against corporate endo-idealism while Federici et al struggled against male endo-idealism. It was male endo-idealism which defined women as the negative image just as it was corporate endo-idealism that defined the corporate worker as the negative image. Furthermore, in accordance with the law of the last circle, many in the workers' movement wanted to fall back to the caregiver circle, the same circle Federici et al wanted liberation from. Solidarity could not be possible under these circumstances.

Endogroup exceptionalism operates independently of individual opinion. A person within the group may hold a person in the negative image in very high esteem and believe they deserve much more than a person in the endo-ideal who they hold in contempt. They will still allocate all benefit to the endo-ideal and all blame to the negative image with such meaningless rationalizations as *That's just the way it is*.

Because of exceptional myths and magical words, the consensus reality of an endogroup is often less accurate than individual reality. The more or less harmless lies escalate as the endogroup membrane thickens until they are so far from universal reality that the lies themselves serve as a secret password for entrance. The Great Revolution of every country, the myth of the 'national character', the fought over public figures and the extreme vilification and discrediting of all unbelievers are common to every nationalist.

The exceptional myth is a measure of the thickness of the group membrane and it is a method of creation of the group membrane. Initial belief in the exceptional myth is usually enforced through a combination of intimidation and guilt, where disbelief is presented as disloyal, sinful or causing harm to the group or the endo-ideal. It may also be presented as metaphorical, allegorical or a revolutionary act to disrupt 'imperial' or oppressive versions of reality. It may be presented as justified retaliation for previous lies of real or imagined oppressors. The meaning may also change daily, or be impossible to ever pin down. Lastly, it will be presented as unimportant and not worth the trouble to dispute with arguments such as, *If it makes them happy, why would you want to hurt them by questioning it?* Somehow, an obvious lie is presented as an exception that must never be examined as universal reality. As soon as the endogroup attains authoritative status, this obvious lie, in all its incoherent and inconsistent glory, will be endorsed by authoritative and institutional expertise and used as a basis for enforcing the laws of endoreality and persecuting outsiders and the negative image. This lie is the tool used to create a variable endoreality which changes at the whim of the endo-ideal.

The feat of convincing others to deny universal reality is an important step in coercing them to defend and strengthen the endogroup. The cognitive dissonance caused by belief in two conflicting realities is painful and traumatic. To avoid this trauma, those who accept an easily demonstrable lie as real must then become dedicated reflectors, shaping an endoreality and defensive endogroup to uphold the lie and shield themselves from cognitive dissonance.

When confronted with universal reality, supporters of endoreality will always insist that it does not matter, and to them it does not. As Hannah Arendt pointed out in *The Origins of Totalitarianism, "The totalitarian mass leaders... could make people believe the most fantastic statements one day, and trust that if the next day they were given irrefutable proof of their falsehood, they would take refuge in cynicism; instead of deserting the leaders who had lied to them, they would protest that they had known all along that the statement was a lie and would admire the leaders for their superior tactical cleverness."*[21] The laws of endoreality dictate that every action of the endo-ideal is a virtue, so it matters not at all, within endoreality, to prove them wrong in universal reality.

The exceptional myth creates endoreality which is fully real in the consequences of its belief within the endogroup. Religion is not delusional if a majority believes in it. Genocide is not criminal if a majority participates in it. Bigotry is not bigotry if the majority accept it. Today, every state in the world (although not all communities) accepts the genocide and ostracization of the poor. The definition of criminal or insane is acting in opposition to the authoritative endogroup defining law and reality so both designations change at the whim of the authority. Authoritative endoreality emanates from the endogroup, national in the case of states like North Korea, the United States or China, international for most, which holds the institutional power to enforce their own endoreality.

The supposed collective consciousness or communal consensus posited by sociologists is not the defining narrative of endogroups, endoreality is. If a person defines their identity as a group, the only remaining question is whether they are the endo-ideal, a reflector or the negative image. That role defines the nature of a supposed collective consciousness because members of an endogroup have abdicated their own consciousness in favour of that of the endo-ideal. Exosocial movements follow ideas and universal knowledge, not endo-ideals or endoreality. It is only in exosocial movements that such a thing as a communal consensus exists, and it manifests through stigmergy.

endo-identity	*A magical word used to set an endogroup off as exceptional and create difference where none exists.*
exceptional myth	*Exceptional myths encourage both unjustified glorification of the group and its endo-ideal and unjustified demonization of the negative images as well as other endogroups and their endo-ideals. The five primary types of exceptional myths address creation, leaders, superiority, persecution and destiny. A purely magical creation, like the endo-identity; its purpose is its function, not its meaning.*
migratory endo-ideal	*When a transcendental endogroup has an overpopulated group of endo-ideals, or they are under pressure, they will begin to swarm by creating a multitude of smaller endogroups at lower levels. This results in alienated societies and in the colonization of negative image groups both within and without the original endogroup.*

The ideal

I saw the Emperor – this world-soul – riding out of the city on reconnaissance. It is indeed a wonderful sensation to see such an individual, who, concentrated here at a single point, astride a horse, reaches out over the world and masters it. - Hegel, on Napoleon[22]

Hegel's impression of Napoleon is reminiscent of Carl Jung's thoughts on Hitler, *"He seemed as if he might be a double of a real person, and that Hitler the man might be hiding inside like an appendix, and deliberately so hiding in order not to disturb the mechanism. With Hitler you do not feel that you are with a man. You are with a medicine man, a form of spiritual vessel, a demi-deity, or even better, a myth. With Hitler you are scared. You know you would never be able to talk to that man; because there is nobody there. He is not a man, but a collective. He is not an individual, but a whole nation. I take to be literally true that he has no personal friend. How can you talk intimately with a nation?"*[23] Both Napoleon and Hitler were, to an extreme degree, the embodiment of the exceptional myth of an endogroup. Like everyone extremely sublated to an endogroup, they were both a partial self and an extended self. Jung also recognized that *"Hitler's power is not political; it is magic."*

The endo-ideal is the idealized part of the self of the endogroup. They define and embody all the good, exceptional and virtuous claims of the group. When an endogroup is strengthened, the endo-ideal is strengthened. A threat to the endo-ideal is seen as a threat to the endogroup and sympathy for the group is sympathy for the endo-ideal. The endo-ideal is the virtue of the group personified.

People who anthropomorphize groups refer to the endo-ideal, not every member. The endo-ideal expands to contain the entire endogroup. The anthropomorphized groups take all credit and ownership from the individuals in the endogroup and reassign it to the endo-ideal. In this way the work of everyone in a corporation is assigned to the 'self-made billionaire' and the efforts of entire states are credited to the head of state. The endo-ideal has the right to define the group and also the right to direct and dispose of the group.

For those in an endogroup, empathy is greater for the endo-ideal than it is for their individual self. This describes the phenomenon of people more interested in celebrities lives than their own and of caregivers who feed their dependents before themselves. It also explains the logic of people who threaten family members to get compliance that they would not obtain if people were threatened directly and the logic of people who agree to sacrifice their own lives in the defence of the lives of others. People killed by the state produce far less widespread trauma and outrage than world leaders killed by citizens. Media coverage often focuses entirely on accused powerful men and their feelings ahead of their victims.

Pain or personal injury to the individual self is experienced with greater intensity by the endo-ideal, perhaps due to the real existential threat of having one self or because they have no external empathic comparison. Alternatively, it could be because everyone's empathy is directed towards the endo-ideal, including their own, so their exclusive concern for themselves is particularly intense.

Endo-ideals are typically unable to empathize or recognize that their experiences are not universal. It is often difficult to impossible to convince a person in an endo-ideal position that others are disadvantaged. Endo-ideals are also extremely bad at remembering names and personal details of those outside the endo-ideal. They often cannot remember even the name of a romantic partner because they see the other as an extra body or reflector for their own self or as their negative image.

This strange outlook is created by the circling of reflectors around the endo-ideal. Not only do reflectors have no self with which the endo-ideal can interact, they block all view of the negative image and replace it with a one-way looking glass, so the entire endogroup has difficulty distinguishing the negative image. The perspective of the endo-ideal is a house of mirrors. They are unable to see another perspective to the point that it is often impossible for them to extrapolate meaning where it is not explicitly spelled out, or discern nuance or humour.

For this reason, everything must be presented from the perspective of the endo-ideal. The effect of power on perspective has been well studied and confirms the fact that a position of power severely limits the ability to adopt an outside perspective.[24] What are referred to in cognitive behavioural therapy as cognitive distortions are simply endogroup perspectives and endofilters and they apply to the majority of people in endo-group states, organizations and professions as well.

The attributes assigned to the endo-ideal are impervious to facts as observed in universal reality. An endo-ideal may stand on a stage bragging and tell the audience they are self-effacing and humble and this will be believed. The endo-ideal is idealized by themselves and others, despite all evidence to the contrary. The negative image are not permitted success and the endo-ideal are not permitted failure. The endo-ideal will claim positives and deflect negatives in themselves and reverse this for their negative image. The negative image deny their own achievements and over-emphasize their failures and shortcomings and reverse this for the endo-ideal. The reflectors amplify this endoreality.

As puzzling as this may be to those outside, it is a natural result of endoreality. Endoreality translates everything as relating to a group self in which all guilt is automatically assigned to the negative image and all virtue is automatically assigned to the endo-ideal. Because all in an endogroup see themselves as one unit, and all identify with the endo-ideal more than their individual self, they are able to sort virtues and faults between themselves in a way that is incomprehensible to those who view them as individuals.

An endo-ideal does not exist except as a group reflection. Endo-ideals repeat real or imagined compliments from others, especially those with endo-ideal status (and the ability to define), to establish and reinforce their self. Both internal and external reflection are what establishes them as the endo-ideal. Their knowledge is a false knowledge, born of the reflectors which can only reflect, but oddly have the power to create false reflections. In endoreality, every failure of the endo-ideal is a virtue. They don't achieve success in art because the greatness of their art is above the audience. They never work because they were created for greater work that they are somehow also unable to do. Anyone who disagrees with them or proves them wrong has simply misunderstood the subtlety of their claims. Accusations of compulsive lying which are often directed at the endo-ideal are simply a misunderstanding of endoreality. In an endogroup, reality is what the endo-ideal says and virtue is what they do.

A king does not ask if he is a king. He and his reflectors inform his subjects that he is the king and then demand reflection of that endoreality. This is one important factor in the establishment of dictatorships. Once a president has been elected, it is a straightforward matter for them to strengthen an endogroup to the point that they can declare themselves president for life, then monarch, emperor or god. Once the endogroup is too strong to resist, their reality is the only reality. They have the power to define, not only themselves, but everyone else as their negative image. Because they are king, or emperor, or god, everyone else becomes subjects, or disciples, and are sorted into the devout and the blasphemous, the pious and the sinful, the reflectors and the negative image. The endo-ideal does not exist without reflection but no one else exists without the endo-ideal.

The endo-ideal have the right to define normative and deviant and the right to shun and include. Law and governance is by the endo-ideal, for the endo-ideal. Others are objects owned by the endo-ideal, theirs to use, buy or sell. States offer captive populations to corporations and set the price as minimum wage and corporate tax just as gangs offer captives to customers at the negotiated rates.

Pronouns are one indicator of social boundaries. A frequent tell of endogroups is their odd use of pronouns, even beyond that which is normalized by the wider public which accepts expressions such as *my company* or *my people.* Endogroup pronouns do not reflect bodily divisions between self and other. Endosocial people will attribute work the endo-ideal was not involved with to the endo-ideal, directly or jointly with those responsible. They will use singular pronouns to claim endo-ideal credit for work accomplished jointly. They will use group pronouns to remove sole credit from a singular reflector or negative image. They will deny blame for any wrongdoing or failure by the endo-ideal and cast fault onto the negative image. Endo-ideals speaking of themselves in the third person or with group pronouns is another indicator that their self has expanded beyond the individual. Their outside perspective of themselves is often indicated in statements that begin from an outside point of view, such as *People often tell me, I always tell people* or *People in my position generally feel.* This displacement may be used even in the most personal statements, such as *I always tell people I love you*. This was an often ridiculed tendency of English upper classes who once commonly replaced *I* with *One.*

Information sorting according to the laws of endoreality is seen in endogroups of all sizes and it is also seen among all members. A parent will attribute work done by a disliked child to a favoured child, or a child will themselves reassign blame and credit. Wikipedia editors will write long hagiographies to caucasian men, especially those from the United States, and delete or obsessively challenge articles about women and those outside the U.S. Social media corporations in the U.S. will give authoritative blue checks to anyone involved in technology in California and leave African heads of state unverified. Both European and Islamic history will claim credit for everything they 'discovered' through trade while every smaller nation will, far less effectively, do the same.

A lot of endoreality is based on filtering out information that would require the endo-ideal to acknowledge a debt. They chronically devalue, dismiss or don't see work done by anyone else just as they exaggerate work done by the endo-ideal. To add to all the strange cognitive tells of an endoself or an endo-ideal, they are both often unable to remember simple numbers, no matter how important, if they relate to time (how long they have taken to do something vs when it was promised) or money (how much they spent vs how much they earned). These numbers will have to be proven to them, or their most devout reflectors, over and over and over again and it is a futile exercise. Even numbers become subjective in endoreality.

The work of those outside the endo-ideal is rarely acknowledged. If it is pointed out, it will be devalued or attributed to someone else, usually both. The work of all employees is credited to the anthropomorphized corporation which is then endowed to the endo-ideal owner. The corporation owner takes the identity of the employee in the form of their external recognition. NGOs adopt endo-ideal positions for the people who provide both their identity and their exceptionalism.

Victimhood is very attractive to both endo-ideals and endoselves. Both will cast themselves as victims, especially where they are perpetrators, and claim martyrdom where they are tyrants. Since all guilt belongs to the negative image, all victimhood must belong to the endo-ideal. Since they are exceptional, their victimhood must also be exceptional. As a result, they continue to feel no empathy for their victims. Their own persecution of others strengthens their exceptional myth of outside persecution.

Rapists who claim their victim forced their behaviour is a constant, recurring, reminder of this trait, as are pedosadists who claim that children seduced them and ruined their lives or the cardinal of the Catholic Church who blamed women for the paedosadism of priests and cardinals.[25] Others have forced their victims to 'confess' their guilt for the rape to the priest who raped them. Catholic priests and other powerful men regularly claim to be victims of a 'witch hunt' by survivors of their abuse and white supremacists in the United States regularly claim to be victims of 'lynch mobs' when people try to confront their abuse of others. They retain all aspects of the situations, including language used by the victims, but shun all fault onto the victim and claim all grievance for themselves. This reversal is the source of both the inability of an endo-ideal to foresee repercussions for their behaviour and their otherwise incomprehensible vindictiveness.

An irrefutable criminal act by an endo-ideal is greeted with denial that the criminal is a 'real' member of the endo-ideal while a criminal act by a negative image is assigned to the collective guilt of the entire negative image. Victimhood and credit can travel through time and space and the bodies of others to alight on the endo-ideal, but any objectionable act by themselves, if it must be acknowledged, is always dismissed as in the past, so no longer part of them. Anything they do has either not happened yet, so will be magically prevented from occurring and anyone doubting this is guilty of a lack of faith, or, once the event has transpired, it is dismissed as in the past and not part of their relevant existence. It is a very interesting trait of the endo-ideal that their self is infinite through time and space when claiming credit or victimhood, but has not enough temporal length for one action when it comes to guilt.

Establishment of an endogroup begins with ownership. Filiality was an attempt to find endogroup equilibrium through a balanced temporal self. Death and birth provided an opportunity for a rolling tyranny. Karmic cycles scaled the filial concept to encompass entire societies of justified inequality through a vastly extended temporal self. In Asia, the endo-ideal was central from the start and emanated from extreme filiality. Reflection of the endo-ideal was the core philosophy of Chinese bureaucratic ideology.

Western thought developed its statecraft to save themselves from each other and the western endo-ideal developed almost accidentally from the formation of endogroups. When Germanic warriors offered protection to peasants in western Europe, it was a relationship, but not ownership. It was not until the establishment of inviolable states, aided by pressure brought by external enemies, that the warrior and other endo-ideal classes became the owners and those within the boundaries became their subjects. This guardian coup d'état was then depicted as eternally necessary for their own protection against 'human nature'.

The very important point in both western and eastern views on statecraft was the idea that endo-idealism extended seamlessly from the lowest up into the spiritual realm. Even the emperors were not the final endo-ideal and they too, were expected to reflect a transcendental, spiritual endo-ideal. The transcendental endogroup has managed to sublate every earlier model of hierarchy, as every revolution has simply failed up into a higher endogroup.

Mo Zi, Confucius and Mencius all recommended a moderate tyranny, governed by the bureaucratization of the endo-ideal in the form of a meritocracy of reflectors. While most philosophers who described filiality or patriarchy recommended a despot be benevolent, the nature of the position removes the need for benevolence. Because the endogroup is a structure to enable the creation and transfer of power, the endo-ideal who refuses to become a tyrant may be forced to become a martyr. All virtue will be attributed to the endo-ideal and all fault to the negative image in either case. An endo-ideal can, as so many do, murder babies and children and their endogroup will respond, *Oh well, I'm sure he had his reasons*. and look to the baby or child for provocation. Any criticism of the endo-ideal results in an attack from their supporters claiming the accuser must support an opposing and vilified endogroup. These aspects make the endo-ideal position greatly attractive to an endoself and results in a particularly lethal combination when they are combined.

Endosocialism is fed by hatred of the outgroup which, in the case of an endoself, is everyone. Largely due to the efforts of psychology, a predatory endoself is often conflated with an endo-ideal. The two conditions are very distinct, however, with separate causes and separate characteristics, despite often being found together and most easily identifiable when they occur in unison. While the psychiatric profession lists many endo-ideal traits under the poorly defined Cluster B disorders of the DSM, an endo-ideal is not necessarily anti-social or predatory.

An endo-ideal, like every member of an endogroup, has empathic conduits which are directed exclusively towards the endo-ideal. An endoself has blocked or inhibited euphoric conduits which cannot access primary euphoria. An endo-ideal may have perfectly working euphoric conduits and an endoself may have perfectly functioning empathy. Euphoria and empathy are two very different things, so the condition of an endoself unable to access primary euphoria and an endo-ideal unable to empathize are also very different things.

A person may become an endoself due to developmental trauma causing formation of an endosocial barrier. They may develop a barrier due to the perception of overwhelming social debt. They may be suffering an existential crisis due to severe environmental stressors. Social interactions are not the sole, or even the primary, cause of endoself creation. Every person addicted to drugs, including alcohol, or sugar, or suffering environmental stressors is at risk of becoming an endoself. It is difficult to state social or environmental causes as the primary factor as either could lead to the other.

An endo-ideal is created by expansion of the self through unbalanced transactions. An endo-ideal is nearly always a social creation, although it is possible for such a self to appear through excessive euphoric transfer from art, discovery, creation or spirituality. An endo-ideal does not create themselves and may not even be a willing participant.

While healthy people may find themselves cast into an endo-ideal position, it is a position craved by endoselves. It is also a position that anyone with a damaged personal membrane is incapable of filling, unless they are only a remote or dead icon. Because they have no self, they cannot provide a self for the group to reflect.

The position of endo-ideal may create endoselves. Like the cilia hairs in a smoker's lungs, euphoric conduits may shrivel up in the presence of environmental hazards. They may also dull from lack of use, making the endo-ideal state a possible contributor to the formation of an endoself. It is very difficult to not become an endoself if your image is reflected from every face. It is impossible to establish an empathic connection with your own reflection, therefore it is very difficult for any endo-ideal to develop exosocial empathy. It is also very difficult for an endo-ideal to maintain euphoric conduits in the face of constant unbalanced transactions in which they are the beneficiary and a lack of opportunity for exosocial expansion through their own initiatives.

The self of the reflectors which surround the endo-ideal are simply mirrors of the endo-ideal. The endo-ideal is thus cut off from any balanced euphoric interactions and also cut off from any other sources of euphoria. Their reflective shield creates an alternate reality for the endo-ideal to live in. As the presence of a queen bee will stimulate worker bees to create a hive, the presence of an endo-ideal will stimulate reflectors to create an endogroup. Like the queen bee who is formed by her hive, the endo-ideal is formed by their fawning reflectors. As they experiment with unbalanced interactions, their devotees happily comply instead of demanding balance.

It is possible to resist these well known effects of power. The creators of hereditary rulers often sought to instil a love of other sources of euphoric connection through spirituality, art, study or creation, and most of the least tyrannical despots did have these other outlets with which to establish euphoric conduits. Most places with longstanding empires included traditions of intense contemplation, daily nature walks or meditation in gardens, study, a love of creation through architecture or other great improvement projects.

There are business owners who care about their employees, patriarchs who receive satisfaction in outside endeavours and so present a happy and content face to their families and so on. The benevolent dictator may be rare, but they do exist. It just requires great care and perfect alignment of the stars to create one and the error of failure is disastrous.

In an endo-ideal who is also an endoself, entitlement is accompanied by vindictiveness, propelled by an insatiable quest for secondary euphoria and protected by endoreality.

It is possible for an endo-ideal to remain exosocial. It is also possible, and even common, for reflectors and negative images to be endoselves. Because endosocial groups create subject-object relationships instead of euphoric interactions, any role in an endogroup may be, and likely is, occupied by an endoself. The stronger the endogroup, the greater the likelihood that the majority of members will engage in cruel and predatory behaviour towards each other or outsiders. Reflectors and negative image can be far more vicious than the endo-ideal in enforcing the laws of endoreality, especially since they usually are the ones enforcing the structure while the endo-ideal often stays above the fray. There is also often no direct conflict involving the endo-ideal while the reflectors and negative image are always vying to stay on top of their see-sawing status. Reflectors and negative image are in a zero sum struggle, as in order for one to keep their head above water, the other must sink.

It is not enough for an endoself to define identity and reality for the entire group. Endoselves will also begin to occupy every thought and action of everyone in the endogroup. From a caregiver-ideal who is never satisfied, no matter how much service or personal support they receive, to a totalitarian dictator with work camps and unceasing propaganda, they jealously occupy every aspect of life in every body they consider their own. When an endogroup becomes filled with endoselves, the most vindictive form of totalitarianism will follow.

When an endo-ideal occupies each new stage they occupy it as the endo-ideal. That is their only ambition. They will only move up and broaden their circle if they can continue to occupy the endo-ideal position. An endo-ideal would far rather stay unemployed than be forced to reflect a higher endo-ideal and they would far rather remain in fantasy role-playing than develop a social circle based on mutual respect. They will only participate in creation or discovery if glory, and probably appropriated credit, accompanies those endeavours. If they are blocked from being the endo-ideal, they will stay in the earlier stage and become increasingly tyrannical in it as they attempt to limit the outward expansion of anyone else in the endogroup.

Caregiver endo-ideals can expand to include more than one spouse or child. At a national, discovery or creation level the endo-ideal can even include entire social groups or endogroups based on identity such as a religion, race, gang, political party, school alumni, club membership, professional status or simply a class, such as 'billionaires'. In these cases, they will act on a perceived threat or insult to anyone included in their endo-ideal self as though it were an existential threat. Oddly, the adult endo-ideal does not need to have had any personal experience of ever being the toddler tyrant. Even women who have lived lives indistinguishable from slavery may eventually seize the endo-ideal place as a mother or mother-in-law and become unforgiving and demanding tyrants themselves. Many who were cast in lesser roles in the earliest circles become tyrants as soon as the opportunity arises in a wider circle.

If an endo-ideal is accepted at a national level, they may use group pronouns and make claims of national uniqueness and superiority but they show little interest in other members of the nation except as potential reflectors to be cultivated or dissidents to be crushed or expelled. They have no interest in creation but are very interested in appropriating credit and ownership. An endo-ideal who manages to progress to a discovery level sees all discovery as their own and will vindictively punish the sources of their knowledge. Because they have the myopic perception of an endo-ideal, they feel they are entitled to the privacy and the experience of others but lack any perspective to interpret the data they feel entitled to. Increasing numbers of studies have shown that powerful people acquire and strengthen endo-ideal traits, resulting in reduced empathy, reduced mirroring and a loss of outside perspective. This lack of empathy or awareness of others leads to an extreme myopia. This is the tragedy of all knowledge fields, from science to journalism, that are established as endogroups.

No one in an endogroup treats all people equally, which is why diagnosing people instead of relationships or interactions is impossible. A lifegiver endo-ideal will typically fixate on one negative image, most often women or a class of women, to bear all of their hostility. They are often the most obedient and dedicated reflectors of whoever suits their endo-ideal image. A caregiver endo-ideal will target whoever offers them any kind of relationship or assistance. Those who ignore them are largely ignored in return and those who offer casual friendship may receive it in return. Even those who treat them with hostility are usually afforded the respect due to a worthy enemy. Those who would be their friends, benefactors, loving family or romantic partners are the targets they reserve the most rancour and vindictiveness for. The endo-ideals of nation, discovery or creation endogroups may treat everyone in their family and social circles with loving kindness while murdering, raping, torturing and destroying the environment and health of their particular negative image.

A threat to an endo-ideal causes them to regress to the previous circle of self. If the predominant interactions that a person has experienced, or allowed themselves to remember, depict them as the endo-ideal of a certain level, any threat to their endo-ideal status leaves them with no identity which they recognize, or are willing to accept, at that level. For this reason, all endo-ideals react with extreme sensitivity to any criticism and respond to sustained or devastating attack with regression. Many caregiver endo-ideals describe the feeling of having their status threatened as feeling *under water* or *drowning*. They may react to attacks on their status by retreating to the inertia of a lifegiver-self, neglecting personal grooming (more than usual), and refusing to do any work at all or even get out of bed. The chronic emptiness that all endoselves complain of becomes overwhelming at these times.

This regression to a lifegiver-self is often diagnosed as depression, which all people experience at times and some people experience chronically. In an endo-ideal, it seems more accurate to depict it as a regression, first because it is experienced in response to an attack on their endo-ideal status and second because it is only a caregiver endo-ideal that regresses to their lifegiver-self. Those who have achieved a national status retreat to their caregiver-self and regress to having tantrums. Those who have suffered a loss of status as discovery or creation endo-ideals may look for fame or political power at the national level.

It is very easy to convince an endo-ideal that they are a negative image, at least until their defences take over. That is the conclusion they leap to when subjected to any criticism as they do not see the self as interactions but as an object, with static, clearly defined attributes. Their knowledge of a self is divided between the endo-ideal and the negative image, or guilt and innocence. It is also possible, as the extreme 'thought reform' practices of Chinese, Russian and various other revolutions have proven, to convince an endo-ideal to act as a reflector within another strong endogroup. The strong man leaders are the endo-ideal of local groups, militias, cartels and gangs. A stronger strong man in the form of a king or a state can encompass the smaller groups and, with state law, weaken the tyrannical power of the local tyrants until the people transfer their allegiance to the stronger membrane.

There is much less evidence as to whether it is possible to change an endoself into an exoself with their own primary euphoric conduits because industrial endo-idealism chooses to create endoselves. There does not seem to be any reason why this would not be possible, especially given the successes of all euphoria producing therapies from gardening to dance to spirituality. The development of an exosocial individual is the natural trajectory. It can only be interrupted by the establishment of strong restrictive countering force. If that force were removed, by remedying the causes of ill health, environmental stress or interactional trauma, and the process of developing euphoric conduits restarted, it may be possible to reestablish exosocial development and expansion.

If it is possible to stop the destruction and cruelty of the endoself through therapy, and stop creating endoselves, that is where the world's primary focus ought to be. Endoselves are the true mental health crisis sweeping the world. The proliferation of endoselves is partly a result of the weakening of lower endogroups under a transcendental mono-empire. It is often suggested that endoselves would benefit from stronger allegiance to such smaller endogroups. The problem, however, is neither the self nor the group but the endosocial membrane.

Autonomy and ownership

When there were any excellences and virtues, they were distributed to the emperor. Thus excellences and virtues belonged to the emperor while complaints and slanders were directed against the subordinates. Peace and joy abode with the king while worries and sorrows were lodged with the officials. This was how the ancient sage kings administered government. - Mo Zi, *The Ethical and Political Works*

The endogroup is the self of the endo-ideal and the endo-ideal truly believes that all the bodies in the group are their own, all labour and ideas, from any mind, are their own, all external relationships are their own and they are entitled to the credit and labour of everyone in the group. If anyone in the group stops contributing ideas and labour or leaves the group, the endo-ideal will often be enraged and seek revenge as though their property has been stolen. Furthermore, the rest of the group will join them in that revenge as they also believe that every body and mind in the group is the property of the endo-ideal. This is a key aspect of the endoreality shared and enforced by every member of the endogroup.

Ownership is a right of the endo-ideal. Everything belonging to the group belongs to the endo-ideal. Everything not belonging to another endo-ideal also belongs to the endo-ideal. Theft is possession of property by anyone outside the endo-ideal without the permission of the endo-ideal. Nowhere is this more clearly articulated than in the Westphalia treaties and international trade agreements.

Rape and imprisonment are both extreme violations of bodily ownership. Directing behaviour and dress, demanding smiles and attention and other attempts to control the moods and thoughts of others, unwanted touching and violations of privacy are other examples of ownership claims over the body and mind of another.

Many people feel that women should be forced to let outsiders occupy their bodies, either through sex or pregnancy. These people feel that the owners or user group of women's bodies ought to include entire families, or even communities or states. They argue that women's ownership of their own bodies is a denial of the right to sex or the right to birth for others. At times, not only do lawmakers not believe that women have bodily autonomy, they don't accept that women have any shared ownership at all in their bodies. These lawmakers pass laws such as those in Saudi Arabia where women are stoned to death for having sex that their body's legal owner did not consent to.[26] In these cases, women have no exclusive or shared body ownership and men have exclusive ownership of multiple bodies.

Body ownership is expressed through laws of sexual consent and laws which block access to birth control. Some lawmakers prioritize the rights to life of an unborn fetus or even an as yet unconceived fetus over the life of the woman. The woman's body in these cases is considered to be an unoccupied vessel that can only be externally owned and the existence, or humanity, of the woman is denied. In the past, body ownership was reflected in funeral ceremonies where wives and sometimes slaves were burned alive along with the deceased man. The perception of women's bodies as empty vessels has also appeared in genocides throughout history where men were always murdered but women were sometimes left alive after rape.

Body ownership by the endo-ideal and body violation of the negative image is the reason why many people are so insistent about refusing access to birth control and abortion when they don't actually care about the lives of babies and children at all. It is also the reason these violations of bodily autonomy are more severe on those women whose children will be the least valued by the authorities forcing their birth. When these authorities are not forcing birth, they are forcing sterilizations and abortion, and when they are forced to allow abortion, they insist on a forced and unnecessary vaginal ultrasound. The fetus is not the issue, the bodily autonomy is. Next to murder, pregnancy and imprisonment, rape is the ultimate bodily violation. The endo-ideal increase their power through continual violations of others' autonomy, through rape thinly disguised by euphemisms such as 'strip searches' and 'cavity searches' and also through undisguised rape. Bodily violations are also effected in the continual assaults on the health of others, through radiation, pollution, deliberately harmful products and more. These violations are neither 'accidents' nor 'security', they are an expression of power.

Establishing body ownership for children has been effected by lawmakers dictating that families are not entitled to profit from the sale (including marriage), labour or body or privacy violations of children, even if they are responsible for the support of those children. The duty of parents has, in many cases, been considered one of ownership. These ownership claims have not disappeared in industrialized societies. Instead, ownership has simply passed to the transcendental endogroup, usually a state or corporation. When these transcendental endogroups insist on the autonomy of children, it is most often so those children can make 'lifestyle choices' that expose them to predation by more powerful endogroups through drugs, rape or other paths towards sublation. At other times, laws force children into state institutions of 'education', 'health' or 'justice' where they are threatened with assault, humiliation, drugs, arrest and solitary confinement if they do not relinquish physical and mental autonomy to an endo-ideal.

The destruction and removal of property of the negative image is a feature of every endogroup. Under wealth endo-idealism, poor people are constantly stripped of their autonomy and right to ownership, whether that is of their own privacy and bodily autonomy through continual surveillance and demands for information, their relationships, such as the constant threat to poor parents to have their children taken from them, or property ownership, such as the theft and destruction of personal belongings of those without homes. They live in cities filled with giant buildings and malls of other people's belongings but it is their few possessions that are declared an eyesore.

Strong endogroups or endo-ideals are both created by allocating credit unrealistically to manufacture superiority and by persecuting or demonizing those outside. Credit is not allocated according to fact but according to power.

Reflective obedience is institutionalized in status that refers, not to the work a person accomplishes, but the credit they are entitled to. Positions such as *assistant, secretary, intern,* or *wife* allow the smooth transfer of credit from the obedient reflector to the endo-ideal. Researchers are called simply *Marxist, Freudian* or *Jungian,* along with claims that they are 'continuing his research', ensuring that their life's work will be anonymously credited to some dead man. The men whose names are always credited also are assigned credit for all non-ideal work that came before or contemporaneously to them.

The saying *you can accomplish anything, as long as you don't mind who gets the credit* is usually true, but leaves out an important point. Credit unclaimed does not disperse. Unclaimed credit will always be used to strengthen an endo-ideal. Credit theft is the first step to enslavement and subordination. Unlike other thieves, a credit thief will never improve with further acquaintance or have redeeming qualities. Credit theft is usually the first sign of a thoroughly malevolent character who will attempt to turn every working group and event into their own personal endogroup.

One side effect of credit allocation in endoreality is that the negative image must always work alone if they want any credit for their own work, while the endo-ideal can freely allocate large portions or the entire body of work to others and be confident of still receiving full credit. The other aspect of this is that no one will assist the negative image in work that is not credited to the endo-ideal. Since endo-ideals never have exosocial goals, this is crippling to exosocial development or any development which benefits the negative image.

Modesty is internalization of the negative image and externalization of the endo-ideal. Modesty is a virtue designated solely for women under male endo-idealism, but is also heavily cultivated in Asian cultures for both sexes. Modesty precludes putting oneself forward to claim credit and encourages attribution of credit to an endo-ideal. Attribution of everything a person does to a god or earthly benefactor is an attempt to encourage the humility required for those outside the endo-ideal to remain selfless.

The repercussions for claiming personal achievement were illustrated in 1661 by the life imprisonment of Nicolas Fouquet and the exile of his wife, Marie-Madeleine de Castille. Fouquet was guilty of ordering the creation of a magnificent garden and château at his home, Vaux-le-Vicomte, at a time he was serving as the superintendent of finances for Louis XIV. Apparently, the king had not yet informed Fouquet that *"l'état, c'est moi,"* but he made it clear by seizing the property and hiring the architects to build the same, but bigger, as the palace and gardens of Versailles. The most interesting part of this history is that the architects, who did not claim ownership despite creating the original, were not persecuted. It was not the creation which offended but the ownership and credit claim. This situation has been repeated throughout history and myth, wherever endogroups existed. In order to preserve creation, credit must be immediately transferred to the endo-ideal.

Quotes that are attributed to Confucius by his disciples are always referenced as quotes of Confucius. Quotes attributed to Jesus Christ are also referenced to him, at least by devout Christians. Quotes which Plato attributed to Socrates are referenced as from Plato as western individualism does not follow teacher endo-idealism. This European exception does not apply to women, however, as male endo-idealism still applies. Women who publish their own ideas are always examined for what man could have possibly influenced her but the reverse was never true until recently.

Voltaire received much of his knowledge from his sixteen years of discussions with his brilliant lover Émilie du Châtelet and access to her vast library, but she is never associated with his ideas. Du Châtelet was a physicist, philosopher and the author of her own *Institutions physique* and a French translation of Newton's *Principia.* She is depicted on the frontispiece of Voltaire's *Éléments de la philosophie de Newton,* which lists only Voltaire as author, in a scene which perfectly depicts the reflective role women were assigned. In the engraving, Voltaire wears a laurel wreath as he sits at his desk. Newton sits atop a cloud beside Mme du Chatelet, who uses a mirror to beam a ray of light from the heavens onto Voltaire's page. She, like every woman depicted as a muse, is considered an empty, transitory vessel or medium from which knowledge is transferred for the glory of men.

To illustrate the extent to which a woman with ideas is viewed under male endo-idealism as a commons resource to be plundered, Voltaire was not the only author who was tutored in Newton by du Chatelet. One year prior, Francesco Algarotti had written *Il Newtonianismo per le dame* following a six week visit with du Chatelet. This time, the frontispiece and book both illustrate the credit reversal process. On the frontispiece, a woman who looks very similar to du Chatelet is having Newton explained to her by a man like Algarotti. Within the covers, a dialogue presents a chevalier explaining Newton to a lady. The situation from universal reality is retained, but the roles are reversed according to the laws of endoreality under male endo-idealism.

The transfer of value explains the paradox whereby women under male endo-idealism are both held incapable of possessing virtue and held responsible for any lack of it in their families. These are beliefs held in endoreality which recognize the laws of endo-ideal ownership, however puzzling that may be from the perspective of universal reality.

Intellectual property is a perfect example of institutionalized endoreality. Under intellectual property laws, endo-ideals from Thomas Edison to Bill Gates can claim the creative output of others as their own and demand that they receive credit for all similar or derivative thoughts in perpetuity. With Thomas Edison, this led to him demanding payment for every movie made as he had been authoritatively credited with the invention of the camera, and with Bill Gates, his claim to ownership of programming languages led him to seek payment for every program anyone wrote with the languages.

The limited empathy and perspective of the endo-ideal, combined with a feeling of debt owed to them, make it very unlikely that they will themselves have great accomplishments. If they are also an endoself, the probability is reduced to nil. Those that do have great achievements prior to fame seldom produce original greatness later.

Ownership of ideas is not a positive claim that grants freedom to the owner. It is a negative claim that removes rights to all outside the endo-ideal. In other words, it is not liberation, it is subordination. Neither does intellectual property credit the creator. Instead, it credits the holder of authoritative rights, granted to the endo-ideal, for the endo-ideal. It is institutional implementation of the laws of endoreality regarding credit.

An endo-ideal is often very attractive to others because they seem to share the goals, interests and ambitions of their new acquaintance as well as being deeply admiring of their beauty, intelligence or accomplishments. They are also often very attractive in their immediate commitment to a joint future. That is because they see the new person as an object they wish to acquire. All of those attractive qualities are about to be credited to their self.

Endo-ideals genuinely believe that any idea that reaches their mind from an unrecognized source, one outside the endo-ideal, must belong to them. This is why they feel entitled to copyrights, patents and other 'intellectual property' as well as ownership over commons property. Reflectors are seldom confident that any idea is their own and believe that some endo-ideal person must have had their idea first. They will look for an endo-ideal to claim credit for their own ideas and they will assert endo-ideal credit over the work of anyone else with reflector or negative image status. 'The greater good' is always used against those outside the endo-ideal when they request credit, along with demands that they suppress their ego. While an endo-ideal will be excited and attracted by the ideas and work of others, and frequently echo that work and opinions as their own, they will not remember any personal details of the source, up to and including the name of a love interest. Their minds erase the person as irrelevant.

Every woman living under male endo-idealism knows that the safest way to reject a man sexually or romantically is by claiming that another man has ownership rights over her. If she does not, her assertion of ownership over the body she occupies will often be met with rage and retribution. The woman has no right to ownership or a self. In the same way, credit for ideas is expected to be on offer. Women with ideas will have their ideas complimented and receive offers from men to claim those ideas as their own and to assume a proprietary position over the woman's ideas. If she attempts to keep the credit for herself, this attempt is met with the same hostility as if she kept her labour or her body to herself. All output of women's lives is claimed as commons property until a man takes ownership of it and a woman seeking ownership of her own self is treated as an interloper attempting to steal from the group or from the man who claimed her self. As male endo-idealism has been subsumed into transcendental endogroups, the same hostility is directed towards states that attempt to keep their resources or ideas from supranational corporate ownership. A state which claims ownership of their own resources is cursed as *communist* and attacked just as a woman who claimed her own body is cursed as a *bitch* and attacked.

Even if other people illustrate that a woman had an idea and stated it before the endo-ideal claimed it, a male endo-idealist will claim that they did not hear or understand her and it was more clear when stated by the endo-ideal. This is a result of the endofilter through which all endogroup reality is viewed. If men are to be believed (and why should they not?), generations of them were driven mad by the sound of a woman's voice in any position of power or public recognition and they were never able to understand or retain what any of these women were saying. Men have also claimed that the presence of women in other endogroups causes them to lose focus on the work of the endogroup and be distracted by thoughts of sex. Again, this is caused by an endofilter which viewed the sight of women as an indicator that the subject is now in a caregiver circle.

Everything that has historically happened in the subjugation of women under male endo-idealism has scaled up to every other transcendental endogroup. The liberation of women, where it exists at all, is simply a symptom of the sublation of a wider group. Equality is the equality of subjugation. Academics and journalists as the endo-ideal exploit the knowledge of those designated as sources and subjects, CEO's exploit the knowledge of the people working for their companies, NGOs and migratory endo-ideals exploit the victimhood of those in need of aid, and so on. Authority is a word reserved for the endo-ideal and it provides an endofilter through which people are ordered to view all knowledge.

The endo-ideal has to lose status. The negative image have to fight for it. A U.S. based social media application called Klout once professed to impartially measure the online influence of people. It changed its algorithm when the U.S. president at the time, Barack Obama, was not credited as the highest ranking person. This pattern of setting the endo-ideal as the standard which everyone else has to attain has resulted in endo-idealist algorithms for hiring, policing, assigning credit and all other aspects of life, both before and after the onset of computing. The algorithms are created to match the endo-ideal, not the other way around. This was also the method with which all societal institutions were designed, including law, governance and economy. Value was assigned to the existence of powerful men and denied to the most arduous and dangerous labour being performed by women and other slaves.

Everyone who wants credit for their work who is not the endo-ideal is fighting against cognitive dissonance, or endoreality. The assigning of credit is an indicator of social approval and acceptance. Endogroups do not assign social approval (including credit) outside their own endo-ideal. The assigning of credit, or social approval, only within endogroups and to endo-ideals is very important in understanding the inherent unfairness of the trade economy as explained in *The Approval Economy*.

Reflectors mirror an endo-ideal, but the endo-ideal often seems possessed by those they seek to possess. The reversal of pronouns and inserting themselves into another person's story by appropriating the other's role, adopting all attributes, tastes and background of the other, mirroring and body-snatching, show how little of the endo-ideal is the individual.

The reflector may simply reflect the endo-ideal, but since the endo-ideal absorbs the entire group, they are often reflecting themselves through the form of the endo-ideal. In this way, a person with far more perspective than the endo-ideal can use the power of the endo-ideal to accomplish their goals, as long as their goals do not involve personal ambition. If the person who has the ear of the endo-ideal happens to be an endoself, they can unleash terror and avoid all blame. This is a much easier feat than achieving exosocial goals as exosocial goals are, by definition, in opposition to the goals of an endogroup. A reflector with exosocial goals will find their work appropriated to create a powerful endo-ideal and a misplaced trust which will ultimately be used for endosocial goals.

Reflectors can now create a social media persona to embody their endo-ideal and work and act as their own endo-ideal. Endo-ideals can go on social media looking for adulation and reflection as well as thoughts to steal. At times the behaviour of all who usually occupy specific endosocial roles is being changed. Both sociologists and psychologists are constantly producing analysis of online social activity as though they were viewing organic social tendencies instead of the activities of well-funded state, corporate and other organized criminal networks attempting to socially engineer populations. No analysis can be worthwhile unless it factors in the trillions of dollars of coercive force being exerted on these populations and the coercive structure of social platforms themselves. Online anonymity was fought against, primarily to assert the primacy of the endo-ideal, and social media itself was created to facilitate the laws of endoreality.

Social media is forming societies with no forethought or transparent intent and is increasingly following the bidding of a totalitarian mono-empire. In mapping the effects of these new methods of coercion, few aspects are as important as allocation of credit and authority. In endogroups, reality is a relative state, subject to the whim of those designated as the authoritative endo-ideals. The structure and effects of these new algorithms is discussed in more detail in *Shaping Reality.*

Secrecy and privacy

Thoughts are supposed to stay and grow in quiet, dark places, like butterflies in cocoons. - Helen Oyeyemi, *The Icarus Girl*

Privacy is ownership of a personal membrane and control over one's own circles of intimacy. It is the ability to establish one's own boundaries of intimacy. Privacy is sovereignty over the most intimate circle of self. It includes control over the body, the mind, the self and life.

Privacy is destroyed by violations of the ownership of personal intimacy. Forced intimacy, or violations of privacy, are a denial of one's ownership of their self and a claim of ownership over their self by another. Invasion of circles of intimacy is a negation of the subject's ownership of their own circles of self. It is thus the first step to sublation.

Each aspect of this most intimate circle of the body, the mind, the self and life, is violated by those who wish to sublate the self. Bodies are denied individuality, control over the body is usurped, creation and discovery is stolen, the mind is continually occupied and internal reality is defined externally. All of the interactions which make up the self are controlled or blocked except the relationship with the endo-ideal. Interactions with people, discovery, creation, nations and spirituality are all intercepted or destroyed. People are both exposed and isolated. Life is attacked with continual assaults on health, including constant stress.

It is not just the physical assault on health, body, mind or relationships that matters. It is the destruction of the will to resist that is the mark of sublation. Those who still resist are the criminal and the insane, locked away to leave a population of fully sublated reflectors as *the normal people*.

These circles of privacy are intensely guarded by the self. Control of thoughts is a form of torture. This is why loud music is used as torture, and call centres are such unbearable places to work. All forms of torture are a destruction of control over the self or bodily autonomy. Torture cannot be described in terms of physical acts as no act is torture if it is performed voluntarily. It is something done to the self by an external force. Torture is the external act which triggers the most extreme defences of the self in resistance to sublation. Torture is a struggle for ownership of the most intimate circle of self, that protected by privacy. If that ownership is lost, the self will be sublated. Torture of the body and mind are designed to encourage dissociation as dissociation is a relinquishing of control which allows the person to be occupied by an external self.

Predators remove the right of the self to tell their own story or have it created through their interactions. Slander seeks to destroy personal integrity through lies about their actions, belief and history, to change the perception of their self that is carried forward and to change their social approval. Lies are an attack on the nature of the relationships which form the self. Denial of a right to tell their own stories is also an attack. Women under male endo-idealism have been constantly surveilled, and not permitted to share secrets among themselves under pain of laws against 'gossip'. Church confessions are a well known institution of thought surveillance, but they are not the first. *Do not lie* is one of the three primary laws of the Inca empire and many other legal systems. A law against lying states that a higher authority is arbiter of the truth and that a higher authority is entitled to your truth. These are demands to know the thoughts of another. Thoughts and knowledge are considered the property of the group or the endo-ideal.

Technology firms are primarily in the business or stripping human dignity and privacy from others, a mass sublation of seven and a half billion people to a data centre in the sea, or the ground. Since the mono-empire has automated its own reflection, all are now the negative image and none are entitled to privacy. The few hundred people ultimately in charge of all that data could never find a use for it beyond its primary use, which is stripping privacy from everyone else. The reasons presented for privacy violations, like the reasons presented for endo-ideal secrecy, are simply part of the exceptional myth propaganda. *You wouldn't mind surveillance if you have nothing to hide* is a statement to sort the obedient reflectors from the negative image and attribute vice to dissenters in order to cast them as the negative image. The only real reason for privacy violation is to usurp ownership of the most intimate circle of the sublated self. The only real reason for endo-ideal secrecy is to enforce acceptance of endoreality.

Facebook was established to destroy the personal integrity of women at Harvard with a ranking system populated by their faces. People are now shocked that Facebook is not respecting their privacy. In 1975, photographer Gary Gross took nude pictures of ten-year old Brooke Shields which were published as a Playboy feature. Throughout the 1980s, Shields fought to prevent the continued exhibition of the photos, by Tate Modern among others, and was unsuccessful. The courts ruled that her privacy was Gross's business and art. Degrading photos of people without homes and people arrested in the U.S. are also ruled to be the property of those who take the pictures, not those whose privacy is violated. As the negative image expands to encompass billions of people, the number of people not entitled to privacy also expands. What so many pundits are calling a *post-privacy world* has never been a world where privacy was accorded to the negative image. It is simply a world where the negative image now includes more people.

A typical stripping of privacy of all outside the endo-ideal is the all-pervasive invasion of privacy conducted by spy agencies and their corporate partners. The renaming of spy agencies to *intelligence communities* is an interesting practice that accompanied the widespread public acceptance of spy agencies targeting the privacy of all people the state claimed ownership over. With the switch from an acknowledged act of hostility towards those outside the endogroup to preying on reflectors and the negative image, people the states considered their own, their role was renamed to claim ownership of the information, not as spoils of war but as an endo-ideal virtue. Spies that once were presented as thieves and violators of privacy are now considered the rightful holders of endogroup 'intelligence'. Everyone's secrets are the endogroup's secrets and the endo-ideal are the endogroup, therefore, everyone's secrets rightfully belong to them.

This has advanced to attempts by nearly every major artificial intelligence technology researcher, including Facebook and MIT, to develop mind reading software.[27] China in 2019 announced school programs in which they strapped electrode carrying headbands onto school children's heads and shared with teachers and entire group chats of parents which children were, according to the electrodes, focused or distracted.[28] The chance that the 'artificial intelligence' software is at all accurate in making this assessment is very low. It doesn't matter, however, because the point is not to assess but to define. Once a child has been identified as unfocused, has been reprimanded by the teacher, punished by their parents and avoided by all the other children on the advice of their parents, the assessment will be true. The endo-ideal has the right to define and have their reality reflected by the entire endogroup, therefore they are never wrong. The 'artificial intelligence' team may just as well walk into classrooms and point at children to designate them as the negative image. The results would be just as final.

There is an added feature, however, in the bodily violations of radiating children's brains and broadcasting their moods to wider society, and that feature is the early appropriating of the most intimate circles of a child before they have any chance of establishing a self. While China is obviously focused on establishing the Communist Party of China as the endo-ideal, their efforts are having another effect. The people under this treatment are increasingly reflective and susceptible to any endo-ideal that comes along. This is how to fertilize the ground for revolution, or for increasing cult membership. While there are only five ideologies recognized as official state religions in China, devout membership in every organized religion is growing.[29] The Falun Gong, an ideology somewhat reminiscent of Scientology which terrifies the CPC has seen membership soar, at least according to the intensity of their subsequent persecution. It is very possible to mould people as uncritical reflectors, but it is then much more difficult to prevent their ardent reflection of ideological rivals. This is a lesson the CPC ought to have learned when they maneouvered the former imperial reflectors over to themselves, but the myopic lens of an endo-ideal seldom learns lessons from their own past.

The surveillance of cognition and emotion which has preoccupied spies and tyrants forever, lately aided by technology, is joined with its twin goal, the control of cognition and emotion. China has defended their concentration camps as *"re-education to stop terroristic thoughts from occurring."*[30] This goal, echoed by similar programs in the U.S. and elsewhere, is the use of multiple selves by the endo-ideal. Not only the labour of a body, but the innermost circle of self is occupied, or occupation is attempted, by the neo-necromancers. This is a dream as old as endogroups, the endoself greed to lead multiple unsatisfactory lives since they are unable to fully live any.

Secrecy is ownership and control over the information belonging to and affecting a group, including information obtained through violation of the privacy of others. Secrecy is ownership of the intimate knowledge of another.

People in some cultures still care very much who is told first about significant life events. Secrets have always been recognized as a form of intimacy and many cultures have, or had, different names for different levels of intimacy, which were secret to all but a few. The sharing, preserving and betrayal of secrets has always marked the boundaries of intimacy. The robbing of secrets is a violation of control over intimacy, a forced intimacy and occupation of knowledge which belongs in the realm of personal integrity. The more secrets a group shared, the greater their intimacy became and the more likely they were to become the dominant endogroup in a person's life, even more dominant than the authoritative endogroup. This is part of the reason authoritative endogroups insist on stripping control and ownership of secrets from everyone but themselves.

People are governed by the information they accept to be true. This is why powerful people refer to management of public beliefs as statecraft and this is why they depict interfering with that management as non-state actors meddling with statecraft. Governance by the people would have all information pertaining to the group transparent, permeable and accessible to everyone. This is completely contrary to endogroups.

Not only sharing information, but also accessing information has been off limits to all negative image groups. Curiosity, speaking, learning and taking to friends were all forbidden to women under male endo-idealism, or slaves and peasants under industrial endo-idealism. Folk tales of people losing their voices as punishment are as common as legal punishments which cut out tongues. There are many examples of crimes which practice guilt reversal through criminalizing the exposure of endo-ideal crimes or even the discovery of endo-ideal crimes. The purpose of all law is to enforce subordination to the laws of endoreality. This is very evident in secrecy laws throughout history which criminalize all accusation or even investigation of the endo-ideal. It is clear in spells which cursed accusers with the guilt they exposed and it is clear in the punishment for curiousity of so many women in legends and myth, from Pandora to Psyche.

Forbidden chamber fairy tales such as *Bluebeard,* where the protagonist discovers the chamber contains the remains of her predecessor wives or *Fitcher's Bird,* where it contains the mutilated remains of her sisters, or *How the Devil Married Three Sisters* where it contains her sisters burning in hell, make clear the horrors outside the protective bubble of endoreality they are encouraged to stay in. In these stories, the bloody key or egg or singed flowers provides the proof the murderer needs to assign guilt to the victim and murder her as 'punishment'. These are all variations of the Pandora's Box theme where the antagonist wishes to cause the girl harm and transfer the blame for it onto her own curiosity. These are all clearly guilt transference myths where the guilt is assigned, not for the deed, but the discovery of the deed.

Such guilt is also evident in the story of the Garden of Eden or the many variants of *Mary's Child,* where it is claimed that the girl was in a heaven-like state and was cast out as righteous punishment for her curiosity. These principles are still reflected in laws and verdicts around the world which punish the victims and witnesses of crimes with accusations such as lese majeste, libel, false accusations, perversion of justice or violation of secrecy.

As always, endo-idealism is a generic structure that will be scaled up and reversed whenever the structure or the nature of the endo-ideal is changed. What happened to women under male endo-idealism is repeated to the poor under wealth endo-idealism and repeated to employees and consumers under corporate endo-idealism and repeated to almost everyone under billionaire endo-idealism. People obliged to fight wars are not permitted to know what wars the endo-ideal are planning. Samsung is permitted to refuse to tell its own employees which toxic chemicals they are working with under the guise of 'trade secrets'.[31] Where women were once cursed as *gossips,* everyone is now cursed as *conspiracy theorists,* called *"just as dangerous as terrorists"* by former UK Prime Minister David Cameron as he attempted to cover up the international child trafficking and paedosadist crimes of politicians and royals.[32]

Official state secrets are discussed in more detail at the end of this book in Appendix A, a transcript of a talk on whistleblowing which was censored by the unironically self-proclaimed *"last bastion of free speech",* Oxford Union. Nearly all official state and corporate secrets and surveillance serve the creation of forbidden chambers to guard against discovery of the crimes of the endo-ideal and punish whoever looks for or accidentally discovers them. In endoreality, knowledge of guilt is guilt. The creation of the forbidden chamber is an automated guilt transference to whoever may seek to accuse the endo-ideal.

Reflection and refraction

Women have served all these centuries as looking-glasses possessing the magic and delicious power of reflecting the figure of man at twice its natural size.[33] - Virginia Woolf, 1931

A reflector is a sublated self. They are neither the endo-ideal, nor the other. They exist as an extension of the endo-ideal or they do not exist at all. In the words of Virginia Woolf, "*she was so constituted that she never had a mind or a wish of her own, but preferred to sympathize always with the minds and wishes of others.*"[34] It is important to note that women were not the only angels of modern society. The process Woolf describes, whereby she murders the angel of domesticity who attempts to guide her and must then discover a new self, is a process which must be repeated by all obedient reflectors. Those include the *dutiful son*, the *hard-working man*, the *responsible citizen*, the *respectful student*, and all members of society who are accustomed to the virtue of having no self of one's own.

The nature of this virtue is an important point. This virtue appears in the form of a debt which must one day be repaid. The contentment of a reflector is found in the conviction of secret wealth. Every pat on the head, every recognition of their obedience, is a confirmation of their wealth. This wealth does not exist in endoreality, and it will never be awarded, due to the simple reversal of credit which characterizes every endosocial relationship. Henrik Ibsen hauntingly described the experience of an infantilized reflector wife in *A Doll's House,* wherein she realizes that, in case of crisis, she will be cast as the negative image by her supposedly protective and loving husband. She also realizes she will never, not even for one event, be granted the credit and approval reserved for the endo-ideal. This is the shock of awakening that lies in wait for every reflector. Rejection of the devastation caused by this realization is the motivator behind all denial of reality and justification of the endo-ideal by the reflector.

The debt is a crucial element in keeping the reflector attached to their debtor. This is based on principles familiar to the proprietors of any gambling den. A couple of early wins are provided to give the victim the taste of euphoria which is then followed by a steady pattern of loss that they will endlessly hope to recover if they just manage to stay at the table. Everyone who interacts within an endogroup or with an endoself will be the victim of unbalanced interactions. The unbalanced interaction is a universal source of extreme discomfort. The promise or expectation of restitution is a great draw in keeping people from cutting off the endo-ideal. Even a fully sublated reflector will retain the secret comfort of their wealth credit in universal reality.

It is easy for an endo-ideal to attract a negative image or reflector. Besides the ease with which they allow their personal boundaries to be violated and the need they share for a wider endogroup with a strong bond, all reflectors and negative images enter every relationship with existing credit. New violations add to the credits owed but to anyone who is already owed from a prior relationship, a promise of repayment is irresistible. A potential endo-ideal has only to promise a romance or business relationship or trade agreement greater than that offered by anyone else to attract a person with pre-existing, unredeemed credit.

Korean pop artist Hyuna described the process of being sublated, or infantilized, in her disturbing 2017 single *Babe*. In the song she describes her transformation, within the bounds of this one relationship, from an invincible 26 year old to a child of undefined age. She also describes her confusion as to the source of her transformation, alternating between asking if the other put a spell on her and ruminating that she must like it and she did not know she would be like this. She describes the very common process of adult transformation quite well and also captures the confusion about agency in what is a social, or multi-person phenomenon. It is an interesting song which becomes far more interesting when read as part of an ongoing commentary by women in the Korean music industry regarding audience and industry expectations of them. The same personal relationship phenomenon is clearly found in much wider social situations.

As Virginia Woolf also makes clear above, the power to reflect is itself a power and the very nature of a reflector is changed to want to reflect. Sometimes a healthy exosocial person will encounter an endo-ideal and be sublated but the reverse may also be true. Particularly in situations where people have been raised to be reflectors or negative images, they will create their own endo-ideal. Anyone in a relationship with them is in as much danger of transforming as a person in a relationship with an endo-ideal.

The process of creating a reflector is the inverse of the process of creating an endogroup. Here, all identity and exceptionalism is erased. As every cult and institution knows, the removal of identity is the first step to creating a reflector. It is impossible to think of a person as a separate entity if there is no word that depicts them as such. Any request by reflectors to have their own word is met with rage or derision that they are not content to be represented by the endo-ideal. While recognition of the identity of the endo-ideal is always depicted in grandiose terms such as a *right to exist,* the same ambition in reflectors is treated as pathetically trivial and childish.

The United States clearly outlined their territorial ambitions and dreams of their 'manifest destiny' to control all of America in their selected name, ambitions which are still tacitly recognized by every European fellow endo-ideal, who calls the United States *America* or its inhabitants *American.* Even without a legal empire, the usage of the word allows for the frequent erasure of 34 other states from global consideration. Once the United States is heard from, the opinions of 'America' are represented, in everywhere from Wikipedia articles to diplomatic circles.

The trouble with allowing human categorization by words that become autohyponyms, or words which refer both to a broad category and one of its sub-categories, is that the subcategory is invariably the endo-ideal and it comes to occupy the totality of the references to the word, erasing the rest of the category. This has begun to be seen with the word Europe as well, which is increasingly used as a reference to the European Union, not the continent. When other sub-categories do emerge, they are awkward and invariably marked as inferior to the generic term. In the latter case, the countries outside the EU are reduced to individual states or the-part-of-Europe-that-is-non-compliant-with-EU-regulations. In America, the very inadequate, incomplete and inaccurate term LatinAmerica is often used which serves more to isolate and divide than unite.

The word *woman* did not exist in Old English. At that point, there were three words: *mann,* which referred to all people, *wer* which referred to men only and *wif* which referred to women only. By Middle English, the usage of *wer* declined and women were subsequently pushed out of the word for generic human. This instantly separated women from all the rights and presumptions of equality which had been established as inclusive of *all men. Wermen* were now the default human and women became an isolated fringe case, or subcategory. As Christine Rauer pointed out[35], in Old English *"wer tends to be used particularly in cases emphasising sexuality, courtship, or respectable maturity"* and wif in connotations of *"mature and official marriage or coupledom ... courtship, sexual approaches and sexual unions"*. In other words, sex was not specified unless it was deemed important which was only in a sexual context and sometimes not even then. *"The suggestion again seems to be that the gender of the people involved is of no concern to the author."* As women were pushed out of the generic term, every reference to them became presented in the context of the sex binary.

Further, women no longer existed at all outside of the sexual and couple connotations of the word *wif,* now *wife* and changed to exclusively mean the marriage partner of a man. This left women who were married included only through their role as part of a man. Women who were not married were assigned negative image terms such as *girl, widow, spinster* or *old maid,* which all describe why a woman is not a wife and were all used as derogatory terms. All women were depicted as reflector or negative image to the male endo-ideal which now represented all humanity. This inclusion of women only as part of men was a large part of resistance against women having the right to vote as it was argued that would simply give two votes to married men. This is well illustrated in coverture and other Napoleonic Code laws which claim that a husband and wife are one person, namely the husband.

Women had to fight to appear again as more than possessions, in the form of *wifmann,* or woman, and that fight was very closely related to their recognition as persons in their own right. Medical research and funding and every other government initiative was still directed at the generic human, *man,* which no longer included women. Even outside of the word man, other person nouns such as doctor, scientists, etc, began to appear with female qualifiers if they were not the default male. In 2013, Wikipedia removed all women from the category *writers* and hid them in the fringe *women writers* category while leaving men in the main category.[36] At one and the same time, women were told that they did not need specific representation as they were included in the general term, and they are excluded from the general term. At one and the same time, modern usage of the word man was reserved for males only but credit for all historical achievement attributed to the word *mann* was incorporated under the new, male-only usage of the term.[37]

With their exclusion, both the rights and achievements of women were erased. With their own word, women ceased to be reflectors but became the negative image, or occasionally, the endo-ideal of their own separate endogroup. For a time, there was no English word commonly used to refer to humanity at large, outside of the sex binary. Although *person* has recently risen to the occasion, it is not nearly as common as the binary terms, man and woman, and the words *they/them*, employed for centuries as a substitute for the once gender neutral *he/him*, are still not as common as the binary pronouns either. The fight to reinstate women thus required a tedious process of mandating usage of alternate terms for every word in English which contained the once universal word man.

All older books were still written with the generic human *man* and *he*, which (unlike the German *mensch*) no longer included women and all still have to be re-examined and rewritten to reflect the modern male-only definition. This is a formidable amount of labour that will never result in clarity since the past was not always viewed in a sex binary and the present is. The introduction of the new sex binary on works from the past is contrary to the intent of the work. The time and energy that could have been (and still could be) spent in reclaiming usage of the word man to its original intent was and is instead spent creating two parallel streams of experience fighting for equivalence. This caused a large amount of universal human reality to be framed in terms of a sex binary which triggered endofilters under male endo-idealism.

This same exclusion from a universal identity and subsequent fight for parallel identity recognition is a feature of every revolution, every genocide and every civil war. It is notable that it was, and is, considered more feasible to change the construction of the entire English language and rewrite history than to roll back the usurpation of the word man. This is a parallel to every revolution. It is always considered more feasible to create a new revolutionary or transcendental endogroup than it is to dismantle the structure of endo-idealism. This is due to the fact that, once a population is existing in endoreality, only an endo-ideal can change that endoreality. An endo-ideal, not unnaturally, promotes endo-idealism and creates new endogroups.

Reality is experienced by the endo-ideal and their experience is reflected by those outside. Much has been written about the inhibition of mirror neurons in the powerful as their empathy with anyone outside has been reduced. Much more needs to be written about the occupation of the mirror neurons of a sublated person, to excessively mirror only their endo-ideal and empathize only with their endo-ideal. This occupation can become so extreme that an ardent reflector will see their endo-ideal in their own reflection and be apparently unable to distinguish their very different situations.

While it is sufficient for an endo-ideal to simply exist, a reflector must act. It is in the job description; a reflector must reflect. While the endo-ideal defines and embodies the ideal, it is the responsibility of the reflectors to create it. It is their duty to reconcile every piece of cognitive dissonance which penetrates their, or others', awareness since it will seldom penetrate the limited empathic awareness of the endo-ideal. Like supportive families of drug addicts, their existence revolves around excusing and rationalizing behaviour the endo-ideal is not even aware of, fulfilling the endo-ideal claims and ambitions, and sheltering them from consequences. The reflectors are the wife who becomes adept at hiding bruises with makeup and they are also the seven and a half billion law-creating and abiding people who permit twenty-six people to claim ownership of half the world's wealth.[38]

Sometimes, reflectors are following the lead of their endo-ideal but often they are just on a voracious quest to acquire as many sacrifices as they can to present as offerings to their idol. In most cases, it would not be possible for the endo-ideal to accumulate their power on their own and they seem as bemused about it as everyone outside the endogroup.

People blaming their tyrants are as logical as a hive blaming the queen bee. Endogroups create their own tyrants, support them and uphold them. The persecution may all be coming from the tyrant, and the cost of resisting them may be great, or even unbearable on an individual level, but the tyrant was still created by the reflectors and cannot exist without them. The power is all with the reflectors.

A cult is not created by a cult leader. Both the cult and the cult leader are created by the cult followers. Like a queen bee or ant, the leader is created through the activities and needs of those surrounding them. With no reflectors, the endo-ideal no longer exists, or exists as a shell of what they once were. The deflated and instantly aged appearance of every toppled dictator and divorced abusive spouse attests to the source of energy they used to sustain themselves. A video of the last speech given by toppled Romanian dictator Nicolae Ceausescu in 1989 shows this energy reversal happen in real time as a break in his staged reflection occurred. There have been many examples since, as such moments are more often caught on video. Typically, the endo-ideal in such moments of reflective breaks do not show fear. Instead, they show extreme confusion and even disorientation.

As the reflectors and negative image are created by euphoric depletion, by negating their individuality and worth, the opposite process is used to create an endo-ideal. This is a deliberate process that has been followed throughout ages in the creation of hereditary emperors and religious leaders, as well as members of dominant social demographics. This is the reason the elite demographics cannot be educated along with the rest of the public, and, as Max Weber pointed out, neither can they attend the same church.[39]

The factors which create a reflector and prevent them from ever seeing or realizing their true power are several, but the most important is endorealiity. The most important aspect to understanding groups who are unable to resist a tyrant, even when they seemingly have all the power, is their sublation to a self that is larger than the individual and controls all aspects of their thinking and reactions. Selfless people cannot define reality or themselves. Without a self, they have no point of reference, or perspective. Therefore, they must belong to endogroups and those groups must contain an endo-ideal to define reality and identity for the group.

The reflector can only live vicariously through the endo-ideal, but that does not necessarily mean the endo-ideal has all the power or controls the relationship. The endo-ideal could be a newborn infant or a spiritual icon or ideology and the effect would be the same. The secret is not in some demonic power possessed by the endo-ideal, who typically appear as empty shells, or at least wholly unremarkable. The secret is the nature of the group self. The endogroup has laws unto itself which transcend any individual will. As Jung pointed out, *"The true leader is always led."*[23]

There is a phenomenon in resistance which has been studied during atrocities and genocides all over the world and throughout history. At the beginning, each person victimized must be outnumbered and overpowered and often receives support from bystanders. As the violence escalates, the endogroup membrane strengthens and creates a more and more filtered version of reality, more refracted selves, and a more intense reflector-negative image struggle. Eventually, a few soldiers can lead off thousands to their own deaths with no resistance. The thick fog of endoreality seems to make the enforcement of its laws inevitable, impossible to vanquish or even challenge.

It is interesting to watch the cycle of blame for creating an endogroup move from all being put on the reflectors and the negative image to all put on the endo-ideal. When the endo-ideal is given the blame for creating abusive endogroups, as is increasingly happening under both male and wealth endo-idealism, that is itself a violation of endoreality and a precursor to revolution. It is also a sign that the reflectors and negative image are acquiring a new endo-ideal, probably another transcendental one. If the previous endogroup members were escaping endoreality altogether, they would be able to see all of the contributing factors to endosocialism instead of simply assigning all blame to one individual or group.

Under industrial endo-idealism in many places, industrial work or unpaid preparation for it occupies every waking hour of a person's life from early childhood. Outside of childbirth, which can itself cause sublation or provide the means for it, women under male endo-idealism are also often isolated from all forms of exosocial expansion, including creation, ideas and external relationships. Reflectors are stripped in this way of any opportunity to create an autonomous personal membrane, or self, and designed to reflect an external endo-ideal. If they refuse the role of reflector, they are outcast and despised as a negative image. Women who are content to create work for others to hold up for public acclaim and employees who brag about the 'self-made billionaires' they work for are fully sublated by these processes. They are created in the form of reflectors.

The oppression of reflectors and negative images is always a precursor to the formation of a strong endogroup. A thin personal membrane creates a need for an endogroup. Child marriage and child rape are among the worst disruptors of the formation of an unsublated self and both are common in strong endogroups. Girls under male endo-idealism and migrants under industrial endo-idealism leave home, change their name to their husband or new culture's, worship ancestors and gods that are not their own and lose all the initial relationships that formed their self. Dissociation is the first step to creating reflectors and the institutions of the industrialized world are all set up to accomplish that. Each transcendental endogroup causes a migration from the network of the earlier self.

The establishment of self is also prevented through all the common methods of institutionalized totalitarianism. As we move out of industrial endo-idealism, work uniforms have become less common, but as we move into a global mono-empire, clothing everywhere is institutionalized ugliness and sameness. All time and thought that used to be occupied by work or school are now occupied by corporate noise as passive entertainment and bureaucracy. From cults to dictatorships, dissociative institutions, busywork, poor health, stress, fear of others, no autonomy or privacy, personal boundary violations, anonymity, existential threats and all the other commonplace methods of sublation are employed.

Those who never have their own entitlement challenged, who retain power in their first caregiving relationships and subsequent early relationships, will develop as an endo-ideal. Those from troubled homes, or those whose social class has challenged their original power at every turn, will look for a larger and more powerful endogroup. Since women and girls under male endo-idealism have been able to simply attach themselves to a more powerful man in a marriage relationship, they have not been so susceptible in the past to attraction for gangs, but were even more susceptible to religions with Great Man figures and demands for service and devotion. Men under male endo-idealism have been expected to display personal power in a romantic relationship, which they had to obtain from strong endogroups at levels which transcended caregiver circles. These men, as well as women who have been rejected as caregiver reflectors or do not live under male endo-idealism, are particularly vulnerable to the most exploitative cult and gang leaders or militias or religions which promise the most extreme power in the leader or group.

Illness makes it harder to establish strong bonds as people become more introverted and solitary with illness. People are stripped of their confidence and self esteem to weaken their membranes. Ideologies teach that everyone is lazy, evil, born with sin and cannot trust themselves or each other but need a patriarchal guide. Those outcast by immutable differences, education or wealth have more faults and weaknesses ascribed to them. Schools teach that those with better grades are better people, more trustworthy and more deserving of authority (which is frequently handed out to students with high grades) and future survival. Society teaches that the wealthy work harder, are smarter and are more benevolent.

The destruction of self leaves a person with only two options available: reflector or negative image. The fight to not be the negative image allows genocide, as each village and street tells each other that they are more peaceful, more virtuous or have better relations with the endo-ideal than their neighbours who just got taken away. The alternative, accepting that they are the same as their neighbours, would mean casting themselves as the negative image, a situation that is in opposition to the existential struggle of a reflector. They exist in opposition to the negative image. They are the good woman vs the bad woman, the respectful servant vs the impertinent servant and the peaceful protester politely requesting reform vs the radical who intends to create change. The reflector survives on the approval of the endo-ideal. Obedience is their virtue and reflection of the endo-ideal is their duty. Perversely, this behaviour increases as people are threatened by tyranny. As their personal integrity is violated continuously, they become more dependent on acceptance into the endogroup and in upholding the righteousness of the endo-ideal.

The 1990s in the Anglo / Germanic world was one of several points in history where society cast the guilt at their shortcomings towards children onto the perennial negative image, the children's mothers. (Specifically, it was a time when growing awareness of child trafficking and paedosadism by institutional authorities triggered a guilt reversal and punishment onto caregivers.) During this period, in which mothers were ordered by child development authorities to prostrate themselves to their children from birth forwards, to crawl backwards holding flash cards in front of the baby and never say *No*, mothers were also ordered to drop to their knees and make exaggerated facial expressions in front of the child while identifying the emotion they were feeling. It is no coincidence that the first entire generation of children raised as child emperors should also be the first one unable to establish enough empathic connection with their mothers to recognize her basic emotions.

The wider society has a very large influence on setting the foundation for who is the endo-ideal and who is sublated at each circle of self. There have been many instances in science and academia where a circle of researchers has tried to credit those outside and been denied by those in power, or in the music industry where artists have tried to credit those outside the preferred demographics and been ignored by the industry. States ensure that every part of the world is only recognized as another state endogroup, placing even uncontacted nations under the ownership dominion of state endo-ideals. Likewise, a woman who is trying to resist being sublated by her family is going to face extreme opposition from a wider male endo-idealist society which insists that wives and mothers be sublated. Caregiver circles are capable of reversing the endo-ideal and negative image, in theory, but pressure from wider society and pre-conditioning of negative image groups makes a reversal far less likely than the status quo.

Who is your source / authority / influence is a demand to see the endo-ideal. Members of the endo-ideal do not need to produce any higher authority. Reflectors are only recognized as reflections of the ideal, as employee / mother / daughter / wife / secretary / student / citizen. A woman who kills her children along with her suicide shocks society as it indicates that she sees the children as her reflectors, as part of herself, instead of as an external endo-ideal which she must protect at all costs. Men who kill their wives and children are so common it is not worthy of note and a ridiculous amount of news media report such stories in sympathy with the man and questioning how the murdered family failed in their duty to reflect him positively. The difference in public response is the difference in who the public perceives as the endo-ideal.

Reflectors cannot act for themselves. Women who gain the power to leave abusive relationships often attribute their new resolve to concern for the well-being of a child when concern for their own well-being did not motivate them to act. The change was a shift of their endo-ideal from their husband to their child, not a change in their reflector status. People also have often depicted themselves as putting their lives together for a romantic interest or child or church, when they would not leave their self-destructive behaviour for their own sake. These people also have simply acquired an endo-ideal, they have not formed a self.

Still, roles are assigned individually for each relationship. A woman who is sublated by her husband or mother-in-law may do the same to her child and demand reflection from that relationship. A man who is cast as the negative image in his caregiver circles may be the endo-ideal in his creation relationships. It is very common for an endo-ideal at the caregiver level to refuse to try to succeed at a higher level and for the negative image of a family to seek validation as the endo-ideal in some wider arena. Research that shows western men as more independent and Asians and women as more interdependent are just recognizing how many western men are endoselves and endo-ideals while women and Asians usually have nation and caregiver endogroups in which they act as reflector or negative image. In an exosocial world, this diversity would allow people the ability to escape destructive relationships. Sadly, wider society often blocks all avenue of escape for those outside the endo-ideal.

Sometimes reflectors are converted. In any institutions of power such as hospitals, schools, military, prisons or places of employment, all identity comes from the endo-ideal. The centre of salvation or achievement is not the self. All credit is assigned externally. The endo-ideal defines the rules and acceptable or normative behaviour. Everyone outside is various degrees of deviant and deviant is defective. They are under forced subordination, judged incessantly. If a child under child endo-idealism is well-behaved, a woman is a 'good mother' but the minute the child screams, she becomes a 'bad mother'. The child has the power to cast the mother from obedient reflector of society to the negative image, as every toddler under child endo-idealism soon learns. The reflectors are made complicit in their own judgment through acceptance of endogroup judgment and norms.

Taboos against women and other lower classes or slaves looking at those above them is a taboo against appraisal. The power to define is an endo-ideal power. The reflectors are permitted to provide no perspective. If the reflectors were given the power to define the endo-ideal, to look at the king, it would be the first step to creating their own self and casting an endo-ideal as their own negative image.

A reflector is someone whose empathic conduits are all vectored towards an external endo-ideal. A reflector can still be largely an endoself, however, and spend most of their time extracting euphoria from other reflectors and the negative image and attempting to siphon any they can from the endo-ideal. Someone with a refracted core is a different case. They don't simply vector towards the endo-ideal, their core self is replaced by the endo-ideal. This is a very advanced stage of dissociation where the individual feels numb to their own emotions and experiences emotions on behalf of their endo-ideal very vividly. In such cases, the person will empathize far more strongly, or even exclusively, with an external endo-ideal and feel the pain of their endo-ideal more acutely than pain to their individual self.

Refraction sometimes occurs as a result of extreme traumatic bonding. Symptoms of dissociation often accompany refraction, especially upon loss of the endo-ideal. Such dissociation is often accompanied by lengthy periods of memory loss and an out of body or surreal experience of life or the feeling of not belonging to their own body. The phrase *keeping body and soul together* very aptly describes the difficulty experienced by those attempting to escape suffering a refracted ideal.

Desire, to an endoself, is always for an object. The desire of someone with a refracted core is for a subject, the master, the endo-ideal, the messiah who can provide a self to those who have lost their own. The reason their own self is lost is usually due to the intense shame which is produced by any attempt to access it. This blockage, which may be imagined as an endosocial membrane around their own most intimate circle of self, inhibits or blocks their ability to form direct euphoric bonds of their own. Unlike an endoself, who is trapped within their own self, someone with a refracted core is trapped outside. Thus, they can only experience interactions vividly through another and their direct experience is muted.

Women who uphold patriarchy, or poor people who uphold billionaires, are upholding their own refracted self. Those who have adopted a refracted endo-ideal defend their own subordination because they are effectively occupied by an external self. Sometimes they receive pats on the head from the endo-ideal, such as telling them they *think like a man* or are *not like others of their ilk* and this is a source of great pride to them just as the reverse statement would be an unforgivable insult to an endo-ideal. The people who have successfully adopted a refracted core are the obedient reflectors, the subservient ones who defend the endo-ideal against any criticism, especially criticism from other reflectors.

The battered wife who attacks her would-be protector, the slave who reports on their liberator, the abused population which fights for its tyrant, are all protecting the only social membrane they have. They all need time in a protected and safe environment to create their own personal membranes and they are all vulnerable to new exploiters until they are strong again. As Niccolò Machiavelli pointed out in 1532, *"when cities or countries are accustomed to live under a prince ... they are very slow to take up arms, and a prince can gain them to himself and secure them much more easily"* [40] in comparison to those who had been accustomed to self-governance and freedom. Children in 'care' institutions are vulnerable to pimps, gangs and other abuse and exploitation. Former populations of totalitarian states become immobilized by the thought of leaving as they have built no personal membranes. These populations are ripe for recruitment into the nearest available endogroup and social media filtering has made it disastrously easy to identify and target them.

The struggle of a reflector is between not existing, or existing as the negative image, as so perfectly described by Roddy Doyle's depiction of an abused spouse in *The Woman Who Walked Into Doors*. *"There were days when I didn't exist; he saw through me and walked around me. I was invisible. There were days when I liked not existing. I closed down, stopped thinking, stopped looking...There were days when I couldn't even feel pain. They were the best ones. I could see it happening. There was no ground under me, nothing to fall to. I was able to not care. I could float. I didn't exist."* [41] A reflector will often say *I don't care*. The alternative to not caring or feeling is the intense pain of the negative image.

Reflectors spend their lives avoiding the abyss of the negative image. This fear prevents most reflectors from discovering that a plummet into the abyss can bring both freedom and strength. As Clarice Lispector wrote, *"It is because I dove into the abyss that I am beginning to love the abyss I am made of."*[42] Freedom really is nothing left to lose, as Janis Joplin sang after her own jump into the abyss. Freedom is difficult to perceive from the position of a reflector as they tend to be focused on the negative image abyss and may, especially if they have a refracted core, have as much difficulty in experiencing the perspective of others as the endo-ideal whose perspective they reflect.

While they may transfer allegiance, it is much more difficult for a reflector to form their own endogroup than it is for a negative image. In addition to a lack of identity, reflectors have additional difficulties in creating an exceptional myth. Any attempt to claim exceptionalism is forestalled by their relinquishment of ownership and credit. Any attempt to claim victimhood will be easily rebutted by their own complicity in upholding the structure of tyranny and their victimization of the negative image.

Reflectors must be quiet, polite, smile a lot, always signal that they are not a threat. This compliance can look a lot like complicity, to both outsiders and themselves. Any failure to reflect will immediately cast them as the negative image, at which point they will be far more blamed for perceived complicity than the endo-ideal themselves is. If their old rivals, the negative image, have succeeded in establishing their own endogroup, they will very likely become the primary enemy of that endogroup, not the endo-ideal which subjugated them both.

This can also be a strength, however. Perceived complicity can provide reflectors with real guilt to drive them forward to seek balance through exosocial interactions. They also have not much hope of establishing an endogroup of their own, so are more likely to avoid the revolutionary endogroup trap that is set for the negative image. They are, however, extremely likely to simply transfer reflection to a new revolutionary endogroup in an attempt to make amends for complicity in the former one.

Subjects and objects

There is not much to be got anywhere in the world. It is filled with misery and pain; and if a man escapes these, boredom lies in wait for him at every corner. Nay more; it is evil which generally has the upper hand, and folly makes the most noise. Fate is cruel, and mankind is pitiable. Arthur Schopenhauer, *The Wisdom of Life*

It is impossible to discuss the self today, or the modern endo-ideal, without a glance back at the Germanic endo-ideals of philosophy and science. These men, such as the embittered and hate-filled Schopenhauer, established the global endoreality we have all been living in for the last several centuries.

In particular, Hegel, who took Kant and Hume's ideas of subjective reality and carried forward the logical implications for establishment of self, has defined how we define ourselves. Based on Kant, Hegel asserted that *"self-consciousness ... exists only as a recognized being" and "First, it has lost itself, for it is to be found as an other essence. Second, it has thereby sublated that other, for it also does not see the other as the essence but rather sees itself in the other."*[43] This is a logical step in the sequence of Germanic thought which leads directly through to Marx, Heidegger, Nietzsche, Freud, de Beauvoir, Sartre, Fanon, Foucault and nearly every extremely influential western philosopher or theorist since. It is hard to find any part of the emerging creation of social sciences, or modern academia generally, that did not have its roots well-soaked in Hegel.

Some may wonder why, in the age of neuroscience and quantum physics, anyone is still bothering to rebut the thoughts from the 17th to early 20th centuries. The reason is, it is impossible for anyone, even neuroscientists and quantum physicists, to formulate thought today without using the words and frameworks established by these men. The DSM[1] still has collections of symptoms which look a lot like Freud's neurosis, including one called narcissistic personality disorder, nazis are still reading Nietzsche and protesters are still demanding redistribution of capital. The United States, home of the post-Germanic endo-ideal, has created an entire academic and political tradition based on the misinterpretation and misuse of Hegel. If Newton is the tap root of western thought, then Kant and Hegel are the trunk. Whether or not the tree has rot, or has been pruned in awkward angles, is still worth examining.

In particular, it is worth examining the nature of those selves who applied their view of the self to all of humanity and were so eagerly endorsed as the authorities. As is to be expected of any person who looks at their own condition and believes they have discovered a universal truth, these thinkers were, without exception, the endo-ideal. As is also typical, they all appear to have strong endoself

1 Diagnostic and Statistical Manual of Mental Disorders (DSM–5).

tendencies. This is most apparent in their unanimous agreement of the subject-object nature of interactions. Although studies have clearly shown the correlation between power and viewing others as objects[44], this rarified and myopic view is still the authoritative view of the universal condition which created the institutions we live under.

Since an endoself has damaged euphoric conduits, the interaction itself is of no interest to them. This leads to their inability to view interactions in terms other than that of Hegel's master-slave struggle and sublation into a larger whole. They can only access euphoria through possession, by obtaining secondary euphoria through the absorption and destruction of their desired object. This extremely unsatisfactory existence, reminiscent of the curses of Tantalus and Midas, explains the other traits shared unanimously by the thinkers above. Their outlook on life is of an existence of horror, of frustration, bitterness, and ultimately, futility. These are the people whose viewpoints we have allowed to define our reality and our existence.

Those of the thinkers above who do not fully occupy an endo-ideal position are the French writers who have missed their craved endo-ideal position by one degree. De Beauvoir was a woman. Fanon was viewed as black. Foucault was viewed as homosexual. All were denied the endo-ideal position by one aspect, but all were trapped in the dance of power, or Hegel's master-slave struggle. They all provide the same image of the fully endo-ideal, German, academic man. They simply view it from a reflector position, each as a specific planet orbiting the sun and craving its power, oblivious to all other planets, much less the universe. Kant's ideas, which he compared to a Copernican revolution, have yet to bring us any understanding of space outside his solar system or the forces which govern it.

Those outside the endo-ideal can only define themselves in relation to the endo-ideal or reflect the endo-ideal. Women can talk about their relationship with the endo-ideal from a feminist perspective. Indigenous people can talk about their relationship to the endo-ideal from an anti-colonialist perspective. Anyone can reflect the endo-ideal. But neither indigenous people nor women are permitted to define universal truth. Philosophy, economy, governance, all the universal truths in the world can only be presented from the endo-ideal perspective. All the feminist critique and cultural critique in the world does no more than reflect the positions of the endo-ideal from a reflector or negative image perspective.

What this means for the world is we have thoroughly examined the nature of endosocialism and are, or ought to be, fully cognizant of the nature of the endo-ideal and their reflectors and negative image. These are presented as the universal human condition and compose the endoreality we live within. This has created the structure of power we live under. The glaring twin spotlights of this struggle conceal both the darkness without and the universal reality outside the endoreality, but we must understand what we are presented with before we can find what we are missing.

If, as Hegel says, *"It is in confronting an other that the I is itself"*,[43] then a rejection or lack of acknowledgement by the other may be seen as an existential threat to establishing a self. Those with an insatiable need for validation will initiate continual power struggles with anyone they meet. There are many strategies employed by endoselves and endogroups in order to ensure their rivals are depleted and will lose the confrontations they initiate. This creation of unequal force is the secret to power, as everyone from cult leaders to masculinist 'pick up artists' have discovered. As Foucault agreed, and credited Hegel as being the first to say, *"Power is essentially that which represses."*[45] To be more specific than either of them, power is the energy gained from an interaction of unequal force. With no power struggle, the endo-ideal ceases to exist. This is why revolution strengthens power structures and resistance starves them.

In Hegel's slightly convoluted idea, there is a confrontation between two selves when they meet. The one who subjugates themselves he calls the slave, or bondsman, and the one who strives for autonomy is the master, or lord. These words are usually translated as master and slave, and the passage is known as the master-slave dialectic, but bondsman is a more accurate term in depicting the fact that the subjugated self is held in magical bondage through the creation of an expanded self. Hegel expands his idea of recognition of self as negation of the other with a discussion of the self-sufficiency of self consciousness and concludes that while the bondsman has plenty of other avenues open to achieving self-actualization, the lord has none. Expressed using the ideas of this book and *Abstracting Divinity*, Hegel essentially agrees that while the slave has access to primary euphoria from myriad sources, including discovery and creation, the master has made himself forever dependant on reflection, or secondary euphoria obtained by subjugation of others. (Hegel doesn't say this but his ideas are roughly compatible.)

If there is no self-identity without recognition from the other, this is far more true for an endo-ideal. While it is possible to be a member of many groups and have a large number of relationships and activities with which to establish your self, a king with no subjects is not a king. Neither is anyone rich if no one is poor, anyone a master if no one is a slave, or anyone white if no one is black. In addition, no one is German if no one is not German, no one is chosen by God if all are chosen by God and Bashar Assad is not a president without a country. For those who have established themselves as the endo-ideals, a weakening of the group membrane, challenge to endo-identity or endoreality, or decreased reflection, are existential threats to their self. Every genocidal dictator or person that murders their spouse and children when they threaten to leave is a new reminder of how seriously that threat is felt by the endo-ideal. Murder is only a reasonable response to what is perceived as a threat of murder.

The endo-ideal refuses to recognize the self of the other, or in other words, they repress and subjugate the other. This is very important to understanding the outlook of a person in the endo-ideal position. The only reality they recognize is theirs, the only self they recognize is theirs and the only ownership they recognize is theirs. The endo-ideal does not view their endogroup as a society with a constantly mutating set of relationships and interactions with each other. It views them as a population, the possession of the endo-ideal, with interactions which should only occur under strict involvement and management by the endo-ideal. As all endoreality is the reality for the entire group, this outlook is shared by the reflectors and negative image who are victimized by it.

Hegel's description, which he considered universal, defines an endoself, which is an object incapable of empathic interaction. Hegel defines the other as the antithesis of the self, which is subject-object recognition. His theory does not apply outside of endoreality. Since an exoself is not a subject or an object but a cluster of interactions, exosocial recognition happens on an interactional basis. Because the exoself is a cluster of interactions in which others are necessarily an integral part, the exoself includes the other. It cannot, therefore, be in opposition to, or the negation of the other. Neither does it require a negative image, or an object for its subject. In an interaction, both the action and reaction are included and form a part of each self involved.

Subjects and objects are a very unique part of endoreality. In an exosocial world, the drive towards exosocial expansion is a drive to create euphoric connections. In these connections, a subject does not simply view an object. There is a mutual euphoric connection. For example, when a person sees their home after a long and hard day outside or years of absence, the home fills them with euphoria. The emotional response is a sign of a euphoric connection between what would otherwise be a subject and object. The same response can be felt when viewing or experiencing art, when playing a guitar that belonged to a beloved friend or family member, when smelling a flower that grew in a family garden and so on. These responses are not subject and object encounters. They are euphoric interactions. They create the conduits that need to be established and maintained for a healthy, exosocial membrane. In an exosocial person, existence is marked by an excitement caused by continual seeking of these moments of beauty and connection.

In an endosocial person, the drive to exosocial expansion is inhibited or blocked. The euphoric attraction that stimulates a euphoric interaction is replaced by a desire to possess what is seen as an external object. Once the object is possessed, the frustration and rage caused by a denial of euphoric interaction will cause the endoself to destroy the object. The cycle of object craving, attainment and destruction will spiral in increasing frustration. Lacan's *objet petit a* describes the insatiable craving of the endoself for objects to consume and the immediate loss of the object upon its attainment. According to Lacan,*"There is something in you I like more than yourself. Therefore I must destroy you"* or *"I love you, but, because inexplicably I love in you something more than you - the object petit a - I mutilate you."* The disappointment of the endoself on attainment of an object is expressed by Lacan as *"I give myself to you . . . but this gift of my person . . . is changed inexplicably into a gift of shit."*[46]

This is the emptiness behind the endless consumerism and destruction of the endoself, presented by generations of endoselves as the inevitable and universal human condition. This is the farmer who killed the goose who laid him a golden egg every day and it is every industrialist destroying the earth they live on. It is not a universal state, but thanks to the power of such theorists to define endoreality, it is the authoritative, governing ideology. This ideology is not even an accurate depiction of the state the theorists themselves were experiencing.

The endoself is capable of obtaining secondary euphoria through a one-way, predatory connection with others. They are not capable or obtaining primary euphoria through balanced interactions. Vindictive punishment of others is their hallmark. To any endoself, everyone is an enemy outsider whose existence poses an existential threat to themselves. There is no possibility of ever being subservient enough to earn their gratitude or loving enough to earn their empathy. In fact, there is no possibility of being perfect enough to cause them to refrain from seizing every opportunity to harm you. Even the thought of self-preservation is not enough to overcome the desire of the endoself to cause harm to their own euphoric sources. While they may often appear loving, kind and concerned with the group well-being, the amount of 'accidents' they arrange for their spouse, children, parents, employees, subjects or others always gives their hatred away. The endoself often rejects this aspect of themselves and prefers to think of their inflicted torment as 'accidents' or 'necessary for the greater good'. If they are an endo-ideal, their perspective is naturally reflected as a group reality, but it never withstands impartial examination in universal reality.

The endoself does exist, very much as Hegel described, and so does the endogroup. The endo-ideal became a subject through the reflection of another and the reflectors and negative image became objects through their possession by another. The subject – object transaction works to cast a membrane over the group and change the nature of the self, from a collection of interactions to an object, with an endo-ideal subject. As Weber pointed out, the creation of an endogroup is a magical act (which is why it was and is performed using magical rites) in that it transforms the nature of those trapped within it. Those trapped within an endogroup become objects and subjects and thus become mortal and faced with an ultimate existential demise. Their drive towards exosocial expansion is replaced with existential dread and a desperation for survival, channelled into an endless lust for secondary euphoria. The many, many stories around the world detailing a lust for power and possession which leads to the death of the immortal soul are good allegories for what happens to those who attempt to achieve immortality through possession of others.

Since all endogroup perspective is from the endo-ideal, those outside the endo-ideal appear only as externally viewed or experienced, judged on their appearance and how they make others feel. The endo-ideal are judged on their own feelings. Women under male endo-idealism set goals based on their appearance or their roles, to be a better mother, daughter, wife, while men set goals to improve their own experience of life, to have a better wife, a bigger yacht, or more respect. In male endo-idealism, an attractive woman is one who can be absorbed to the glory of the man, her ideas, virtue, and beauty all adding to his own virtue through the laws of endo-ideal ownership. An attractive man is one who can be reflected to the glory of the woman, who will become the famous Tolstoy if she spends enough nights writing manuscripts out by candlelight or the great Einstein if she tutors him through school and does all 'his' math. Under wealth endo-idealism the same relationship plays out between an employee and business owner. In filial relationships, the parent absorbs the child, in other groups it is elders or shamans. In endogroups, the endo-ideal is the subject and the rest are the objects.

No object, and no self, can exist, or can be proven to exist, except as an interaction. Objects are experienced visually through the displacement and reflection of light. They are experienced kinetically as matter resisting matter. They are experienced auditorily as sound waves. An external self is experienced through shared empathic conduits.

If a person can only exist in space and time, then a person can only be an action, as only an action can move through time. That act must also be an interaction to be externally recognized as a self. If that self is to be known in different times and spaces, it must be a cluster of interactions. The exoself is not recognized, it is experienced. Hegel's synthesis is already present in every interaction, as an action and reaction. The endoself exists only through external recognition. The exoself exists through its effects on others, through euphoric transfer and empathic connection. The endoself is mortal and will cease to exist when its reflection ceases. The exoself is immortal and will always exist as a part of every self it interacted with. The interactions that make up an exoself will always exist in the time and space they occurred in. The endoself is seized with constant existential dread while the exoself follows an ever-expanding force.

An endoself lives in a permanent hell through the fear of existential threat and the chronic anxiety which accompanies mortality. For an endoself, being and appearing are the same. They cannot exist without reflection. They are, therefore, the slave of their slaves, as Hegel pointed out. Complete freedom is not mastery, after all[47]. Borders create a prison for oneself and mastery is dependence. Like the occult demons who can only appear and maintain power within an unbroken circle, any weakening of the group membrane is a loss of power and life to the endo-ideal. Ironically, the experiential self is less dependent on others than the reflected self.

An endoself is never reconciled to their body mortality as their self is stuck in their body. They will fight mortality to ridiculous extremes. A world given over to prolonging the lives of a few old men while billions suffer is a picture of the exceptionalism and blocked growth of an endoself. This entitlement is normalized and institutionalized by the trade economy and property ownership and their enforcement. Hegelian thought, as well as the similar ends arrived at through Confucian and other forms of filiality, do not describe universal truth. All ought to be called endo-idealism, or endosocialism when the reflector or negative image perspective is considered, as they describes human relations solely within the extremely filtered reality of the endogroup. Endo-idealism is the basis of modern governance and economics. The only alternatives presented are within the paradigm of endosocialism as that is what is currently accepted as universal truth.

Endosocialism is the natural home of the endoself, so not only hierarchy, but cruelty and exploitation are inherent in the structure and increasingly encouraged in their own right. As Hegel pointed out, existential struggle is the only possible relationship within a subject-object paradigm. As discussed further in *Great Men, Commoners, Witches and Wretches*, power requires action of unequal force. It is never inert and never benevolent for long. If interactions are painful and unbalanced, they may be blocked. If enough of these euphoric conduits are blocked, the self becomes contained in an impermeable membrane. If the unbalanced interactions continue, the self with less power will be subsumed into the more powerful self. The self with more power (Hegel's lord or master) will then attempt to block all contact between its prey and outside sources of euphoria so that every unblocked transaction they are capable of is a transaction with the master-predator. In this way, the weaker self is consumed.

While parts of Hegelianism are parallel to the thought presented here, there is also much disagreement, primarily around the inevitability of the struggle for subjugation and existential angst. These are the ideas behind the *war of all against all* thought which pervades Germanic and many other streams of philosophy and justifies the supposed need for subjugation to a state to control supposedly natural impulses. The primary difference here stems from the fact that Hegel (following Kant's line of reasoning) felt that self-actualization was found in external recognition and the opinion put forth here is that the self is created by direct and uninhibited access to euphoric conduits. Following from this, Hegel also feels that the goal in subjugation is to obtain reflection and is universal, and here it is suggested that the goal is to obtain secondary euphoria, and is only by those who are unable or unwilling to obtain primary euphoria.

Hegel's conclusions lead to the inevitability of endless power struggle and natural masters and slaves, and here the alternative to endless struggle is to allow development of healthy, permeable membranes and exosocial expansion and to resist interactions of unequal force, or power. To an exoself, there is no battle to the death as Hegel and Fichte describe the meeting of two selves. There is simply the establishment of a euphoric bond and each self becomes a small part of the other. This is possible without sublation because each self is not an indivisible object but a cluster of events.

In exosocial development, thought is neither the first, nor the most important sign of self; empathy and euphoria are. Without the empathy and euphoric bond which attracts every newborn mammal to their mother, none would survive. It is our knowledge and experience of empathy and euphoria that we ought to examine in search of the nature of exosocial knowledge, not objects. We can prove the existence of anything we share a euphoric connection with by the damage to our self if they are lost and we can prove that damage through our own experience of pain. We can also prove the existence of things outside ourselves by our attraction to or repulsion from them and their ability to change or affect aspects of our self. If a self is a composite of interactions, the other selves within these interactions are a part of the self, which explains the pain felt when they are lost. This pain is not experienced by an endoself.

An endoself cannot enjoy objects they do not possess They may covet their neighbour's couch but until they possess it, they do not enjoy it. In fact, they hate it. As all objects they possess become part of their own endoself, so do all objects they do not possess become part of a rival endogroup or negative image. Ownership is a result of the desire of the endoself to make objects a part of their self. Once an object is joined to the self, it acquires higher subjective value, a well-known phenomenon often exploited by marketers who suggest potential customers picture themselves owning an object.

As in all parts of social group formation, the internet has had many effects on traditional subject-object relationships. There has been a large change on social media in the last decade or so, from subject voyeurism to object display. By objectifying themselves, the objects have seized the endo-ideal position and demanded reflection from the viewers. The former subjects have become the reflective objects and the former objects are now the endo-ideal subjects. The right to define decides who is the subject. The pre-2015 revenge porn and creep shots that filled the internet and created the voyeuristic porn industry is replaced by social media where the porn actor is the creator and idealized subject. The self-objectified subject is a growing phenomenon as endogroups disappear in favour of endoselves. This requires a new examination of what porn is and what its effects are since the objectification has been reversed.

Conjunct to the rise of auto-objectification in pornography has been the rise of the massive global industry of fully sublated victims of trafficking, drugs and ever-younger children whose torment has replaced much of earlier porn. If it was ever unclear that a large subset of porn was primarily marketing sublation, not sex, it is increasingly impossible to ignore.

The new auto-objects are, like Sartre's masochists, trapped in a paradox. As Sartre pointed out in *Being and Nothingness*[48], as soon as the masochist orders another person to objectify them, they become the subject and objectify the other. Any masochist who pays or coerces others to degrade them is still degrading and controlling the other, so no masochist can ever be sublated by the process. It is unlikely that a masochist can be said to exist under these terms, or, if they do exist, they will never be fulfilled. As Hegel said, in sublating the other they found their own self, so self-sublation is impossible.

In any case, the new auto-objects tend to display all the characteristics of both an endo-ideal and an endoself. The populations where they are most obvious are on social media, probably because it is designed for auto-objectification. With its forced self-identification in terms of avatar and name selection, image manufacture and staged, performative quality of communication, social media may even be considered to be making auto-objectification compulsory. Auto-objectification may also be more prevalent among all endo-ideals and endoself populations. Certainly celebrities, politicians and self-proclaimed thought leaders all gravitate to such auto-objectifying social media platforms.

It is worth further examination into whether people who begin activity on social media with a dominant tendency to act as reflectors or the negative image of others, transition into auto-objectification over time. It would also be very interesting to examine whether such a transition carries over into real life interactions, as this seems to be the case[49] and to what extent this is related to the relative importance of the social media endogroup. A significant factor to be considered is whether there is something in electronic exposure in itself which causes the development of an endoself which could be the precursor to auto-objectification or, conversely, whether an endoself gravitates to electronics._Whether social media formed its population or vice versa, the dominant preoccupation on most platforms appears to be the shaping of an idealized self, or auto-objectification.

The role of social media in creating auto-objects may not be seen as a concern in a culture which has devoted itself to encouraging development of endoselves and endo-ideals. Indeed, auto-objectification may be a very liberating process for those trapped in reflector or negative image roles. However, the rarity of exosocial interaction in the design of social media must be a concern for anyone who sees a healthy self as an interactional, experiential drive instead of a subject or object. The only solely online interactions that were once exosocial were those conducted anonymously and an increasing effort has been made to fully eradicate such interactions.

Hegel was hardly the first western theorist to depict life as a struggle for dominance. Thomas Hobbes was famous for writing just that in the *Leviathan* in 1651, and many others have proposed the same before and since. It is Hegel, however, whose timely treatises inspired generations of academics who founded social sciences and institutions in emulation of his model. In order to progress, it is necessary to look back at this Hegelian thought, or thought which has been justified through the use and misuse of Hegel. If people who meet are in instant and inevitable struggle, what purpose would this serve? If this basic premise is false, then the foundation stone of almost all of the founding German academic men, and the French writers reacting to them, and very nearly the complete body of academic thought in the social sciences of the United States, is sand. This thought is underlying every modern institution created in the last two centuries, globally.

What if Hegel simply described an exceptional circumstance which was neither universal nor optimal for daily life? What if its daily implementation was disastrous? Imprisonment, as one example, punishes the exosocial self while preventing interaction and expansion necessary to develop an exoself. Economics enforces the structure and nature of endogroups, as does representative government, history writes exceptional myths and justice systems enforce the laws of endoreality. We need historians, archaeologists, anthropologists and others who are willing to look in places outside of endo-idealism before we can claim knowledge of any universal social truths based on the perspective of endo-ideals and endoselves.

Alternatively, we could look at the present. The abstractions of the trade economy have allowed those closest to the endo-ideal to live in a simulated environment which mimics a state of autonomy. This group is dependent on neither social approval nor an endogroup membrane. This group of people, equipped with powerful passports and full bank accounts, have increasingly shown tendencies to exosocial expansion which neither dominates nor allows itself to be dominated. This is an artificial result of sufficient money and power to simulate unlimited social approval, but it is nevertheless valuable insight. Even outside of this demographic, people are increasingly valuing experiences over objects, another sign of the growth of an experiential exoself.

If these exosocial people are at least partly able to provide a good model for development, how would we create a structure of institutions which enable this type of development without the exploitative nature of trade and passports? And what would be the role and nature of families, nations and communities? What would the world look like if it were based on the freedom of balanced interactions and allowing uninhibited exosocial expansion instead of the world of Hegel's master-slave sublation and Lacan's possession-destruction desire? It is the examination of these questions which this series will attempt.

The negative image

When you light a candle, you also cast a shadow. Ursula K. Le Guin, *A Wizard of Earthsea*

In Hegel's terms, identity is the identity of identity and non-identity.[50] For an identity to exist, its negative image must also exist. In carving David, Michaelangelo also created the scrapings that were not David.

The negative image has externalized the endo-ideal and internalized the negative image. As two bodies experiencing one reality from one perspective, both the endo-ideal and the negative image uphold the endo-ideal and oppress the negative image. It is humiliating for the endo-ideal to be referred to as the negative image but a compliment in reverse. The endo-ideal defines what it is to be human and each deviation is progressively more dehumanized. The endo-ideal is the normative model which all others are measured against.

While the endo-ideal defines the negative image, the endo-ideal is never the sole source of power in the endogroup. The negative image may force their own definition by consistently refusing opportunities to succeed or receive credit, reward or any self-affirming attention and consistently behaving in a manner which has been defined as negative. Just as reflectors and the endo-ideal support endoreality, so do the negative image. The entire endogroup polices everyone's behaviour, including their own, to ensure they all play the roles assigned to them. In the negative image this has many names, such as internalized oppression, but it is simply the same support for group endoreality that everyone in the endogroup supports.

In endo-idealism, the endo-ideal have the power to define themselves and to define the negative image. If the poor could refuse to be poor, the wealthy could not be wealthy. Neither the positive nor the negative space can exist without the other. However, the nature of endoreality denies the negative image the ability to define. The punishment for going against endoreality is external punishment through shunning and internal punishment through the cognitive dissonance that arises from challenging endoreality. Both can be overwhelming threats to a person already depleted and with no strong self of their own or external euphoric conduits.

Endoreality is always a binary reality. It consists of the endo-ideal, which incorporates the sublated reflectors, and everything else cast into the negative image, as an indistinguishable mass. As long as it does not acquire an endo-ideal of its own, the negative image exists as a passive lump. The individuality of the negative image is denied. They live and die as big round numbers, as populations and demographics, and as the rejections of the endo-ideal. *The Poor, The Elderly, The Homeless:* these adjectives which have become nouns are all negative images which cannot yet act as an endogroup. Their resistance is not romanticized with an exceptional myth, their struggle and oppression is not named as a civil war, they have no reflectors and they have no external endo-ideal validation.

Liberation that works would restore or create an exosocial structure. Instead, most efforts at liberation simply establish a new endo-ideal with a new identity which is almost always the negative image identity established for the group during ostracization. The picture of the negative image is the silhouette of the endo-ideal. The identity of the negative image upholds the endo-ideal and is still trapped within the endoreality. It is not enough to simply address the endo-ideal and starve the endo-ideal of reflection. As long as there is a symbiotic need between the negative image and the endo-ideal, they will continue to recreate each other.

The most noticeable difference between the negative image and reflectors is that the negative image is always given a name. Reflectors never have a name of their own. All of their experiences and ambitions are subsumed into the endo-ideal, as the identity of all of America was subsumed into the United States, and the identity of women was once subsumed into man. When the world speaks of America, they do not mean Bolivia or Belize, and neither are Bolivia or Belize asked for their opinion. Non-ideal countries are represented as Victorian children, seen but not heard.

In contrast, Africa is named, but exists as an indiscriminate mass, where vast diversity is all melded together into one word. Africa, the birth mother of all humanity, has an identity but it is only as the negative image.

From the Sahara Desert to the Kilimanjaro, from M'Hamid to Lagos, every region or state in Africa is frequently called simply 'Africa', with no individuation or recognition of the immense diversity between and within the 54 states. This melding of the negative image into one mass, along with the erasure of reflectors, is the method used by endogroups to create an artificial binary reality.

Some people in the U.S. have recently gone from ignoring all the other 34 countries in America as simply their identity-less reflectors to casting them as their negative image, still as one indistinguishable mass. A banner on Fox News on March 2019 was ridiculed for calling El Salvador, Guatamala and Honduras *"three Mexican countries"*[51] but it has always been a source of pride for some in the United States to not be able to distinguish between outsiders. People south of their border have often been depicted by people in the U.S. as all *speaking Mexican*. The inability to distinguish between outsiders is a mark of the endo-ideal and therefore a point of pride for those who aspire to be the endo-ideal. When some in the U.S. ceased calling the rest of America nothing and started calling them Mexicans, they signalled that they had stopped considering them as obedient reflectors and started considering them the negative image.

The negative image has attained the first step to becoming its own endogroup, through their possession of an endo-identity. They could be conceptualized in an image, even if it was the negative image of another. This identity came from the endo-ideal, however, and any attempt to establish that identity as a tool of liberation will only reinforce the former endo-ideal.

Without an endo-ideal, their identity is simply a curse. Since only the endo-ideal may define endoreality, any revolutionary endo-identity must come from an endo-ideal. Since a negative image is externally defined, no negative image can self-identify as the negative image without becoming an endo-ideal. This is why new endogroups are usually formed from various intelligentsia endo-ideal revolutionaries, from a migratory endo-ideal or the endo-ideal of other endogroups who are attempting to sabotage the current endo-ideal. The presence of an endo-identity tends to attract migratory endo-ideals and it is the first step to revolution and civil war, as opposed to genocide.

- *An endo-ideal defines, and in so doing they are the endo-ideal.*
- *A negative image is a negative image if an endo-ideal defines them as a negative image.*
- *An endo-ideal is a negative image if they define themselves as a negative image.*

This triptych contains a paradox. An endo-ideal can define themselves, but once they define themselves as a negative image they can no longer define themselves. They must define themselves and demand reflection as a negative image, from the negative image, an ability that makes them no longer a negative image. In order to resolve this, they must use the endo-identity of the negative image to create an endo-ideal who retains the ability to define themselves. In this process, the negative image becomes their own endogroup with their own negative image and reflectors from within the population they are defining themselves as.

Since a negative image is externally defined, no one can self-identify as the negative image without becoming an endo-ideal. Sublation is the external occupation of ownership of the innermost circles of self. Self-sublation is impossible and self-oppression is impossible.

Migratory endo-ideals are often welcomed by the negative image due to their power to create an endogroup and due to the promotion of the supportive negative image to reflectors. This process always creates a schism between those of the negative image that accept the migratory endo-ideal and benefit from their new position as reflectors and those that reject the new endo-ideal and have their former equals turned against them in a new reflector-negative image struggle. The reflector-negative image struggle is the primary struggle within an endogroup. It is of paramount importance to those outside the endo-ideal to avoid the pain of guilt transference and punishment suffered by the negative image. This struggle is very useful to the endo-ideal, both in dividing the rest of the population and in depicting this struggle as the source of oppression. The reflector-negative image struggle allows the endo-ideal to occupy the position of necessary authority, peacekeeper and judge.

The defining feature of the negative image is that they are not the endo-ideal. They may be opposite each other in every way, they may be far more like the endo-ideal than each other, but they will always be defined as an indistinguishable mass. Women and children are one and the same under male endo-idealism, and both are only acceptable when silent and contained. Well-meaning people born in the endo-ideal image who attempt to defend or represent oppressed people are usually still incapable of distinguishing between individuals or ideas in the negative image. They will insist that anti-state anarchists have *solidarity* with totalitarian statist communists and order feminists who defined gender and patriarchy as the structure of their oppression to be *intersectional* with genderists and patriarchal ideology.

Women under male endo-idealism are given the task of solving the relationships with everyone and everything exploited by the endo-ideal, from the environment to children to poverty, all addressed, if they are addressed at all, in one lump referred to as *the opposition* or *feminism*. All human rights have traditionally been considered women's issues up to the point when they become an industry with an endo-ideal. The result is that even something as universal as a demand for clean drinking water is depicted as opposition to the endo-ideal and not something that ought to be supported by any endo-ideal. If women are the negative image and they are lumped in with children and health, then a proper endo-ideal must despise and work against children and health.

Manichean binaries are not a realistic basis of classifying the diversity of people on earth. They are created from the endoreality which sees only the endo-ideal and its negative image. If there is man, all else must be woman. If there is good, all else must be evil. If there is white, all else must be black.

Once, when words were recognized as magical, a person would be cursed, and thereafter they would be referred to as some form of *the accursed one* which recognized and accepted their shunned status. Likewise, people were outcast by having their names no longer spoken and their likeness or photographs banished. Today, words and images are no longer recognized as magical and no one admits they are used for shunning, but the effect is the same.

An endogroup is a magic circle in which words have the magical effect of creating reality, at least within the circle. The importance of name-calling is to cast someone as the negative image. Group solidarity may cause people to defend another member of their group, but that solidarity disappears when they are called a different name. As soon as someone becomes *The Poor, The Homeless, The Disabled* or *A Single Mom,* they belong to a separate group and are no longer entitled to wider group solidarity. Furthermore, they are the negative image of the obedient reflectors, portrayed as *The Honest Hardworking Man* or *The Taxpayer*. As the negative image, they are targets for abuse.

As soon as someone is called a name during an argument, they are identified as part of a separate group which then can be cast as the negative image. In an endogroup, it is far more effective for an endo-ideal to call someone a derogatory name than to attempt to discuss their arguments, as debating their arguments validates their right to an opinion and identifies them as an endo-ideal. Those disagreeing with the endo-ideal are already advertising their status as the negative image simply through their disagreement. This may be referred to by onlookers as objections to their *tone* or *disrespect* but it is simply the act of disagreeing with endoreality as defined by the endo-ideal which is causing discomfort. The laws of endoreality dictate that the endo-ideal is always correct, so any opposition, especially an effective one, is breaking the law and threatening the entire endogroup..

All the endo-ideal has to do is trigger additional associations of their opponent with outcast groups to win the crowd's support. Their opponent has the far more difficult task of removing the endofilters that are rejecting everything they say before they even say it. If the endo-ideal rejects that method and debates points, they are recognizing their opponent as a member of the endo-ideal who has a right to debate and define reality. This is why people with ostracized beliefs, such as paedosadists and white supremacists, are so fixated on acquiring opportunities to debate with possible converts. The inclusion in debate, in itself, facilitates their entry into mainstream society.

In 2015, Volkswagon produced an ad entitled, *"Three Old Wives Talk Dirty."* This ad portrayed a demeaning caricature of three old women to discredit the supposed *old wives' tales* that diesel produced heavy pollution. According to a 2015 interview, Pete Favat, chief creative officer of Deutsch North America *"believes that the commercials work best when a young, good-looking man is the counterbalance for the ads."*[52] This is Endosocialism 101. To defend a bad argument, or no argument, cast the protagonist as the endo-ideal and their opponents as the negative image and the public's endofilters will do the rest. The same derisive *your mom* casting has been used by advertising, especially in technology and other masculinist fields, since its inception. An ad of only a few seconds does not present arguments. It simply associates an idea or product with an endogroup role and endofilters do all the work.

This ad ran during a period when Volkswagon was producing up to 80 times the allowable rate of pollution and cheating on pollution tests. Like a person who cannot lie without moving their hand to their mouth or face, many people cannot commit acts which bring them guilt without transferring guilt for the same act to a negative image. An endo-ideal will very often address their own guilt through this transfer and the endgroup will very often then consider the topic dealt with, despite the fact that the wrong person is accused and punished. Despite the subsequent proof and admission that Volkswagon was lying, it is still 'old wives' and environmentalists who are discredited.

This automatic transfer of guilt to the negative image is useful to the endo-ideal in other ways. Proposed laws are almost always associated with negative images by propagandists who want to implement tools to crush opposition. Some are even named after people, especially in the U.S. A public that is unable to think of a principle without aligning it to an endo-ideal or negative image is a public trapped in a strong endoreality.

The negative image have internalized guilt and do not feel they are worthy of escape. The drive to unnecessary self-martyrdom, inexplicable to those outside endoreality, is a symptom of this overwhelming guilt and the need to balance it. They, like everyone else in endoreality, have also internalized the ownership of the endo-ideal. If you compliment a person cast as the negative image, they will deflect, reject the compliment for them and transfer it to someone else, usually an endo-ideal.

Endogroups will never produce equity or social equivalence because endosocial individuals will always prioritize the endo-ideal over others. Rational choice theories depend on the perspective of the individual's self, which is often not found within the individual but resides in an external endo-ideal. Endogroup structures make it impossible for police and justice systems to defend the interests of the negative image against the endo-ideal. Rational choice theories were created by the endo-ideal, from the perspective of the endo-ideal. They were later rationalized by the endo-ideal according to the laws of endoreality which explained that people support billionaires and kings ahead of themselves because benefits sometimes trickle down. Benefits in an endogroup follow a centripetal force. They do not trickle down, they siphon up, and there has never been a time when this was not evident. Analysis which produced such claims was itself clouded by the laws of endoreality which attribute virtue to the endo-ideal.

Since empathic conduits in an endogroup are directed towards the endo-ideal, for empathy to exist, the victim must be someone the observer recognizes as a member of the endo-ideal. At the very least, the victim must not be a member of the negative image, to whom all guilt is attributed. A man may not feel the need to reject a man who rapes a woman but may react violently if the same person rapes a man. The same revulsion may not be felt against the rapists of women or children as they carry no threat to male endo-ideals. People who threaten corporations and governments are called terrorists and receive international response, but people who rape and murder children are depicted as victims of a sexual orientation which just needs understanding, even when they make up the world's largest organized criminal industry. The easiest way to convince people to allow atrocities is to convince them that the victims are not a part of their endo-ideal. If the victims are successfully portrayed as the negative image, they will be assigned the guilt for their own victimhood.

Men kill dark women, or light women, or indigenous women, or women who have sex, or women who won't have sex, or women who fail to uphold patriarchy or women who fail to intersectionalize their feminism obediently enough. This is why the terms *bitch, slut, whore, feminaz*i, etc., and racial curses are important. They indicate that a woman's behaviour or status have opened her up to shunning and no one, not even *good* women, should defend her when she is killed. Men also kill children, and the more pressure that is put on societies to accept women as part of the endo-ideal, the more children are exploited, raped and murdered. Men also kill men and those murders are also very often negative image killings, when they are not between endogroups to strengthen solidarity.

It is not enough to ascribe male violence to *toxic masculinity* without recognizing that killing is shunning of the negative image and, under endo-idealism, the endo-ideal is authorized to assign guilt and inflict punishment. Men may kill people under male endo-idealism but industrialists kill people under industrial endo-idealism and the wealthy kill people under wealth endo-idealism. It is not masculinity that is toxic, it is endo-idealism.

In countries with a dominant endogroup centred around anthropomorphized society, or a state, both self-immolations and self-mutilations are common acts accusing wider society or power of guilt. While people in these countries see such acts as a sign of individual strength and resistance, this is unheard of in the individualist parts of the world which prefer mass killings, typically of the most vulnerable. Both the endo-ideal and the negative image punish the negative image upon assignment of guilt.

People don't kill up. They don't even punch up, hence the tendency to blame poor people for everything caused by rich people. Murder and assault are nearly always against a negative image. This is one reason why Mikhail Bakunin's *propagande par le fait* suggestion[53], interpreted as a call for targeted assassinations of the ruling class, caused such horror in the endo-ideal and shock in all who heard it. The disparity in shock, anger and sorrow caused by the murder or death of an endo-ideal relative to the negative image is a measure of the extent to which people experience the endo-ideal as their own self. To kill your own idealized self-image is akin to killing your self, or far worse. It is something that is only possible if the killer has adopted a new endo-ideal or if the killer is 'crazy', the medical interpretation of a person who does not accept the dominant endoreality.

The western endo-ideal, which has established over many centuries that Anglo / Germanic, academic, males have the right to define reality and no one else does, accuse their challengers of 'identity politics', for all the world as though it was not identity politics which placed them in the seats of power. Their continuing ability to define the rules and reality around them have created an opposition that plays their game on their terms, a perpetually losing strategy. An opposition that organizes itself within endoreality is both providing the negative image for the endo-ideal and supporting the structure which created them. The only thing such an opposition could possibly win, if they ever won, is a world organized exactly as before but perhaps inverted. In drawing the non-ideal, it is impossible to avoid redrawing the original endo-ideal.

The negative image is not in opposition to the endo-ideal. In every binary debate between opposing but indistinguishable endo-ideals, the true opposition is the unspoken topic ignored by both. Debates between the thought of the east and the thought of the west profess to create a universal picture but leave out the thought of Africa, the origin of all human belief. In opposing political party debates, rule by the people is never acknowledged as an option. Media discuss the relative merits of two sides of a war while ignoring all the people terrorized by both sides. In Manichean ideologies of the last few millennia, opposition is between good and evil gods to cover the sublation of animism. This structure is so common that binary debates may be viewed as a method of concealment. The representation of two inverted options presents an unopposed depiction of the endo-ideal, represented by both the picture of the endo-ideal and its negative image. All of these binaries are simply endo-ideal poles which erase almost the entire world, as a spotlight on two performers erases the entire audience.

The negative image has both an endo-identity and the victimhood to create an exceptional myth. This can only be actualized into an endogroup through the colonization of the negative image by a new endo-ideal, however, a choice which only moves the existing negative image from a position of negative image to a precarious position as reflector. A revolution for liberation of the negative image can be fought, and has been fought many times with results that have become monotonously predictable. Revolutions bring new tyrants, new endoreality, new negative images and new violence to create and strengthen the endogroup.

The negative image has far more valuable gifts. One is the sense of guilt, or debt, which increases their exosocial drive to attain balance and may ultimately lead to a much healthier self than that possessed by any other endosocial roles. While reflectors are trapped by their existing credit and the belief that they will one day be compensated for their subservience, the negative image is driven outwards by the need to balance their internalized guilt. Another gift is the ability and expectation that they will act in opposition to endoreality and defy established convention, which gives them limitless paths of expansion.

Reflectors and endo-ideals must uphold the endoreality which establishes their own virtue and exceptional myth to avoid the shame that would come with acknowledgement of their own guilt. The negative image is the only role that has nothing to lose by shattering endoreality. The negative image experiences both shame and sorrow, and both provide very strong motivation to further exosocial expansion to heal themselves. Because of these gifts, nearly all endosocial change will ultimately come from the negative image, even if it is credited to an endo-ideal. If they can resist the pull to create a revolutionary endogroup or be co-opted by one, they are the source of all endosocial progress and they have the best chance of exosocial expansion and liberation.

The reflector-negative image struggle: Commonly called 'competition', the reflector-negative image struggle is the primary struggle within an endogroup. It pits the obedient reflectors against the ostracized negative image in a zero-sum struggle for the approval of the endo-ideal. It occupies all force that may otherwise be directed towards the endo-ideal.

The revolution or liberation choice of the negative image: Identity and victimhood may be used to create a revolutionary endogroup or guilt and sorrow may be used for exosocial expansion and liberation.

The gifts of the negative image: Identity, victimhood, guilt and sorrow.

Guilt deflection

My illness, my weariness, my guilt, my crime, my sin, my transgression, The illness that is present in my body, my flesh, my veins, Be peeled off like this garlic so that
The fire-god, the burner, consumes today! May the curse leave so that I may see the light! – Šurpu V–VI, 1350-1050 BCE, Mesopotamia

Every person and endogroup has internalized accounting which demands that transactions between people are equivalent and involve no unbalanced force. Where that force exists and is used, every person and endogroup feels an urgency to balance the transaction before the punishment of shame and shunning arrives. This awareness of an unbalanced accounting is guilt. Guilt signifies a debt that must be paid, sooner or later, by someone.

In the *Šurpu*[54] above, guilt is described as both an illness and a curse. It is clearly transferable, in this case to garlic, which will then be burned. Guilt plays a large role in whether a curse will be effective, as it is usually necessary to detail the recipient's guilt during the invocation of the curse. The guilt is often seen as providing the force to the curse, or sometimes the curse may be seen as the manifestation or assignment of rightful guilt. This is the same guilt-curse relationship still seen in modern courts where the judge acts as the magician, cursing people with verdicts of their supposed guilt. Then, as now, the assignment of guilt does not necessarily, or even often, correspond with the perpetrators of the acts of unbalanced force. The victim is often the one punished, as courts today punish poor people for their poverty, in accordance with the laws of endoreality.

As seen above, this guilt has the power to make its holder very ill. A very large proportion of spells around the world dealt with the transference, purification or retribution of guilt and a very large proportion of mental strain today is related to guilt. Hand washing is one behaviour that features prominently in purification rituals from the past and in guilt-related obsessive compulsive behaviours today. Pacing in circles and cursing and assigning guilt to the self or other are also prominent in both.

Guilt can be externalized onto objects, as seen in the *Šurpu* above and as seen in daily expressions in every language. *The bus left me,* or *The economy won't give me paid work,* are deflections onto objects and abstract concepts which allow distancing of fault from the self and also from more powerful figures such as the bus driver or employers. These are useful incantations for guilt avoidance among those who do not use other people as their scapegoats. Guilt can also be transferred to the negative image. Those same outcomes may be blamed on the secretary who did not remind them or the parent who did not force them to get an education.

People use mental gymnastics that allow them to process guilt reversals every day. Mantras such as: *They could have money if they worked. They brought it on themselves. There is nothing I can do about it. It's God's will. They probably deserved it. Helping would just make it worse.* are used internally and between people, to ward off guilt. The overwhelming amount of unbalanced transactions people are now forced to live with every day would cause crushing guilt if it was not constantly deflected.

In many cultures, any war had to be followed by an accounting and atonement of all the losses and injuries on each side before peace could be expected. Peace treaties were counsels in which every death would have to be balanced by another death or enslavement and any destruction or injury would require compensation. Until this process was complete, people could not be expected to recognize each other's humanity and resume sharing and social interactions. This is true of all nations which maintained exosocial relationships, as they must be balanced.

Today, those in power prefer to simply maintain the division. In order for international trade and other exploitation to exist, people must be permanently and irrevocably divided into separate endogroups. Between endogroups, no balance is required and no guilt is experienced. Guilt does not traverse endosocial membranes. If there is no empathy, there is no guilt. Both the rise of states with the rise of trade and the explosion of sub-national endogroups within unequal societies are a result of this permanent state of unbalanced transactions.

In exosocial relationships, guilt can only be balanced on an interactional basis, between two people. Allowing unbalanced transactions to continue causes an accumulation of debt and accompanying guilt. This will encourage the debtor to attempt formation of an endogroup to sublate their creditor and alleviate their guilt. This cause of endogroups is probably the primary cause today. Unbalanced transactions are compulsory to function in endosocialism. In addition, many people today are endoselves, unable to balance interactions due to upbringing or health inhibitions. These reasons necessitate the formation of endogroups to facilitate the chronic power imbalance.

In an endogroup, there is one self and all guilt is assigned to this group self, not individuals. Balance is not necessary within one self, whether that is a political group, a temporally infinite filial self or a karmic cycle. Guilt within a self is a shared property which can be allocated to the negative image. The purpose of the creation of the negative image is to absorb this guilt. In an endogroup, the negative image is already depicted as a shameful creature, so all guilt is immediately and sometimes even automatically transferred to them. Within an endogroup, transactions are not balanced, they are sorted according to endoreality. The guilt produced is absolved by punishing the negative image.

Where people are bonded as one endogroup, they must designate a negative image to absorb all guilt transference and punishment for the unbalanced transactions which are the hallmark of endogroups. The negative image must be punished for all guilt, which is why The Homeless can't have homes and The Poor can't have food and it is also why human rights disasters are larger with every level of empire. The current mono-empire has such extreme imbalance it apparently requires a global genocide to absorb all the guilt. The global hatred of, and otherwise incomprehensible spite towards poor people is a symptom of their role as the scapegoats of wealth endo-idealism, expressed in their punishment for all unbalanced transactions. Women under male endo-idealism and indigenous communities under industrial endo-idealism suffer the same fate.

Politicians gain popularity by attacking the negative image in the form of welfare 'cheats', criminals, women giving birth, or not giving birth, the 'unemployed', etc. The more cruel and outrageous their treatment of the negative image, the more popular they will be as the endogroup becomes intoxicated on the secondary euphoria. This is not simply a strengthening of endogroups through violence. It is absolution from guilt for the entire endogroup. Children may blame parents, siblings or imaginary friends for any behaviour of theirs that causes guilt. Sibling rivalry, especially from an idealized eldest, could be partly a result of this transfer to a negative image. This transfer and punishment is seen at every level of endogroup. The subjugated are always the sacrifice.

Guilt atoned by the sacrifice of negative images was often written into laws. This is still practised in many places today, in institutional courts and the court of public opinion. This is a very common scenario in cases of rape. Rape is itself a denial of bodily autonomy in an attempt to sublate another person, therefore, any victim of rape is perceived as sublated, or cast as the negative image. As the negative image, they are the holders of guilt in the self which the rapist created between them. They will thus be punished for their own victimhood, by the rapist, by wider society, and often by themselves People are punished, shunned and sometimes put to death, for the act of rape committed against them, all over the world. The difference between rape and most other crime is the effect of joining and sublation which is more easily effected through rape than other crimes. This is not, as it is often depicted, an act of simple male endo-idealism, as the same guilt reversal occurs in all rape cases, including those of men by women.

Guilt is usually established through a quasi-judicial enumeration of wrongs and detailing of the event which are accurate in all respects except that the participants are reversed. In this way, those in poverty are accused of being parasites on the society which cast them out, mothers are accused of not contributing to the workforce they birthed and raised, and priests and other powerful men who are accused of inhumanity towards women and children claim they are victims of *a witch hunt*. Rape victims are accused of robbing their rapists of free will by seducing them. Victims of corporations hold the guilt for being sick, not those who destroyed the environment which made them sick.

In 2006, the murders committed by the U.S. military at Guantanamo[55] were first depicted as suicides, then the suicides were depicted as an act of aggression against the U.S. military. The U.S. commander stated that the murders (depicted as suicides) were *"an act of asymmetrical warfare waged against us"* by the murdered men. Israel president Netanyahu made similar claims in 2014 regarding the children and babies the Israeli military murdered in the Gaza strip. He said they were *"telegenically dead"* that Palestinian grieving parents were using to make Israel look bad. In 2013, Myanmar claimed the same victimhood over their genocide of Rohingya, claiming not only that the Rohingya had voluntarily burned their own villages and disappeared, but that they had done so to make Myanmar look bad. The guilt transfer is so much a feature of every atrocity that denial was recognized as the last step in a genocide by Genocide Watch.

The reversal is also a part of everyday life outside of crimes. The terms employer and employee assigns the benefactor position to the employer instead of reflecting the work the employee gives. The employer is claimed to have *provided jobs* or given people *the opportunity to work*, as part of an imaginary exchange to disguise the one-sided transaction that allows the employer to control and benefit from the employee's time and labour. Billionaires believe they provide jobs and deserve gratitude when in universal reality, they have stolen the labour and lives of all their employees and the resources of nations and earth and intercepted all communal interactions and will never be able to repay any of it. The Taxpayer describes the only category of worker paid for their labour, and depicts them as paying for everyone else instead of benefiting from everyone else's unpaid labour. Caregivers of all kinds are all accused of parasiting by those who parasite off of them.

The endo-ideal of any endogroup does not retain their own shame or guilt. If an endo-ideal experiences shame it is a temporary threat to their position which will be violently resisted. Women under male endo-idealism are the public holders of shame and guilt for both couples and families, regardless of their position within the caregiver circle. Wider society will transfer the guilt for all behaviour in the couple or family onto the wife, mother or girlfriend under male endo-idealism. If the woman holds a more powerful position within the caregiver endogroup, the guilt they received will be transferred back onto the child or spouse as soon as they are back in the caregiver circle. In these cases, the woman is not the final destination of outside shame but the family conduit for it.

The cognitive dysfunction of endoreality extends beyond a lack of empathy. In endoreality, middle aged men can accuse toddlers of seducing them and that endoreality is endorsed by judges and media. This is not an isolated occurrence but is something that has happened again and again, and has been reinforced by academic and political circles. The victimhood asserted by the endo-ideal is reflected by all in their endogroup and blame and guilt are cast to their negative image by the entire society. Endo-ideals can commit terrible acts because they displace guilt and their entire endogroup will enable and support them in this. If the endo-ideal feels shame or is holding guilt, a negative image must be sacrificed to remove the guilt. The entire fields of psychology and economics, not to mention law, are part of a vast institutional apparatus designed to create endoreality and effect guilt transference.

It is not that the event does not exist in endoreality or that they remember it incorrectly or that they project blame. The event exists inside their wider self, and they allocate victimhood to the endo-ideal and blame to the negative image regardless of which body performed which action. This process is impervious to the external reality which sees the perpetrators and their victims as separate people. Predatory behaviour in endogroups will never change as the endo-ideal is never guilty as long as their status remains unchanged. Just as a body relies on its liver to clean up the effects of toxic substances even though it was the brain that decided to ingest them, an endogroup will continue to punish the negative image as the holder of all guilt, including for actions committed against them.

This is why a 'jury of peers' is never going to fairly assess social behaviour and neither is the endo-ideal judge. Being a victim of an endo-ideal makes the victim the negative image. Guilt is always cast onto the negative image. This is the root of the shame victims feel.

Everyone who has ever loved an endoself or endo-ideal is familiar with the experience of waiting in vain for a sign of contrition, only to find that the event in which they were wronged is blamed on them in the mind of the perpetrators. They will be accused of doing what was done to them, their victimhood will be attributed to the perpetrator and they will be punished for their own injuries. At times, this reversal of universal reality is so blatant, and so well endorsed by others in the endogroup, that the victim will begin to think they may themselves be losing their minds. This phenomenon is so common it has its own term, gaslighting, in reference to the Hitchcock film by that name.

This often comes as a shock to those who were used to being treated with respect in the early stages of a relationship and cannot comprehend the abrupt difference which accompanies whatever threshold the endo-ideal has established for considering them an extension of their self. If an endo-ideal does eventually take any responsibility for their own guilt in a relationship, it will be long after the relationship has ended, if they have managed to separate to the point that they no longer see the other person or people as a part of their self. Only then can the effects of the endofilter and its automatic reassignment of guilt and credit be lifted.

If the endo-ideal does admit guilt, or it is proven against them, the guilt becomes a virtue. They are said to have done it for their family, or their people, or their confession is so noble it outweighs the crime, or the crime somehow becomes a virtue in itself, a *'crime of passion'* or *'child love'* instead of rape and murder. If that is not possible, the focus is placed on the *'brilliance'* or *'skill'* of their *'fascinating'* criminality. In the face of the endo-ideal's indisputable guilt, the accuser is held guilty of making life difficult for them with the troublesome accusations. The word *'claims'* is very often used in reference to allegations against an endo-ideal instead of the more neutral 'stated'. In English, 'claims' is the name of a crime if the statement is false. Prisons around the world are filled with those whose crimes consist of accusing the endo-ideal.

The nature of victimhood is reversed in the same way. Even if the victimhood is acknowledged, it is often asserted that the victim *'liked it'* or *'wanted it'* or *'if they didn't want it to happen why did/didn't they ___'*. The endo-ideal is often presented as the victim of their own crimes by headlines placing them as the subject and asserting that they are *'under attack'*, *'facing down claims'* or *'hit by accusations'*. Media write that the perpetrator is *accused, pressured, hounded, facing an onslaught of criticism, pursued by accusations* and *haunted by their past.* Instead of headlines stating *Child murdered by man,* they are written as *Man accused by court in child murder case,* which completely reverses the victimhood.

In the end, the endo-ideal is depicted as sacrificing themselves for the endogroup. Militaries torture children to *'keep people safe'* and corporations destroy the environment to *'give you jobs'*. In this way, instead of creating a debt from the endo-ideal to society, the actions create a debt from the society to the endo-ideal. All of the tactics employed are attempts to transfer guilt or negotiate the amount of guilt down.

Endogroup responses to accusation against an endo-ideal follow a predictable pattern:

1) *Accuse the accuser.*
2) *Vilify the accuser as the negative image who can't be trusted to tell the truth.*
3) *Assert that due to the exceptional superiority of the endo-ideal, all of their actions are justified and too subtle for common understanding.*
4) *Assert that due to the exceptional victimhood of the endo-ideal, all of their actions are justified as their 'right to exist' and any criticism is a wish to kill them.*
5) *Downplay the effect of their actions on the victim.*
6) *Exaggerate the effect of the accusation on the endo-ideal.*
7) *Assert that the guilt was a sacrifice the endo-ideal made to benefit others.*

Guilt is an acknowledgment of debt for unbalanced transactions. Because guilt is transferred to the negative image and the endo-ideal is free from guilt, the endo-ideal feels no compulsion to balance debt. On the contrary, with every guilt reversal, they feel more deserving of compensation. Escalating violence and escalating consumerism are both features of the guilt transference. With every object the endo-ideal acquires they feel deserving of more to balance this skewed accounting. With every act of predation they commit against another, in order to effect guilt transference, they must further punish the other.

The feeling of being owed compensation which the endo-ideal carries instead of guilt, can be immobilizing. An endo-ideal will often refuse to participate in any activity that their internal calculator does not estimate will bring them benefit. In this way, they refuse to establish or maintain their own euphoric conduits and become increasingly dependent on secondary euphoria. They also become increasingly trapped by the same feeling of credit owed which traps reflectors. This is a phenomenon that is quite easy to measure through the simple expedient of asking them to do something. If their response to such a request, no matter how trivial, is to refuse, display sudden incompetence, immediately find a reciprocal task the requester must carry out in exchange, or to punish the requester, they are harbouring a feeling of credit owed. This will also be evidenced in endless attempts to get others to perform pointless tasks for them or in making work for others unnecessarily.

The guilt assigned to a negative image, conversely, brings great motivation to balance their debt through increased exosocial interactions and altrusitic interactions. This provides an expansive energy to the negative image that the endo-ideal can never match. Alternatively, the negative image may seek justice, repayment of debt and atonement or redemption through proving universal reality. Their need for this closure is a powerful force keeping them orbiting the endo-ideal, at least until they have fully internalized the guilt assigned to them or renounced it by severing ties with their accusers. The acceptance of guilt and debt is the mark of a negative image and the wait for atonement is the mark of a reflector.

If the negative image has internalized or accepted guilt, they may refuse gratitude or reciprocity, leaving others with no path to seek balance except through devaluing their gifts and punishing them for them. This has been the case for many child-ideals whose parents refuse to ask or accept reciprocity and it has been the case for corporations who are neither expected nor have any way of reimbursing communities for their resources or environmental or community damage. If there is no path for redemption, self-preservation forces the debtor to transfer guilt.

There are two very well documented behaviour patterns following abuse. One is overwhelming self-hatred or shame by the endo-ideal who is momentarily caused to see themselves as the negative image. This extreme contrition may or may not manifest publicly, but it is either replaced or immediately followed by the so-called honeymoon phase where the abusive partner enacts the perfect, considerate partner. It is far more likely that this is an attempt to re-establish their own self-image than any desire to make amends to their partner. In fact, subsequent abuse is usually progressively worse, possibly due to the added sense of entitlement by the increase in disparity between how nice the endo-ideal was and the blame for the abusive action which is now added onto the negative image. As the abusive relationship continues, the honeymoon phase will stop appearing as the abusive partner becomes more adept at immediately casting guilt onto the abused partner and the discrepancy between endo-ideal and negative image becomes more defined in endoreality.

The person who is the victim of the unbalanced force is often further punished by those who are guilty, in order to affect guilt transference. Punishment can follow any offence but is more common after an accusation by the victim. The perpetrator may have eliminated or rewritten the event in their endoreality, but once guilt has been established, punishment will follow, and it will not be directed towards themselves. A victim who has congratulated themselves at finally establishing that the offence existed is often dumbfounded at this turn of events, but it is logical in the mind of the endo-ideal and very predictable.

Academic and scientific literature consistently portray guilt denial, vengeance on the victim and perpetrator claims of victimhood as deliberate, contemplated and premeditated behaviour in the so-called sociopath, but there is no evidence that supports this in any of the proliferation of material which claims it. DARVO, an acronym for deny, attack, reverse victim-offender, is a term popularized by Jennifer J. Freyd to describe *"a strategy"* employed by perpetrators of violence *"to confuse and silence their victims"*.[56] While the behaviour described is familiar to most people, the term strategy and the assignation of a perpetrator motive seem premature and not justified by available research. There is no perpetrator school where people study this technique, which can be seen throughout history and around the world, sometimes in very young children. It is an instinctive response in many perpetrators of violence and may therefore reflect a genuine depiction of their own perceived reality. It is more reasonable to assume (if assume we must) that the proliferation of unbalanced transactions an endoself participates in produces overwhelming guilt which requires compensatory behaviour to avoid shame. The compensatory behaviour is easily affected by guilt transference in a group self.

It is a short step from articles claiming knowledge of intent to the websites written by psychiatrists which claim a significant portion of the population are *experts in mind control*. Such a view is used to explain the fact that all members of an endogroup uphold endoreality, nearly always when the endo-ideal is not even present or aware of the situation. However, there is again no supporting evidence to indicate such mind control. There is a great deal of evidence to show that endogroups act as one entity and allocate guilt according to the laws of endoreality.

Every day, people are forced to work for corporations in jobs which they know are destroying the environment, harming people's health and contributing to a terrible society. The overwhelming guilt caused by the majority of corporate jobs requires a scapegoat and plenty of scapegoats are conveniently provided in the form of those victimized. The employees can pretend that corporate victims somehow deserved shorter lives or that it is somehow better for the greater good. They may even start viewing their victims as an enemy outgroup. A side effect of this phenomenon is that employees at the most destructive corporations display the most hatred and the least empathy towards their victims and are often convicted of extra-curricular crimes against their victim populations. Clear examples of this behaviour are found in mining corporations, all so-called care organizations, including NGOs, and corporations creating toxic consumer goods. It is possible that they demonize their victims as the only way to maintain a perception of themselves or their employer as good or to alleviate their own guilt and shame.

The guilt transfer is very important in endogroup relationships for another reason. Despite the transference, the innate desire for a balanced transaction remains intact. With the transfer of guilt, the endo-ideal will be in a permanent state of victimhood as, with each offence they commit and transfer the guilt for, they become more entitled to compensation for that guilt. If the partner does not share this endoreality, this results in relationships where both parties feel abused and aggrieved and entitled to compensation.

This very common reversed accounting manifests in endless spiteful, destructive and seemingly pointless acts of abuse the endo-ideal will direct towards those they have wronged. First, they will take all their victim's money and then they will, for no discernible reason, tell all their victim's friends that the victim has a sexually transmitted disease. First, they will manipulate their victim into supporting them for years, then, for no apparent gain to themselves, they will burn their victim's house down. First, they will beat their victim, then, when their victim leaves the relationship, they will kill them.

This additional punishment of people they have wronged is a hallmark of those commonly called sociopaths. They will even hurt themselves in the pursuit of this overwhelming need for vengeance which can only be explained by their reversed accounting. The most dangerous points in an abusive relationship are immediately after victimization, accusation or attempts to punish (including by leaving the perpetrator) because of the final guilt reversal and punishment. This is why ends never justify means. If the means include unbalanced transactions, the ends will contain final guilt reversal and punishment.

The endoself or endo-ideal will destroy gifts, preferably in front of the giver, to ensure they are devalued, and later they will deny they received any or accuse the giver of stealing them. If someone pities their perpetual unemployment and offers them work, they will cast that person as their negative image and do everything to sabotage, slander and deride their employer while doing as little work as possible and stealing or causing the employer to lose additional money. This is the case even if the employer was a friend until the employment. If someone provides them with free room and board they will make extra work, destroy the house and tell everyone their benefactor is a terrible host. If someone pities their lonely state and offers to run errands or visit them, they will find themselves put to the most inconvenience and expense they are willing to endure and, sooner or later, will also discover that the person they thought they were helping has slandered them to everyone around, accused them of stealing, of incompetence and of somehow benefiting monetarily or socially from their kindness.

If a gift is not used to compensate for an imaginary debt, the gift itself will be turned into a further debt that the giver will be punished for. This punishment is most often effected through use of the gift itself. A loan of a valuable item will be punished through loss or destruction of that item, an appointment to an important role will produce sudden incompetence or outright sabotage in the role, trust with a confidence will result in use of the confidence against them, introduction to a friend will result in sabotage of the relationship with the friend and so on. If the endo-ideal is a corporation head, this still applies. They will take all the water for free and poison what is left. They will destroy the land and then murder the residents. They will appropriate resources and use them to create products which create horrible illness. They will become overnight billionaires by doing nothing and use their billions to install global totalitarian surveillance. There is no rational explanation for their behaviour except reversed accounting.

Vindictive victimhood is found beside exceptional invincibility in libertarian utopian fantasies which predict the fall of the state and the fall of government control over currency and business. Somehow, these fantasies avoid foreseeing the fall of corporations and accumulated wealth itself. These utopians can conceive of a world where they no longer obey their government or pay tax to it, but they cannot conceive of a world which ignores their money and no longer labours for them. In their fantasy world, intellectual property is respected without national laws and militaries enforcing it and the peasants they leave outside their walls to die will refrain from sending in a few homemade drones. They foresee an end to national control of currency but do not expect that people will create an economy that benefits community instead of destroying communities to benefit the erstwhile wealthy. In short, they believe that they will remain the endo-ideal of a world that is no longer an endogroup. This type of magical thinking is a hallmark of both the endoself and the endo-ideal. Because they push all guilt onto their negative image, they naturally expect all consequences to befall the negative image as well and are shocked and outraged when this is not the case.

A lack of gratitude is another hallmark which can be explained by the feeling that anything they receive is simply compensation for debt owed. Chronic unemployment, a tendency to create work, stress and humiliation, and using up all available time, money and energy are more examples of seeking compensation or vengeance for a debt which is incomprehensible to anyone else. There is abundant evidence that punishment does nothing to change the behaviour of so-called sociopaths. How could it, when it just adds to their inner tally of grievances?

Violence usually requires some sort of assertion of the guilt of the target of violence. Looking at the causes of violence necessitates examining this accounting system and guilt allocation at least as much as any other factor. The fact that violence is often widely considered justifiable when it is a part of court proceedings, and courts of justice are dispensaries of violence, does support the idea that vengeance and retribution is at least a factor in other violence. There are studies which support this idea. For instance, Clark McCauley and Sophia Moskalenko highlight *"the importance of personal grievance as a motive for terrorism"* and give examples of both personal and endogroup victimization used as justification.[57] Terrorism is another example of guilt transference, from an individual onto an entire endogroup. The need to balance the perceived injustice is strong enough that the terrorist will happily die themselves to kill unrelated people upon whom they have transferred guilt. Terrorists are obviously not alone in this, as state militaries will do the same.

When this common acceptance of retribution violence is combined with reversed accounting, it almost certainly results in the same justification of violence and may also contribute to the inability to anticipate consequences for malevolent actions. Not only does violence increase endogroup barriers, it increases the depiction of the victim as a member of a negative image, and it increases the negative perception towards that group, through the reassignment of guilt. If the guilt has been transferred and the endoreality modified, there is no reason for the perpetrator to anticipate consequences toward themselves, which may explain why an endo-ideal is usually both shocked and outraged if consequences occur.

One of the great powers of guilt is the ability to transform an endo-ideal into a negative image. This is how it has been used in revolutions throughout history. An itemization of the crimes of former endo-ideals, often entrenched in museums and national education, are a key component of every revolution. This is a power which is available to anyone in a society through journalism and working justice systems, which is why these are two of the most frequently co-opted components of society. In 2014, the OpDeathEaters movement[258] set out to catalogue and present all instances of paedosadism and child trafficking by the endo-ideals of every society and how these instances were covered up by the entire supporting society. This movement is similar in goals to Bakunin's *propagande par le fait* but far more effective. Assassinating an endo-ideal may shock a society but they are just as likely to create a martyr as to revolt. Removing the invisibility cloak of endoreality and revealing their guilt is a far more thorough and long-lasting remedy.

If guilt can be made to stick to an entire class of endo-ideal, they will no longer be the endo-ideal. This is why endogroups fight so strongly to pretend every endo-ideal that is irrefutably guilty is not a 'real' member of the category. This is why authoritative powers attempt to block their opponents through assignment of guilt. And this is why truth and reconciliation, or a proper assignment of guilt and retribution which does not pander to whichever side is the dominant endo-ideal, is an essential aspect of every attempt at lasting peace.

Open science and journalism which do not reflect endoreality have another great power. They have the ability

2 The OpDeathEaters campaign is one of several movements initiated by this author with a goal of combating endoreality and changing perspective and audience empathy around topics which were and are the target of heavy state and corporate manipulation.

to usurp the endo-ideal's right to define. This was another strategy employed by the OpDeathEaters campaign above which changed the language and the depiction of crimes against children from the narrative produced by the authoritative endo-ideals in science and journalism. This movement and other similar initiatives were described in Michael Salter's 2017 book *Crime, Justice and Social Media.*[59]

The law of balanced interactions: All interactions must be eventually balanced or they will result in guilt which will be punished by shame and shunning. Small amounts of imbalance are a sign of a wish to continue a relationship, as they provide a need to continue interacting.

The law of guilt transference. Guilt can be transferred from the person who incurred the debt by a variety of means.

Th law of reversed accounting: Guilt transference will create escalating abuse as every wrong committed by the abuser will be added to the debt owed by the victim, resulting in victims continually and increasingly punished for their own victimhood.

The law of unredeemed credit: Those who feel they have accumulated credit, including the endo-ideal, due to reversed accounting, will be greatly attracted to opportunities to redeem that credit through unbalanced interactions benefiting themselves or punishment of others.

The law of debt: Those who have accepted debt or guilt will be compelled to atone for the imbalance through unbalanced interactions benefiting others or self-punishment.

Shame and shunning

Shame is the power we give others to wield over us. - Chinelo Okparanta, *Happiness, Like Water,* 2013 .

Guilt relates to an unbalanced interaction. Once the imbalance is remedied, guilt is assuaged. Guilt is an exosocial, or interactional product and so can be in opposition to, or independent of, endoreality. Shame relates to endogroup status and is associated with the state of the negative image. Guilt is a universal feeling of discomfort. Shame is solely an endosocial condition. Shame relates to the ancient feeling that debt unpaid results in bondage. Debt can create an endogroup through its creation of a negative image.

Shame is punishment. Shame is a fear of shunning and can result in shunning oneself to avoid pain. Guilt results in remedial action; shame frequently results in shunning the person who caused the feeling or withdrawal from society. Shame is a deeply painful and sometimes crippling emotion that can even cause such extreme shunning as murder and / or suicide. Shame can result from social rejection such as a romantic rejection or shunning from the dominant endogroup and it can be experienced vicariously for someone. Shame can be felt by all reflectors on the humiliation of one and by all negative image on the humiliation of one.

Shame is the experience of being shunned and the internalization of the perception of the self as the negative image. Shame reflects the status of the self in the endogroup. Speaking in public is overwhelming for many who both perceive themselves and are perceived by the audience, as the negative image. Any public appearance for a negative image is a public shaming. Shame is expressed, or punished, by contempt, both internal and external. Evidence of shame is, in itself, enough to cause shunning by others who will often reject a social interaction with someone who is exhibiting signs of shame such as blushing or stammering, behaviours which increase in the presence of a person the speaker perceives as an endo-ideal. Since achievement by a negative image frequently results in shame instead of pride, it is part of the reason members of a negative image strive to hold each other back from achievement.

Shame is the feeling that destroys face, a fact illustrated perfectly by the act of blushing. Face is a concept very close to a personal membrane. Shame is a condition of the faceless negative image with a very thin or damaged personal membrane, and is inimical to the endo-ideal. The value of face accorded to the endo-ideal vs the negative image is seen in every aspect of an endogroup. The function of endoreality is to preserve face in the endo-ideal by protecting the endo-ideal from shame and guilt. Humiliation of the endo-ideal is typically responded to, not with shame, but with rage, by the entire endogroup.

The endo-ideal is extremely sensitive to the experience of shame and will react violently and in desperation to avoid it. Since guilt is a factor of unbalanced transactions, and the laws of endoreality prevent balanced interactions, guilt is a constant by-product of endogroups. A correct allocation of guilt would cause the endo-ideal to lose face and be in violation of the laws of endoreality, so guilt must be constantly monitored and transferred. For the endo-ideal, shame brings instant fear of being shunned as the negative image.

Shame in an endo-ideal is externalized as humiliation and outside people are blamed. Endo-ideals typically have a vindictive response to humiliation. If it is by someone they feel ownership over, they may kill them to remove an offending part of their self. If it is perceived as an external threat, they may attack or exact revenge in some way to ensure endosocial separation and enemy status for a person who may previously have been a friend. Shunning the accuser, possibly to avoid the pain of shunning, is a common response.

In times like the present, where several lower endogroups are being sublated into a transcendental mono-empire and many endo-ideals are suddenly exposed without the protection of authoritative or dominant endoreality, the surge of guilt assigned to these soon-to-be-former endo-ideals puts them under severe mental strain and in an existential crisis that makes them very dangerous. This is seen first in the swarming of migratory endo-ideals, who are attempting to avoid collective guilt by dissociating from the former endo-ideal (and using their endo-ideal power to define to do so). This part of the cycle manifested in several of the past decades as the most powerful sector of society insisted they were actually oppressed 'nerds' and has progressed as this sector has attempted to colonize nearly every negative image on earth.

In whatever manifestation they appear, they are marked by their vicious punishment of real negative images for crimes that look a lot like what was done to the real negative image. The rage to return and establish themselves as the endo-ideal of the last real or imagined endogroup is particularly very dangerous for anyone they consider their former negative image. Without understanding the incredible power of guilt, the drive to balance interactions, and the transferability of guilt, the extreme danger this creates for all negative images in times of upheaval is always overlooked. To accuse the endo-ideal is to activate punishment of the negative image.

The endo-ideal outlook is illustrated by the hugely exaggerated descriptions they give of the mildest criticisms of them. A mild request to balance an interaction is seen by an endo-ideal and their reflectors as an attempt to cast them as the negative image. Any assignation of guilt in endoreality is a designation of negative image status and so, understandably, produces a violent reaction which seems inexplicably exaggerated in universal reality. The extreme binary endosocial outlook interprets the mildest criticism as shaming and so the endo-ideal react with violent anger to reestablish their position. The common myth, initiated and perpetuated by psychiatrists with no supporting evidence, that so-called psychopaths do not feel guilt, fails to account for their recognized and acknowledged actions to deny, diminish and displace guilt. If they truly did not feel guilt, they would have no reason to avoid it, much less create elaborate defense mechanisms against it.

People who are diagnosed by authorities or others as experiencing no shame may actually have an overwhelming shame response, or at least great sensitivity to shame. The lack of visible shame could be the result of no shame existing, or it could be the result of an immediate and effective response to the threat of shame. Typical behaviours are usually associated with those diagnosed with no sense of shame, such as laughter, anger, denial and rejection of empathy with their victims, frequently manifesting as further punitive violence towards their victims and projection of guilt. These behaviours indicate that shame is both present and recognized, at least subconsciously, and the behaviour is a defensive response. Otherwise, there would be no need for any reaction.

It would help to measure the ability of an endoself to process shame and ascertain whether environmental stressors have contributed to the development of a rapid defence or inhibited the ability to process shame. Alternatively, it is possible that shame is overwhelming to the endoself due to the volume of guilt they experience as a result of their abundance of unbalanced transactions and their inability to remedy the imbalance. In this case, study should focus on the need of an endoself to rely on secondary euphoria and the reasons they are unable to access primary euphoria. This would help to understand why a lack of shame, empathy or responsibility for guilt develops in those who are beneficiaries of power, or constant unbalanced interactions. Gaslighting and bragging may be used to rewrite facts so they do not feel the pain of shame.

Lastly, guilt is an exosocial emotion which acknowledges a relationship. Feelings of guilt may be a catalyst to widening a social group to include those formerly mistreated as outgroups. Establishing empathy for outgroups can result in guilt over their mistreatment, so it is also possible that guilt is rejected in order to preserve endosocial barriers.

In any case, shame is the result of guilt which accompanies unbalanced transactions. Any attempt to get an endoself or endo-ideal to acknowledge guilt or experience shame will meet with strong resistance if it is seen as an attempt to cast them as the negative image. It may be more helpful to attempt to establish paths to redemption, through traditional truth and reconciliation processes, rather than the more modern attempts to simply identify 'the bad guy' and punish them.

The negative image can be made to feel shame and increase the well-being of endo-ideals through their shame even when there is no specific guilt to transfer. This is a common phenomenon in filial cultures where children and descendants are routinely made to feel guilty with no particular fault ascribed to them. It is also seen in the regular police harassment of the negative image of every state and in the contempt heaped on poor people of every country in the grips of wealth endo-idealism. This serves the dual purpose of entrenching the sublation of the negative image and providing secondary euphoria to their harassers.

Some U.S. academics, building on Ruth Benedict's 1946 work in *The Chrysanthemum and the Sword* [60], have asserted that the west has a guilt culture as opposed to a shame culture in the east. The primary premise of the depiction is based on a fairly blatant U.S. endo-idealism which claims that people in the U.S. are guided by conscience while people in Asia are guided by public appearance. Beyond this, however, it asserts that so-called guilt cultures focus on law and punishment while so-called shame cultures focus on pride and honour. So-called guilt culture is simply an endoself or endo-ideal outlook which leaves it up to the individual whether or not to accept guilt and typically allows only law courts as the sole external authority, which is the opposite of a society guided by conscience. The difference between so-called shame and guilt cultures is that the family and society is the dominant endogroup in a so-called shame culture and the state or economic ideology is the dominant endogroup in a so-called guilt culture. The addition of a fear-power structure by recent academics is simply an addition of a dominant caregiver or nation group.

All of these theories are endosocialism, just with different levels of dominant endogroup. Supposedly, guilt is assigned through authoritative, institutional (church or state) justice systems, shame through social shunning and fear through physical threat. These classifications are not at all useful in understanding social dynamics, much less in creating endogroup cultural stereotypes, as guilt, shame and power are all present in all societies. Anyone who does not think the west has a shame culture has never been an indigenous, single mother on welfare. Anyone who does not think Asia has fear-power relationships has not been confronted by Asian police. It is far more useful to examine these emotions and their responses as the universal elements of humanity they are. Guilt is a product of all unbalanced transactions. At every level of endogroup, guilt is assigned to the negative image and it is shame that keeps these designated negative images from refusing to absorb society's guilt. Fear facilitates the transfer of power which creates every endogroup.

Contempt is an emotion directed downward, from the endo-ideal to reflectors and the negative image and from reflectors to the negative image. Contempt serves to increase the separation between the person experiencing it and the humiliated person or group. Shame is felt vicariously upwards, as empathy is directed upwards. A patriarch who claims to feel shame because of a family member really feels it because of their community and transfers it down to a family member who may or may not have the power to transfer it further.

Shame is the punishment for guilt which, as we have seen, can be transferred. *They have brought shame onto our family.* This statement does not allude to any act the person has committed. It alludes to shame which has arrived which they, as the guilt holder, must be punished for. The statement of guilt above is simply an incantation to effect guilt transference and is no more true than such incantations usually are. So-called honour killings, which are really shame killings, are a result of strong endogroups or families which share shame from the transcendental endogroup and jointly allocate that shame to the negative image. The effectiveness of this transference is evident in the fact that the victims of unbalanced force feel shame and the perpetrators and witnesses seldom do, at least in strong endogroups.

While the negative image bears all punishment for the endogroup self, the pain experienced by the negative image is not primarily physical abuse and deprivation. The primary pain is the result of the twin tortures of shunning and shame.

Shunning without an endogroup is a remedy against predators. Shunning within an endogroup is a form of torture. The extreme effects of such shunning, as well as assignment of guilt, are easily observed. They have been portrayed in culture from ancient fairy tales to modern teen dramas and are clearly evident in behavoural studies. The only reason the effects are downplayed or ignored is the fact that they are exclusively directed at the negative image. It is far more lonely to feel isolated in a strong endogroup. Both pain and joy are far greater in endogroups, which is their attraction.

With no society, there is no self. One of our most overwhelming impulses as humans is to belong to a society. The pain of shunning is the most powerful coercive tool we employ against each other. Shunning can motivate people to take their own lives or the lives of others. Solitary confinement can rapidly destroy mental health. An infant left without human contact can have all of their physical needs met and still grow up with severe physical and mental damage. The need to belong can be used to overpower principles, deep rooted morals and self-interest. History has repeatedly proven that the majority of people can be coerced to do almost anything to themselves or others by the need for social inclusion.

The desire to be a part of something bigger than themselves is frequently expressed as a motivation for action, and duty to society is a frequent excuse for compliance. The desire for inclusion in a bonded group is supported by the exclusion of anyone outside societal borders. Shunning and inclusion are the primary methods of coercing extreme human behaviour. People will risk their lives instead of leaving an endogroup. People also die taking dares as they would rather risk their lives and health than their reputation within an endogroup.

Reflectors and the negative image both have an internalized image of an external endo-ideal and the negative image also have the self-hate that goes along with the knowledge that they are the negative image of that ideal. It is shunning and shame that divide the reflectors from the negative image and encourage the reflectors to do almost anything to avoid the pain of the negative image. The reason shunning appears to be torture is that it destroys the ability to form relationships, which is part of the most intimate circle of self. Shame appears to have the same effect by making interactions painful and difficult.

This is why the last act of a predator that does not kill their prey is to simply leave, preferably taking as much of the other's social circle or life with them as possible. A fully depleted person, left with no means of restoring themselves through balanced interactions, will often complete the job of self-destruction or the surrounding predatory society will do it for them. The lack of resources to deal with the final guilt allocation that would be triggered by separation is one reason so many people are unable to leave abusive relationships. The exposure to wider society as a negative image is another. Society that is supportive of a person they see as an obedient reflector will immediately attack anyone who is revealed to them as a negative image. This is especially true of any society made up primarily of endoselves, as their predatory tendencies are aroused, but all reflectors see it as their duty to uphold endoreality and punish the negative image.

So-called 'honour killings' are really shame killings and they are closely tied to endogroup ownership. Sometimes shame killings, including so-called 'crimes of passion', are permitted because of a family's endogroup ownership of women and children. A state death penalty is simply a state shame killing. If all were truly equal under the law, transcendental endogroups would have no more ownership of people than lower endogroups. If a family cannot kill, why can a state? The only difference is the level at which authoritative endoreality resides.

Shame killing is the killing of an insubordinate reflector, since insubordination causes the endo-ideal to feel shamed within the transcendental endogroup. Shame is the experience of being shunned. For a negative image to refuse an endo-ideal often produces a shock at their audacity and shame, which in the endo-ideal is always seen as an attempt to cast them as the negative image. This is why so many endo-ideals will act as if they have suffered a great injury on being rejected or treated with contempt by the negative image. To lose face by someone perceived as beneath you is a bigger attack because they have less power so reduce the rejected person even more. So-called 'crimes of passion' are also shame killings. The endo-ideal almost never commit suicide, but they will commit mass murders when confronted with their guilt or any other perceived humiliation.

The idea that certain people are possessed of evil or can have evil transferred to them and must be purged from the rest of society to purify the whole has its roots in ancient animism. Anyone from an old woman to a newborn baby to a powerful priest may be assigned the guilt for the entire group and killed to purify the entire group. This belief was by no means universal to all humanity but it is globally widespread and very, very old, quite possibly originating from a time before the great migration out of Africa.

The itemization of guilt is extremely important. This is why an endo-ideal or endoself will go to great lengths to interrupt and immediately deflect any attempt to assign them guilt. It is also why, once the action has been stated out loud, they will counter accuse the accuser of the same action or depict the accusation itself as the greater injury. Violence is usually accompanied by the itemizing of guilt being assigned to the victim and violence is nearly always accompanied by magical words designating the victim as the negative image. Words such as *bitch, whore, cunt, slut, witch,* or *feminazi,* terms which all refer to various forms of insubordination in thought or action, are used to announce that these women have ceased being considered obedient reflectors and are now the shunned negative image. This naming has been extremely important in denunciation and spell-casting in every society which practiced either.

Earlier taboos clearly stated that all of the older words above were curse words. These curses are now all acceptable in almost any mainstream conversation because it is perfectly acceptable under male endo-idealism to curse women as the negative image and assign them the guilt for their own deaths. Their acceptability in mainstream conversation coincided with the fight for women's liberation in the 1960s, when women were widely accused of negative image guilt for their opposition to endoreality and their insubordination as reflectors. None of these words are recognized as hate speech because laws are created to uphold endoreality. The modern taboos against uttering such words when they relate to men, and referring instead to *the n-word* and *the f-word* are recognition of the magical powers they possess to transfer guilt to the victim of violence and to justify the violence to wider society.

The words above, including the words no one is permitted to write because they have been used to depict men as the negative image, are convenient spells as they contain both the accusation and the negative image designation. The notable feature of a curse is that the type of insubordination used to assign guilt is included in the word. This is a feature retained from ancient curses which were accusations made against another in the hope that punishment could be invoked against them. The guilt of a former reflector being cast as a negative image is always insubordination against endoreality, such as a refusal to reflect, a claim of autonomy over thought or body or a demand for credit or liberation. These words rid the perpetrator of guilt and are frequently accompanied by a further attack against the negative image which atones for the punishment as well. An attack on a negative image is an act of purifying the self and warding off shame.

Another form of curse reverses a crime of the endo-ideal to cast blame upon the victim. In this manner, trafficked children may become *prostitutes* and victims of environmental hazards become *parasites on society* as do caregivers of all kinds. Corporations taking everyone's control over lives, work and resources and living in a borderless world curse immigrants as *illegal* and taking jobs. The curse is always an accusation of guilt but it does not always reference any act by the accused. The accusation of insubordination is always a part of the curse but it does not have to be true or even plausible, as seen in words that accuse children of being prostitutes.

These curses are in no way an attempt to communicate with the accused or even the wider public. They will be used even when no one is around or alive to hear them. A person in extreme distress will often start speaking, or even screaming, to themselves and that is nearly always done to effect a guilt assignment. People who curse at strangers on the street (usually the negative image), executives who randomly yell at employees and anyone who suddenly starts pacing (often in a circle) and muttering to themselves are all attempting to curse someone with a guilt transference or indicating that they have themselves been transferred guilt. This is why curses are so often used by those who are themselves the negative image. The women who scream *"Cunt! Slut!"* at other women, like the person trying to survive on the street who curses passing negative image strangers, are trying to rid themselves of the guilt they have been assigned. The curse transfers communal guilt and the subsequent violence punishes it.

Honour killings, crimes of passion and *paedophilia* are all expressions that attribute virtue (honour, passion, love) to the perpetrator and ignore the experience of the victim. In stories about these crimes, the perpetrator is explained and often justified at the expense of the behaviour of the victim, who is cast as the negative image and assigned guilt with words such as *slut, whore,* or *rent boy,* or at least words which establish the perpetrator's ownership rights over them such as *wife, lover,* or *prostitute*. In all of these expressions, the victim is blamed for provoking the perpetrator's reaction. The terms themselves attribute blame to the victim. On a state level, those persecuted by a state are all cursed with negative image words such as *criminal, terrorist, dissident, traitor* or simply *illegal,* another adjective converted to a noun to define a category of humanity instead of describing an event. In the case of genocides perpetrated by state leaders, cries for *sovereignty* against possible *regime change* assert the property rights of the president over the lives and personal sovereignty of hundreds of thousands or millions of people.

The steps of negative image creation and punishment are as follows:

Identification: This becomes most evident when the verb or adjective becomes a noun, such as The Poor, The Disabled, The Immigrants, The Homeless, The Sick, or The Environmentalists, or the reflector gets a name describing their insubordination. Like the endogroup itself, the negative image is an abstract concept with no basis in universal reality so it requires an identity to exist.

Melding: There is one negative image. Disparate, or even fundamentally opposed groups are bundled under one umbrella and bear group accusations and guilt assignment. In this way all opposition to a state or corporation can be depicted as terrorism if one person has been accused.

Threat: All negative images must be seen as a threat to the endo-ideal and the group they represent. The Poor are after your money, The Single Mom is both a bad parent and probably depriving corporations of her labour, The Homeless will bring down property values, and so on. The threat is simply a part of the guilt curse which casts someone as the negative image, so it does not need to be consistent or correlate to any facts in universal reality. It can hold two or more opposing assertions at the same time, such as immigrants are criminals who do not contribute to society and they are taking all the jobs and women need to stop having both babies and birth control.

Guilt: All guilt is assigned to the negative image and the negative image is treated as one entity where even infants are guilty of the transgressions ascribed to any member.

Curse: The power of the curse was far more widely recognized in earlier times than it is today, when people struggle to define what hate speech is. The proper definition of hate speech is a curse. A curse is an otherwise meaningless word that serves to both condemn a person to the negative image and assign guilt to them for whatever bad actions are taken against them. Curses are notable for the frequency with which they are screamed at someone who is being murdered or assaulted.

Shunning: The negative image is ostracized from the rest of the endogroup in order to prevent any sympathetic or empathic connections from forming.

Punishment: Every act committed against any member of the negative image is depicted as collective punishment for the guilt assigned to the entire group by any member of the endogroup. This collective grievance is often depicted in the phrase 'debt to society' which depicts society as an anthropomorphized, wronged endogroup.

Final guilt reversal for the punishment: The last stage of shunning is to transfer the last guilt to the negative image. This time the guilt is for their own punishment. This continued reassignment of guilt is the root of the cyclical nature of all endosocial abuse and inequality.

These eight steps, identification, melding, threat assignment, guilt assignment, curse, shunning, punishment and final guilt reversal for the punishment are also the steps of both genocide and imprisonment as these are both forms of guilt assignment and shunning. Justice systems meld all they accuse into criminal categories and enact a final guilt reversal through a criminal record. The famous ten stages of genocide (formerly eight) identified by Genocide Watch founder Gregory Stanton are classification, symbolization, discrimination, dehumanization, organization, polarization, preparation, persecution, extermination and denial.[61] An extremely important aspect left out of this list is the assignment of guilt and the nature of genocide as a collective punishment. This is essential in presenting the act as a balanced transaction and bypassing the tremendous guilt such an act would otherwise produce. Guilt for their own punishment is also assigned to their victims which is the cause of what Genocide Watch recognized as the last stage of genocide, denial. It is usually a further transfer of guilt, this time for the punishment enacted against them.

Another weakness of the Genocide Watch document is that the first stage states that mixed societies are less likely to have a genocide than bipolar societies. In fact, all societies are mixed until the last moments before genocide when the endo-ideal and negative image are each solidified into bipolar categories. For instance, Myanmar is a very multi-ethnic state which yet managed to commit a genocide against the Rohingya by depicting them as outside invaders from Bangladesh instead of one of many ethnic or religious groups. Hitler clearly hated a vast many different groups of people, but, as he explained, it was necessary to present them as one enemy.[62] Few outside people could look at the United States and discern *black* or *white* people, but that is the endoreality polarity much of that society lives in, with near-daily lethal consequences. Facts in universal reality, like the fact that race does not exist, have little to no effect on the perceptions of endoreality. The binary reality of endogroups emerges from the process of creating an endofilter, not from daily evidence.

Genocide Watch also states that all cultures have Us and Them divisions, which is not true. It is only endogroups that have such divisions and culture is independent of endogroups. This misplaced belief leads to the Genocide Watch recommendation that transcendental categories be encouraged. The extreme ineffectiveness of such a strategy, despite the globalization of society, is easily shown in the continual genocide of everyone poor or weak under transcendental wealth endo-idealism and the fact that we are facing a planetary extinction, our biggest genocide ever, as we move to a mono-empire. The ineffectiveness of transcendentalism is also clearly illustrated by the law of the last circle, the fact that as soon as any transcendental endogroup is weakened, all the endogroups sublated to it immediately reappear.

Genocide is built into endogroups. It is neither a feature nor a bug, it is a key structural component. There is no endogroup without a negative image and there is no negative image that is not a genocide in the making. At best, the negative image becomes a rival endogroup and the result is a civil war instead of a genocide. What those who care about humanity ought to be recommending is that all endogroup categories be challenged and discouraged.

All organizations are endogroups so all organizations consider outsiders to be their enemies and all organizations transfer guilt onto their negative image. Thus hospitals punish patients, bureaucrats torment clients, corporations poison consumers, schools destroy the futures of students, and governments impoverish citizens. This occurs at every level of organization. There are no exceptions to this rule. An organization is created from inclusion and there is no inclusion possible without shunning outsiders and a negative image.

In the last step of guilt assignment, the person assigned guilt is punished. Often this is through 'accidents'. Creating accidents is what every corporation and world leader is doing constantly. They are killing and torturing people, deliberately, and continually reassigning the guilt. The guilt is the people's fault for being *stupid* or *poor* and the killer is a great person and genius for *creating jobs* or *boosting the economy*. Victims have to prove which company directly caused their cancer and pay for their own cures, which usually make them worse. People facing the extinction of the planet by corporations are told to stop polluting, just as people are told to tighten their belts for the economy while billionaires hoard all the world's wealth and resources.

In the most sublated negative images, they will enact their own punishment if guilt is internalized. This was clearly illustrated in the 1980s when women were tortured by themselves, by the decree of society, for the insubordination of demanding paid work and female washrooms in work places, an end to the economic and architectural segregation of women to caregiver circles. An entire generation of women spent their lives barely living, and sometimes dying, in misery in response to a social judgment that they ought to be five calories from starvation at all times. Those who accepted the most torment were then ascribed even more guilt through medicalized attribution of 'their condition' as an aspect within themselves, not society. Although extreme versions of this behaviour is not unrelated to physical conditions, the fact that it is not an epidemic now indicates that it was far more of a social phenomenon that appeared at a time when women were fighting to reverse the endoreality laws denying them credit and payment for their own work. It is also no coincidence that the fashion for anorexia was dictated by modeling agencies which were fronting for global child trafficking and paedosadism rings. The loss of body ownership, reliance on outside assessment from one source, complete obedience and the reflector – negative image struggle with those girls deemed *not perfect enough* for a life of abuse and slavery, is key to the sublation of trafficking victims.

The same phenomenon was apparent slightly earlier with the rise of the punk movement at a time of particular hatred for poor and 'unemployed' people. The punk movement, with its graphic depictions of self-mutilation and self disgust, ably assisted by the disgust of wider society, may be viewed as a negative image public self-flagellation, no different from those which have occurred during other times of turmoil and societal guilt.

Self-punishment is also seen in boys and girls from lower classes who sign up for militaries. This acceptance of guilt and reparations owed to society immediately changes their status from negative image to obedient reflector in some countries, and they are fawned over as trophy wives are fawned over, groomed with the approval of the endo-ideal and desperately proud of their achievement in gaining that approval. Suicide bombers are an extreme case of this family or community redemption through suicide. Self-punishment also appears very often in the self-sabotage of individuals cast as the negative image. Although there are multiple reasons for drug use, including to dull pain, repair a self membrane, or alleviate endoself boredom, it can also be part of self-destructive behaviour used by the negative image seeking to balance their guilt and eradicate shame, through death if necessary. At the most extreme end, there are those who admit to crimes they did not commit, apparently under the conviction of their own guilt. Several people in history and even in modern times have either pled guilty to witchcraft accusations they did not do or volunteered to be burnt as a village sacrifice.

This seemingly voluntary and self-induced punishment has appeared at various times in history in large populations. Widespread asceticism, self-flagellation, penis amputations and other bodily mutilations throughout history have been associated with purification from guilt. The current medicalized body mutilations and bleached skin appearing with the social endorsement of 'beauty' are simply different manifestations of this. Both 'beauty' and 'sin' are euphemisms for guilt and its punitive remedies. Because of the last stage of punishment, assigning the guilt for the punishment to the negative image, the result of such self-sabotage is usually an instant relief followed by even more crushing guilt.

Judgment and punishment are also assigned to the negative image by institutional endo-ideals such as those in law and psychiatry who diagnose subjects as the negative image, often due to their recalcitrant compliance with endoreality, and then punish them with life-destroying pharmaceuticals and inhumane prison terms. Punishment follows guilt. Those that say the negative image 'attract' bad luck onto themselves are individualizing, and assigning guilt to the negative image, but they recognize a real phenomenon. The negative image are the first to get diseases and the first to suffer misfortune. It would be more accurate to say that society punishes the negative image rather than the negative image attracts punishment, but the results are the same.

Despite the prevalence of counter accusations, it is not difficult to ascertain who is the negative image and who is the endo-ideal in an accusation by looking for dread or excitement. The endo-ideal has confidence in the guilt assignment and obtains euphoria from the thought of punishing the negative image. The negative image feels dread at any accusation, including ones they are themselves making, as they are the designated recipient of guilt. Such responses ensure that the endo-ideal *looks innocent* and the negative image *looks guilty*

It would be interesting to discover whether people can discern a damaged membrane empathically where there is no cognitive evidence and whether that ability is stronger in an endoself. Certainly, endoselves are extremely attracted to vulnerability, and even less predatory people may become very predatory in the presence of vulnerability. This is yet another reason why people are often unable to predict the behaviour of others towards the most vulnerable. Guilt is truly a curse which attracts misfortune. In the collective sub-conscious, there are no accidents.

The eight steps of negative image creation and punishment: identification, melding, threat assignment, guilt assignment, curse, shunning, punishment and final guilt reversal.

Anger and fear

They were more severely infected than the men, because while men were always getting furious, they calmed down in the end; women, who appeared to be silent, acquiescent, when they were angry flew into a rage that had no end. - Elena Ferrante, *My Brilliant Friend, 2011*

Fear is anticipation of an attack on a euphoric source. In a primarily exosocial person, the feared attack is on a euphoric conduit. In a primarily endosocial person, the feared attack is on an endogroup. Endosocial fear is a result of aversion to damage of a protective membrane, whether that is through physical assault or an assault on dignity or honour or an endo-ideal, a violation of the laws of endoreality, a denial of exceptional myth or an attack on any of the things that strengthen the endogroup. Fear can be sought out, especially among people who are seeking exosocial expansion and wish to challenge their existing boundaries.

There have been many cultures in history and at present in which fear of the individual in defence of the endogroup is no more evident than it is in bees or ants. Even in industrialized societies, such 'selfless' defence of a wider self or external endo-ideal is seldom considered worthy of comment when it occurs in a mother defending her child. This same behaviour in defence of wider society is often seen in times of crisis or emergency. The endo-ideal and endoself are both often resistant or impervious to fear. Anger has been shown to reduce fear. Anger lowers assessment of personal risk[63], possibly due to an endofilter which causes them to expect all punishment to be assigned to their negative image. In a situation which would inspire fear in most people, the endo-ideal is often impassive or angry.

Anger can be *defensive, dominant* or *predatory*. Defensive anger protects a euphoric source or membrane. Defensive anger is against external threat and can be experienced by anyone. Dominant anger occurs within an endogroup and is used to sublate another. Predatory anger is a mark of an endoself and is used to obtain secondary euphoria through the stress response of another.

Defensive anger can be created from fear in the self or others. It can be produced by a protective instinct, the *mama bear* response in reflectors who never experienced such angry reactions in themselves until it was in defence of an endo-ideal. Predatory anger can also be produced by fear felt by others, as the stress response provides secondary euphoria[64] to an endoself. Dominance anger is used to create fear in others. All three forms of anger are seen to a marked degree in dogs, who will both leap to attack an outsider if they smell fear on their own family and will sometimes be attracted to attack those who experience fear. Dogs, like humans, can be induced into an attack frenzy by the presence of fear.

Defence, or self-preservation anger results from an existential threat such as an attack on an endosocial membrane. Anger from jealousy is an attempt to protect social standing within an endogroup. A person who becomes overwhelmed with rage in reaction to a perceived slight to a company their spouse works for or a university their daughter attends has a refracted endo-ideal and is attempting to protect their endo-ideal. A reflector could be perfectly accepting of insults to themselves but not to their endo-ideal.

Anger is stronger in a group with more strength[65], and anger is associated with power[66], so anger identifies power as well as creating it. Studies have shown that participants both attributed status and showed support for an angry person over a sad person.[67] Since the person with anger is usually the endo-ideal and the person with sadness is usually the negative image, this shows people using these emotions to implement the laws of endoreality. Studies have shown that the ability to associate with another perspective is inversely correlated with anger[68][69]. The ability to associate with another perspective is significantly lower in an endo-ideal, as has been shown in many studies of power and perspective. Anger will cause the person experiencing it to attribute its cause to external provocation because anger also causes the perspective bias of an endo-ideal. Anger puts the angry person in the position of the endo-ideal and distributes guilt and victimhood according to the laws of endoreality. Anger creates an endofilter and both creates and identifies an endo-ideal.

Fear and anger are symbiotic in that the fear of one causes the anger of another and the anger of one attracts those who are afraid. Dominant anger is the property of the endo-ideal and fear is the property of reflectors and negative image. Dominant anger in one outside the endo-ideal is a challenge to the endo-ideal and will be met by greater anger. Anger causes fear in an entire endogroup if it emanates from a reflector or negative image as that is a precursor to revolution. This is why reflectors and negative image are always coerced to be smiling and calm and any display of anger in them is met with severe overreaction by the entire endogroup. The greatest display of anger wins endo-ideal status and the one to show fear is sublated to the endo-ideal.

Anger and fear are also symbiotic in that the anger of one drains power from the other, sometimes to the point of leaving them immobilized and causing severe physical stress symptoms. Since it is a fear response to seek out a powerful person and it is a power response to drain euphoria through fear, this is a self-perpetuating cycle that results in endogroups.[70] The anger-fear symbiosis is the most common cause of endogroup creation, aside from its recent usurpation by the need for guilt transference.

Anger-fear symbiosis is very likely the reason humans evolved with the ability to create endogroups, or the method by which they were created. The endogroup is a special defence system that causes all of the group's power to be transferred to the endo-ideal. When endogroups are maintained and enforced institutionally, this causes people to pour all of the world's power, resources and money into a few billionaires, even at the cost of destruction of earth itself. This behaviour is illustrative of the fact that this symbiosis is an emergency powers act which knows no limits, as it is designed to meet an existential threat to the group.

Anger is a frequent result of a parent, including non-human animals, seeing their child testing their fear boundaries by engaging in risky behaviour. If a parent reacts in fear, they will be sublated in the relationship. If the parent reacts in anger sufficient to cause the child fear, the child will be sublated. In first age nations, where the national bond is encouraged to be greater than the caregiver bond, parents are schooled to show no reaction to such provocations or to turn their backs or walk away. In cultures where parents are expected to be sublated, they are subject to extreme social coercion to react with fear to such provocations and in cultures where the child is expected to be sublated, parents are coerced to punish them. The anger reactions correlate with the location of perceived ownership of the child.

Dominance anger is used to repel an endo-ideal challenger or cast a reflector as a negative image. In a child endo-idealist society, anger from either a child or parent instantly causes the parent to be transformed from obedient reflector to negative image in the eyes of the society while the child remains the endo-ideal. In a parent endo-idealist society, anger from either a parent or child causes the child to be transformed from obedient reflector to negative image in the eyes of the society while the parent remains the endo-ideal. The same is true under any endo-idealist structure. Anger from employee or employer shames the employee in an employer endo-idealist society. Anger from a monarch or subject shames the subject in a royal endo-idealist society.

Public anger is a chronic condition in societies full of endoselves but remains the fastest way to lose face in most of

Asia, where the endo-ideal is at a higher level. Anger of men towards their wives or parents towards their children is still very common in Asia, however. Anger suppression and redirection towards safe targets is a symptom of its role as a tool of creating power. This behaviour is not at all limited to people and can be found in most animals which are prone to endogroup formation, such as horse herds.

Anger is often part of guilt transference. It is used to enforce the transference through rapid punishment before the accused has a chance to deflect it and also to create the negative image in order to transfer guilt.

Anger is an essential tool of anyone trying to create or maintain endogroups. Once an endo-ideal has established themselves as the primary or sole euphoric conduit for others, they can use rage to threaten the rest of the endogroup with a loss of that conduit. Insubordination or violation of the laws of endoreality will bring retribution and anger from the entire endogroup. Any attack on an endogroup will strengthen the endo-ideal who rises up in anger, attracting all those frightened by the attack. Fear causes bonding to both the group and the endo-ideal, an effect studied by many researchers in attachment theory and evidenced by a daily diet of fearful news and angry Thought Leaders.

Fear is used to keep people sublated to the endo-ideal. This is seen in states which profess to protect the populations, it is seen in parent-child relationships and it is seen as a tool of male or wealth or any other type of endo-idealism. The anger-fear symbiosis is the key to the guardian coup d'etat. Scary movies in the past were not scary at all for men, as they almost universally showed women as victims and men as perpetrators and defenders. They served to tip the balance of power between men and women on a daily basis. Women were driven to fear media, to fear the dark, to fear strangers and to fear being alone, in short to fear life outside the protective membrane of the male-female couple. Women were socially encouraged to show fear and socially shunned for showing anger.

The negative image is conditioned to feel fear and there is strong social discouragement against them showing anger. Instead, they are preyed on by endogroups in search of captive reflectors and euphoric sources. Propagandists target those showing self-damage because they are vulnerable to suggestions of existential threat and because strong group membranes have great attraction for them. For the same reason, people are subjected to personal membrane destruction to encourage their attachment to an endogroup.

Power is energy acquired through interactions of unequal force. Addiction to anger is addiction to the substance produced by others in response to anger. It is reasonable that members of a group self should be able to transmit such energy to the strongest during crisis, and they do. It is quite possible that pain and other trauma and stress responses also contribute to power for the same reasons. Sometimes fear appears quite irrational, such as a fear of spiders. Fear can be experienced empathically. Spiders have an extraordinary degree of empathic sense. It would be interesting to discover whether, instead of a simple irrational fear response in humans causing arachnophobia, if spiders have the ability to trigger that response in some way that is not immediately obvious in order to boost their chances of survival. In any case, people sometimes have phobias that are even more irrational. Perhaps fear becomes chronic in the negative image as part of a punitive guilt response or as a side effect of extreme vulnerability, or perhaps it is continually triggered in them by a predatory society.

Stress is the physiological effect of environmental and situational demands as they become overwhelming. Stress and depression both kill. The constant inundation of stress by one person onto another, is a long term form of murder. An endoself feeds off of the stress response of other people. They will seek out people with acute stress response and they will cause them stress, even if that stress incidentally harms them as well. This can be seen in family situations where one person is chronically unemployed, late or missing essential items, and it can be seen in the world powers destroying the earth we all live on and creating wars.

Fear produces pheromones which can be spread throughout groups of people. It is possible that pheromones or some other response to fear or existential threat replaces euphoric connection in endoselves and causes them to seek out and create this traumatic emotion in others. Endoselves also have very low fear response compared to wider populations, possibly because fear is related to loss of euphoric conduits and they have none, or few. A doctor associated with the North American NXIVM cult conducted 'studies' in which women were forced to watch videos of rape, dismemberment and self-cannibalism.[71] This is one of many examples of behaviour in cults and other endogroups which show an extreme attraction to the fear and revulsion responses of others. On an individual basis, the same predilection is evident in attraction to paedosadism, rape, gore sites, horror movies and disaster tourism.

An endoself only derives excitement in response to imminent disaster and much of their anger is directed towards those who seek to minimize stress. Any outside attempt to cause them stress, however, whether that is through consequences for their actions or their same behaviour reversed on them, is likely to meet with rage. If the stress is something a person is asking them to voluntarily assume, they simply won't. Sometimes they just refuse and sometimes a selective incompetence prevents them. Relieving the stress of others is something that they are rarely capable of, even when they superficially want to.

An endoself can feel obvious, intense stress which drives them and the people around them to alleviate their stress, but it is nearly always in pursuit of goals that are the mirror image of what other people would seek. Their stress is caused by anything that stands in the way of harm that may befall them or their 'loved ones' or anyone else. It is a response to anyone who attempts to stop them from destruction or attempts to push them to prevent some easily preventable disaster.

Anger has well-established side effects of impairing both empathy and objectivity[68] and increasing object desire.[72] The desire to possess is an endoself trait, as is a lack of empathy. Anger aids in the creation or strengthening of an endoself. An endoself seems unable to anticipate bad consequences to themselves and instead feels excited in the presence of danger, as though they are anticipating harm to an enemy instead. A situation which results in fear by others causes excitement in an endoself. For instance, they may drive dangerously to make other passengers scream and they may also jeopardize the health of their families or the security of their companies to produce stress and fear in others.

An endoself sometimes displays dispositional anger, where anger becomes a part of their general personality. Endogroups and endoselves both externalize guilt so they externalize anger as well. The resultant anger helps to strengthen their endosocial membranes, creating a self-perpetuating cycle. Anger is an attack to cause submission of an object possessed or retreat of a challenger. Every outside criticism or challenge to their endoreality is an existential threat to an endoself. A severely depleted person, either a negative image or someone experiencing a health crisis, may also display a long-term tendency to anger. This may be the condition of an endoself as well. An endoself may sometimes be simply a person suffering a severe health crisis.

While any person will feel anger at an attack on a euphoric source, a recovering negative image may feel anger at any depletion at all. Rage is a defence against extreme predation, especially when it occurs in a severely weakened self. They, like those suffering from illness, may use anger to seek emergency euphoric replenishment, as an endoself does. The well-known correlation of suppressed anger with some forms of disease or self-destructive behaviour indicates that anger suppression is a part of, or triggers, the self-punishment of guilt acceptance in a negative image.

If a person is under relentless attack from abusive relationships with parents, spouse, children, employer, landlord and other members of a society determined to deplete them of any euphoria or sense of self, they will naturally not have the available membrane to protect themselves from the existential threat posed by even the mildest threat or stress. Anger may therefore be more frequent in someone trying to recover from abuse and put themselves together again after long term depletion. Anger is also much more necessary after long term depletion as outsiders are more likely to see a depleted self as prey. Such suffering is seen as an open tray of blood in a street full of vampires, particularly to a society of endoselves.

Anger is the emotion that builds membranes and prevents encroachment by others and external anger can be used to destroy such membranes. Anger can occur against inanimate objects on bodily violation. Toddlers and teenagers use anger to both remove and establish boundaries. Amicable divorce is very difficult in couples who have become one abusive endogroup because the sublated person needs anger, even hatred, to create their own individual membrane again and destroy the former endogroup. The negative image needs anger to stop their fear response and stop the feeding frenzy on them, both within the couple and from society at large. Recently divorced couples and recently separated states both benefit from a time out and wider external interactions to lessen the intensity of the bond. Until the separation is strengthened, great care is essential in preventing violence due to both the growing anger of the negative image and the remaining ownership claims of the endo-ideal.

The anger felt by a reflector or negative image when they begin to repatriate their self is a crucial phase. It is progress, in the sense that they are rejecting the sublated role and developing a protective membrane, but it is also a trap, as they are using rage to create their own endosocial membrane. Prolonged rage is not a path to an exosocial being. It may be initially necessary, in order to create and defend a self, but it will eventually make that membrane impermeable and endosocial. A tendency to dwell on victimhood may lead to development of their own exceptional myth. This is especially true if they have a reflective circle offering, or being forced to provide, power through unbalanced transactions and reflectors of their own endoreality, which is why some people will aggressively seek out such reflection during recovery.

An endoself is formed in response to severe euphoric depletion and inability to access primary euphoria. A recovering negative image is at risk of forming an endoself membrane and predatory tendencies in their efforts to protect themselves, a tendency reflected in what is usually referred to as a cycle of abuse. If a person finds it too difficult to establish exosocial relationships with other people, they can attempt to access euphoria in other ways to aid their recovery, through creation, discovery, spirituality, etc. Society that blocks all such avenues continues to create angry and embittered endoselves who revictimize others.

Laughter

We can only feel sorry for ourselves when our misfortunes are still supportable. Once this limit is crossed, the only way to bear the unbearable is to laugh at it. - Marjane Satrapi, *Persepolis 2: The Story of a Return*

Laughter is a reaction to the experience of euphoria or awareness of endoreality. From an infant laughing at a game of peek-a-boo to comedy audiences laughing at exposure of cognitive dissonance in their daily lives, laughter is a reaction of shock at a sudden awareness of endoreality, a challenge to it or a defence of it. Given that people also laugh at the experience of euphoria or in order to share euphoria, this second cause may be an attempt to obtain euphoria to repair any damage caused by cognitive dissonance.

Neither an endoself nor an exoself will laugh at endoreality, the former because they cannot escape or perceive it and the latter because they have none. As a result, an endoself is left with no understanding of humour and an exoself is left with the laughter of joy or excitement. An endoself may still laugh a great deal, but it is a part of the emotion-aping behaviour they are prone to adopt and the laughter is without humour. An exoself usually laughs a great deal, but with them it is a method of sharing euphoria, often referred to as *cheering people up*. Pretending to understand jokes and learning to fake laughter is a hallmark of an endoself as spontaneous, uncontrolled laughter and highly developed sense of humour is common to very exosocial people, including babies. A baby will also laugh or cry at unexpected appearances or actions which are violations of group membranes and their endoreality.

To the world within endogroups, the boundaries of humour indicate the boundaries of endosocial membranes. Within endogroups, no joke is as funny as an inside joke. The joy of laughter is the joy of social belonging. Laughter both inspires fear and is a symptom of fear. Laughter is a social corrective. It teaches the bounds of society. It shuns those outside or on the fringes and it recognizes inclusion of those inside. Laughter shuns behaviour that is not acceptable. In this way, it strengthens endogroups and makes them less permeable to outside relationships. But laughter can also be used to open an endogroup if it ridicules those barriers themselves.

Early Protestants hated levity, as did many Greek and Roman philosophers. Both considered first age nations to be childlike partly because of their ready laughter. This is probably more of a reflection on the endoselves dictating reality than a popular opinion, in either case. In most of the industrialized world, humour is rare and even embarrassing. In Asia, laughter and smiling are feminine or lower class indulgences and in Germanic or Slavic nations, even rural people don't smile or laugh often. In the United States, people both smile and laugh far more than most industrialized cultures do but the laughter is seldom from humour. It appears more of a social defence, like the broad smile they offer upon meeting someone new. These are all a great contrast to most less industrialized societies around the world, where ready laughter is the norm, at least within communities.

Laughter upon anticipation of euphoria, whether the primary euphoria of an exoself or the secondary euphoria of an endoself, is common. In both cases, it is a reaction of excitement. Laughter is also used to establish euphoric bonds or to strengthen group membranes against outsiders. Besides simple experience of euphoria, these are the six types and uses of humour.

Self affirmation: An endoself will typically react to any criticism of themselves with a soft laugh, as if to themselves, a very disturbing reaction in serious cases as shown in media accounts of smiling or laughing mass murderers. Following that first reaction, they tend to become violently angry at continued criticism, as if to an existential threat, so it is not amusement that provokes the laughter. The solitary laughter of someone in a severe mental crisis is also a sign of a self attempting emergency repair to their protective membrane. Like a cat which purrs when it is content and also when it is in severe pain or dying, people laugh when they are happy and also when they are in severe psychic distress.

The laughter of a baby or child, or even an adult in extreme distress, which alternates with crying, is another sign that laughter can accompany extreme distress. The Asian habit of smiling profusely or laughing on receiving negative social feedback is probably another example of this reaffirmation of self upon loss of face. The 2019 BBC Newsnight interview with the UK's Prince Andrew[73], questioning him on his connections to paedosadism and child trafficking networks, featured at least one example of self affirmation laughter, when he laughed while affirming the death of his close friend Jeffrey Epstein. His strong identification with Epstein in the interview is shown in a pronoun slip when he says "I" instead of "he" and may also be found in the tie he wrenched tighter just before the interview (Epstein died by hanging or choking).

In *Laughter: An Essay on the Meaning of the Comic* [74] Henri Bergson claims that mirth needs to be shared as part of a social group. The exception which proves his rule are those once considered 'mad' and their solitary laughter was considered a mark of their madness. The definition of insanity is not sharing the same endoreality as the authoritative endogroup defining sanity. If laughter cannot be shared across endosocial barriers, it stands to reason that those outside the endogroup must laugh alone.

It is an interesting point that neither Bergson's rule nor its exception are as obvious today. People may giggle or laugh out loud, oblivious to their surroundings and it causes no more note than when they talk and smile seemingly by themselves. Technology has broken down the barrier between those considered mad and those considered sane by allowing people to participate in virtual endogroups and ignore the ones in physical reality. This same behaviour was also sometimes acceptable in cultures where communication with surrounding spirits was normalized. The rule noted by Bergson seems to have been more of a taboo than something inherent in the nature of people. It is reasonable that endogroups should discourage laughter which is not shared within the group as that is a sign that the group is relatively unimportant.

Self affirmation laughter can also include a variety of strategies to obtain affirmation from others, including humour that seems like endogroup submission but is used in a context where it will certainly be negated by affirmation from others.

Self destruction: Laughter can be used to aid in the destruction of an individual through ridicule, by self or others. This type of laughter is described by Bergson, *"Laughter is, above all, a corrective. Being intended to humiliate, it must make a painful impression on the person against whom it is directed. By laughter, society avenges itself for the liberties taken with it. It would fail in its object if it bore the stamp of sympathy or kindness."*

There is a moment in the 2018 Italian film *Happy as Lazzaro* when the village women are all teasing a little boy, telling him that his mother has killed herself because she dislikes him so much. They then laugh that he is so ugly when he cries. His mother arrives and joins in the laughter at his gullibility. This scene is reminiscent of Lady Macduff in *Macbeth,* telling her son that his father has died to entertain herself.

Such casual cruelty seems shocking in most industrialized, third age cultures but teasing children about the death of their family members is not uncommon within the extreme teasing of many strong endo-nations. Such traumatic teasing ensures that a child's first membrane is insecure and intensifies their bonds to the wider group and their reliance on the nation. Weakened membranes between a mother and child make sense in first age nations which suffer high mother and infant mortality, in order both to lessen the trauma to a young child if the mother dies, and to strengthen an outer bond which can be there for them in the event of such a tragedy. It also ensures their loyalty to the nation over their family. Such teasing is typically more extreme when directed towards boys in highly gendered cultures and may also serve to drive the boy from the caregiver circle.

The once popular 'roasts' on television illustrated the social function of older television comedy. An endo-ideal was 'roasted' or ridiculed by a panel of their peers to reduce their personal membrane and then they were built back up by compliments from their peers to strengthen the group membrane. A roast was never conducted by those below the subject's strata. This is similar to 'hazing' employed by other social groups such as boarding schools, militaries, gangs, clubs and traditional endogroups that seek to break down personal membranes in order to strengthen an endogroup membrane.

Hazing is typically employed before endogroup acceptance to strengthen group bonds, just as ascetic rituals have often preceded group acceptance. Hazing, or extreme teasing, is also often a reaction of a group to the good fortune or achievement of one of their number. Those who have more, those who may feel pride, those who may need to be reminded to be considerate or may need to have their loyalty or humility tested are teased in order to bring them down to the level of the rest of the group. Self-deprecation serves the same purpose but is a pre-emptive and self-inflicted measure to ward off extreme hazing. If this is not done, or if the teasing is rejected, particularly with anger, the target will leave or be shunned out of their endogroup or they may be accorded a new status as endo-ideal.

Individual destruction is used as part of shaming, either as a corrective against those who are not accepting cultural norms or a punishment against those to whom guilt has been assigned. Extreme teasing can have another affect if it is accompanied by shunning. Shunning can cause people to accept the group's negative image assessment of themselves as their own truth. These people may kill themselves or ensure that they live lives of misery and failure. Their acceptance of endoreality demands their agreement that they do not deserve happiness and provides an internalized method of social policing. Sometimes a strong child is tormented to the point that they dissociate from their own community and its endoreality instead, and seek reflection or exosocial interaction from another group. The upper strata of celebrity, wealth and power are filled with people craving reflection to prove their internalized tormenters wrong.

Shunning is not less in third age societies but a wider endogroup makes those shunned more invisible and those with the power to shun more distant. Those with poor health or tragic lives, those who do not conform at school or industry, those who are without money, certification, or now in China, *social credit*, are eliminated by algorithm with little social contact required. The shunning is more inescapable and cruel but dissociated from communal involvement and laughter.

Social affirmation: Social affirmation laughter can be an attempt to socially include an outsider, frequently by pointing out interesting differences in their appearance or behaviour from that of the group. Awareness of diversity is neither xenophobia nor endo-idealism. Isolated villages that comment or laugh about the appearance of outsiders or even follow strangers, touch their hair or mimic them, are not hostile or harmful. They are attempting to increase familiarity through laughter. Laughter can also be in response to recognition of shared similarity, within a group or with a stranger. This laughter is an offer to share a euphoric bond.

A group of people pointing and laughing at a stranger can be either shunning the individual or offering euphoric connection. Typically, endogroups use laughter as a precursor to stronger ridicule and shunning and exosocial people use such laughter as a precursor to acceptance. The latter is often attempted through an inside joke, such as 'tall tales' which everyone in the community knows are fiction but are used to trick an outsider. This shares a quality of hazing, in that the reward at the end is that the stranger has an added bond through being privy to the secret joke. Groups that use such teasing tend to highly value the ability to laugh at oneself as an indicator that the person does not put themselves above the group. The teasing is meant to ensure that the group membrane remains stronger than the individual membrane. This is typical behaviour of highly permeable groups. Strong endogroups, which employ humour as ridicule for exclusion, tend to simply smile (excessively) or laugh without humour, or show no sign of humour, to indicate acceptance of strangers.

Social affirmation laughter can also be from friends at the embarrassment of an included individual. This is not an attempt to shun but reaffirmation that the person is still a valued member of the group despite their personal embarrassment. This type of humour can follow bouts of individual destruction, where included members are alternately ridiculed and then affirmed as a means to strengthen group bonds while simultaneously weakening individual ones.

Social affirmation laughter is an often misinterpreted type of laughter, particular among industrial culture tourists who claim locals in various parts of the world, but particularly Asia, are laughing at them during disputes. Such laughter is far more likely to be either the self affirmation laughter of someone being publicly shamed or the social affirmation laughter being offered to a tourist who is embarrassing themselves, at least in the eyes of the locals, with a public temper tantrum.

Social affirmation humour can also include any kind of shared situational humour. Making people laugh is a path to social acceptance, partly by pointing out cognitive dissonance in exclusion and partly through the bonding experience. According to original *Saturday Night Live* comedian Jane Curtin,[75] her co-star John Belushi thought that women were innately not funny and should not be on the show. This was a show where Curtin played a news anchor whose weekly broadcasts were always responded to by her co-host saying *"Jane, you ignorant slut."* People such as Belushi and skits where the negative image were the comedic foil, were attempting to preserve social barriers. Most comedy from the endo-ideal is limited to that which strengthens endoreality, not that which challenges it.

Making people laugh is an important asset in breaking down social barriers. Comedians with negative image attributes use humour to combat bigotry against them and humorous strategies such as a funny 'pick up line' are sometimes employed to approach strangers when no other option presents itself. A sense of humour, so often cited as an essential trait of attractiveness[76], may be a reference to social openness or the permeability of a healthy social membrane.

Social exclusion: Social shunning by ridicule includes the huge genre of jokes based on ridicule of groups by negative image attributes and it includes online 'trolling' or workplace 'ribbing' that only targets those who the perpetrators want excluded. Social exclusion laughter is frequently also social affirmation laughter as the shunning of an individual strengthens the group membrane of those laughing. This is the type of humour described by Thomas Hobbes as *"The passion of laughter is nothing else but sudden glory arising from sudden conception of some eminency in ourselves, by comparison with the infirmity of others, or with our own formerly."*[77] An example would be a man who, seeking to exclude a woman at his workplace, makes a derogatory joke about women which his male co-workers are expected to laugh at. If any do not, he may subject them to a *'white knight'* or *'cuck'* type of joke as a challenge for them to leave or join the group which is shunning women. The introduction of a magic word is a threat to cast him as a negative image along with the woman, and any accompanying jokes are an attempt to shun him as well. There are a variety of negative image terms designated for defenders of most negative image groups which are used for this purpose.

Empathy develops from shared emotion and mirroring. If a group is laughing at an outsider, as part of shunning, and the outsider joins the laughter, the group will typically stop laughing and escalate to stronger forms of rejection. If they fail to respond in this way, the shared laughter may succeed in forming a bond.

Causing a person to laugh at a joke ostracizing another person or group encourages them to subsequently devalue the person or group. This can happen through an attempt to repair cognitive dissonance. If the person feels they would never laugh at an unfair characterization, they must then start to believe the characterization is true. In addition, if they feel guilt for laughing, they may then transfer that guilt to the victim. Laughter can also be used to normalize behaviour the subject feels guilty about. Guilt is then lessened by making the behaviour seem sanctioned by the group, or at least widespread.

Humour can also be used to break down social aversions to ideas the group have already rejected, such as bigotry towards another group or unaccepted behaviour. Rape jokes are an example of this type of boundary pressure, as well as jokes about other violent or sexual taboos. Jokes which encourage people to laugh at a tragedy serve to minimize the tragedy while forbidden jokes or refusal to laugh enforce endogroup mourning. Laughter from an audience is a shared bond which indicates the barrier has been at least weakened. Shared euphoria makes the audience more empathic with the source and less empathic with anyone who opposes their interaction with a euphoric source. Opposition to a joke may stimulate anger instead of empathy as it seeks to block euphoria. Recognition of this power to weaken taboos and social boundaries is the reason political censors are so wary of comedy[78]. Laughter is a reflection of a reality which may be in opposition to the authoritative reality.

Endogroup domination: This type of laughter is the ridicule of others who are accepted in an endogroup. This is the same as social exclusion except the subject has a choice of being shunned or accepting a negative image designation. Social humiliation is a part of learning to take one's place in a hierarchical society when the endogroup acts at a community level. Targets are, however, sometimes permitted to react angrily. It may have been sometimes acceptable for an ethnically Irish boy in the early United States to punch someone who laughed at him, to challenge the exclusion of being Irish from being socially acceptable. An ethnically Congolese boy would not likely have been permitted the same right to challenge their exclusion. They would be left with the options of leaving (being shunned) or joining the laughter (accepting their position as negative image in the group). This right to anger allowed the United States to stretch their endo-ideal from WASP (white, Anglo-Saxon, Protestant) to 'white' but no further. An expression of endogroup domination is '*They may be [negative image designation] but they are my / our [negative image designation]*', a statement which affirms both the negative image designation and the group acceptance.

A great deal of what was once considered comedy is now considered bullying. Many situations which would have a crowd laughing uproariously a few generations ago are not seen as humorous at all now. In particular, it used to be very common to laugh at children, women and a laundry list of variable negative image categories. The social humiliation has remained but the humour is gone, possibly because the audience has intact personal or group membranes and will not laugh when humiliated or perhaps because endogroup inclusion has been abstracted beyond community acceptance. The dominance is not less in industrialized society but the excluding society is far removed from community laughter.

Endogroup submission: A person designated as the negative image may be expected or coerced to laugh at a joke deriding their own negative image category in order to demonstrate their loyalty to the dominant group endo-ideal and their willingness to persecute others who share their categorization. This is the humour that separates an obedient reflector from a negative image. A requirement of this laughter is there must be a name to call those who refuse to join in the laughter, as the name is the magical curse that casts them out from the group reflector status and into the negative image.

Self-deprecating humour is an offer to lower one's own membrane protection in exchange for social group acceptance. This is often essential for reflectors and the negative image who must indicate their awareness and acceptance of their social roles before being admitted into a group. Among the negative image, a continual self-deprecating narrative is expected but it does not have to be humourous. Those fighting for reflector status are the most likely to employ this humour.

Laughter is often used as ridicule of self to indicate acceptance of a negative image status as a condition of acceptance in a group. This type of humour can be group-specific. The same individual may not use endogroup submission humour in another group or to people they do not recognize as being above them. Women who may laugh at themselves in front of a man will aggressively defend against such humour from another woman. The ready laughter of women, children and lower classes around the world is often of this type or individual or social affirmation. These groups are often ordered to smile and laugh in the presence of the endo-ideal.

This type of humour is also employed as satire by people with negative image attributes who speak in dominant positions, such as professional comedians, to ridicule and weaken strata boundaries. Groups containing people of different power, such as a teacher in a classroom, may use humour effectively against themselves to weaken the social barriers and ease communication[79]. A 2006 study suggested that the use of humour by men could increase their desirability by women, but the same was not true in reverse and neither did women prefer women who used humour as potential relationship partners[80]. It is possible that humour's power to define endoreality is taboo when it is used outside the endo-ideal or that it makes those in the endo-ideal more relatable or sympathetic to those in the negative image, possibly by weakening endoreality dictates that the endo-ideal is infallible.

Endogroup submission humour may be employed by members of the endo-ideal who wish to be seen as relatable by subordinates. The depiction of women in high executive positions as being humourless is probably related to the fact that they are already perceived as the negative image and self-deprecating humour would not work for them in the same way it does for their male colleagues. Pointing out weakness in the negative image does not weaken endoreality, it strengthens it.

Humour has been long associated with both physical and mental health[81]. Exosocial laughter is a means of sharing euphoria. Endosocial laughter is a means of strengthening endosocial membranes which contain endogroup euphoria. All people may laugh in anticipation or experience of a euphoric interaction. Laughter seems to be a method of sharing euphoria or establishing euphoric bonds. Laughter may often be tinged with fear as establishing euphoric bonds always carries the risk of harm to the membrane, or perhaps it is only when cognitive dissonance is also present that laughter and fear appear together.

Humour can point out vices in the endo-ideal by giving them the virtue of being funny. It can also ascribe virtue to the negative image in the same way. In this way, humour has an endoreality-defying power. The cognitive dissonance anxiety usually caused by defying endoreality is released and its damage is repaired through socially acceptable laughter.

A theatre is an enclosed (temporarily endosocial) group which indulges in laughter and tears as a group. It is common for theatre goers to enter as strangers and exit feeling as though they now share a euphoric bond. This unifying aspect may be part of what makes the theatre a valued part of so many societies. What then does it mean when the theatre of the street, the stadium or the closed opera becomes internet streamed entertainment at home? Societies bond on a far more broad scale due to modern media, but they do not typically share the outlets of laughter, crying, fear, anger and more.

Social media has provided some of that wider expansion, but because of the need for commentary, the shared emotion is possibly more often endosocial than exosocial. This wider shared experience, especially globally shared humour, is a crucial part of creating exosocial bonds. The tendency of people online to create globally accessible jokes to share their experiences is a very important aspect to creating shared euphoric bonds which can then encourage formation of empathic bonds to share sorrow, fear and other experience as well. The design and control of these online platforms is the single most important aspect of both implementing and combating global totalitarianism today.

The quality of humour as a means to establish both euphoric conduits and endosocial membranes is interestingly shared by violence. Every one of the above uses for humour also apply to violence. The shared euphoria from sports is an exosocial joy. Asceticism is used in times of severe personal crisis as self affirmation. Shared violence is used as social bonding and an offer to fight or undergo an ascetic ritual or play a violent or at least competitive and physically demaning sport is a precursor to acceptance in many endogroups. Extreme stag parties and other rituals ensure endogroup loyalties on occasions it might be weakened and violence is as much a part of such hazing as humour. Violence is also used for individual destruction and social exclusion as well as endogroup domination and submission.

Furthermore, humour is often used in place of violence and vice versa. If a person is being ridiculed, they are likely to retaliate with a punch and if they are punched they will likely retaliate with ridicule. Often, people develop one attribute to compensate for a lack in the other. Whatever quality is present in humour seems to also be present in violence. Both have been declared taboo in social situations where they were once normal, as the authoritative endoreality is discouraging bonding at lower endogroups.

Pride, envy and jealousy

Once you're here, you're ready to give everything, or almost everything, to stay and play a part in the great theatre of belonging." - Valeria Luiselli, *Tell Me How It Ends: An Essay in Forty Questions*

Every emotion is anticipation or experience of access to euphoria or anticipation or experience of an attack on a euphoric source. Even guilt and shame are related to shunning and inclusion from a euphoric source or protective group membrane. If the person is primarily exosocial, the emotion relates to a euphoric conduit or source. If they are primarily endosocial, the emotion relates to an endo-ideal or an endosocial membrane. The presence and allocation of pride, envy and jealousy is a reflection of endogroup boundaries and roles. These emotions, all felt in response to acclaim, achievements or attainments of another or oneself, are very different depending on the presence of assigned endogroup roles.

Outside of an endogroup, pride is solitary or shared euphoria over achievement. Within an endogroup, pride is an antonym to shame, depicting the status of a person as the endo-ideal of an endogroup. The laws of endoreality allocate pride, along with all credit, to the endo-ideal and shame to the negative image. If the endo-ideal acquires external credit or a coveted object, it is a source of pride for the entire group. Members of an endogroup also feel pride when a member of their endogroup behaves in a manner which adds to the exceptional myth of the endogroup.

Parents often feel pride at the external valuation of their children, as North American bumper stickers which brag about the academic standing (or product grading) of children attest. Nationalists may also feel pride regarding national monuments or royal possessions, even if they are never allowed near them. Pride is a feeling of well-being or euphoria resulting from the achievements of an endo-ideal or the strengthening of a shared exceptional myth, which in turn, strengthens the endogroup. This is why people in an endogroup are often shocked by the suggestion that the success of the endo-ideal does not benefit anyone else in the group. Their displaced and shared ambition and pride makes them unaware of the perception of their individual condition in universal reality. Conversely, an endosocial person may feel confused or threatened by an exosocial statement of pride in their achievement as it feels to them like a claim of ownership or dominance.

Aristotle's definition of pride in his Ethics, described a man who *"thinks himself worthy of great things, being worthy of them."*[82] The baked-in subjectivity of this definition is evidence that it refers to the social status of an endo-ideal. Aristotle's definition of hubris, in his Rhetoric, is, *"to cause shame to the victim, not in order that anything may happen to you, nor because anything has happened to you, but merely for your own gratification. Hubris is not the requital of past injuries; this is revenge. As for the pleasure in hubris, its cause is this: naive men think that by ill-treating others they make their own superiority the greater."*[83] This is the display of endogroup pride which is the partner of endogroup envy. It is the pride that promotes the endo-ideal at the expense of the negative image.

Pride may be seen as the domain of the endo-ideal who has achieved authoritative status and hubris, like vanity, is attributed to one outside the endo-ideal, where authoritative society does not agree with their self-assessment. Whether or not pride is considered merited is simply a measure of how much the self-assessment aligns with authoritative endoreality. When the authoritative endogroup agrees, there is no need for the boasting and reflection-seeking of hubris or vanity as ample reflection is being provided. This relative, or endosocial, quality of the definition is supported by the frequency with which pride is attributed to a national endo-ideal and hubris and vanity to women and lower classes or to mortals in the presence of gods.

In order for a reflector to avoid the accusation of hubris and associated punishments, they must immediately credit their work to the endo-ideal, whether that is a god, master or king. In more industrialized societies, it is the employer or the mythical 'group mind' that must be assigned credit for any extraordinary achievement from the wrong source. The punishments for disobeying this dictum are seen in punishments for hubris throughout mythology and history or the vilification for 'ego' in a negative image today.

Honour is related to the exceptional myth. Any challenge to the exceptional myth is seen as an attack on honour and requires either an external endogroup aggression or the sacrifice of a negative image. Honour can contribute to face or a personal membrane but seldom in a good way. A lack of honour harms a membrane and defence of honour harms its permeability. Someone who would murder their daughter to save their honour could not be said to have a healthy membrane, one which is resilient, permeable and strong through relationships. The word honour is an endosocial term as it is a hierarchical measure of approval. It is replaced in an exoself by dignity, which refers to the preservation of ownership over the inner circles of self which creates personal integrity and strength.

It is interesting to contrast the well-known emotion of pride, seen in sports stadiums everywhere, with the expression of Medusa in Argentinian sculptor Luciano Garbati's brilliant reversal of the tale. There is a divide in the reaction to personal victory which reflects endogroup status. The reactions are dictated by whether the achievement is fulfillment of an endo-ideal destiny, an offering by an obedient reflector to an external endo-ideal (such as god, king or master), an achievement that will bring rage and retribution upon the head of a negative image, as beautifully depicted by Garbati, or an exosocial euphoric achievement which does not affect endogroup standing.

The endo-ideal experiences what is typically thought of as pride, a surge of power and affirmation of their endo-ideal status, for which they need reflection. The reflector experiences anticipation, anxiety or satisfaction in an offering to their endo-ideal. The negative image is reminded again of their status, fears retribution, and experiences shame, sorrow, guilt and resolution in parts dictated by their own situation. Finally, the exoself experiences simple achievement euphoria. It is easy to see why these very different emotions produce very different rewards for achievement and lead to very different motivation. In terms of energy, pride brings energy to the achiever, the reflector offering brings energy to the endo-ideal of the achiever and the negative image will have the victory energy released against them, entirely or in part, through envy and shame. Studies indicate that stress in those outside the endo-ideal increases on achievement[84] and this discrepancy in energy transfer explains why.

Envy is the response felt by members of an endogroup if the external acclaim or a coveted item is held by someone outside the endogroup or its endo-ideal. Envy combined with anger and vindictiveness is felt if such credit or ownership is allocated to the negative image or a reflector and such allocation is often felt to be an injustice. Since the purpose of justice systems is to uphold the sublation of the endogroup to the endo-ideal and enforce the endoreality laws which allocate all credit and ownership to the endo-ideal, this is a reasonable endogroup response. Credit allocation in an endogroup is a zero sum game. Envy is a solely endosocial response and it is the wish to right what is perceived to be an injustice in the allocation of glory and to restore the pride to what they perceive as its rightful owner. The correlation between feelings of envy and subsequent joy in the envied person's misfortune reflect this demand for restoration of endogroup order through punishment of the fortunate.[85]

Envy can be used to discern a person's perception of the endosocial role of another. When hearing of the achievement or victimhood of another, do they ignore, refuse eye contact or change the subject? Immediately, or soon after, do they find someone else with claims of similar achievement or victimhood and demand the first person empathize with or reflect the new claimant? (If they are the endo-ideal it will be themselves they present as the new claimant.) Do they diminish the achievement or victimhood? Do they sabotage or punish the person? The above behaviours are all indications that they see the person as the negative image or a reflector, unentitled to recognition or empathy. If achievement is acknowledged, they may attempt to assign guilt and turn the achievement into a vice, usually with accusations of dereliction of duty in the person's rightful place. A woman with achievement in creation or discovery may immediately be assigned any caregiving duty that can be found or invented, with the strong implication that she must have too much time on her hands. In addition, she will have her caregiving status critiqued along with any higher recognition.

While approving responses to achievement vary greatly by culture, even the most restrained cultures will make direct eye contact (where that is unusual) to indicate strong approval, even if it is a completely impassive stare, or they will ignore the achievement but make something nice happen for the person. Even the most restrained cultures will also respond supportively to victimhood through physical proximity (a tactic used by many animals as well) and making nice things happen for the person.

Eye contact appears to have bonding effects, as seen in the tendency of infants to stare at their caregivers and everyone to stare at a new love. Eye contact is also avoided as part of decorum in more restrained cultures and in those who have trouble bonding. Direct eye contact is often forbidden towards an endo-ideal. Eye contact appears to have both dominance and self-recognition, or bonding, qualities. In the case of achievement, eye contact appears to be recognition of achievement, perhaps manifested in the tendency to place people on stages and stare at them as achievement recognition. Avoidance of eye contact appears to be a refusal to recognize achievement.

In Aristotle's Ethics, envy is described as *"the pain caused by the good fortune of others" and "those who have what we ought to have."*[82] Kant defined envy as *"a reluctance to see our own well-being overshadowed by another's"*. [86] Neither Kant nor Aristotle nor anyone since has been able to explain why we would feel pain at the good fortune of others at some points and pride in others. Parents of children in competitive sports consistently prove that their self has expanded and their endo-ideal has refracted into their child in whose destiny they now place all their ambition and envy. It is also proven in any endogroup where reflectors labour and lust for power for a dissociated endo-ideal, whether that is in politics, sports or industry.

This cannot be dismissed as simply people expecting residual benefit from belonging to a group as envy is just as strong in people who are fully aware they will never reap any benefit from the power of their endo-ideal. Envy is a lust for greater power on behalf of an endo-ideal, whether that endo-ideal is internal or external. It results in hatred of those outside the endogroup or in vindictiveness to non-ideal members of the endogroup who are perceived as trying to claim achievement instead of giving it to the endo-ideal. A lot of vindictiveness towards successful reflectors or negative image is this sort of refracted envy. Many people who have no ambition of their own outside of their reflector roles are enraged by the thought of other designated negative image or reflectors succeeding in wider fields. They feel no resentment towards endo-ideal success, however, and they will do their best to redirect the credit they are envious of back to the nearest endo-ideal.

A similar feeling of injustice and the impulse to even out advantage is seen in many or most cultures when inequality is perceived. In these cases, those perceived to be unfairly advantaged will be strongly or even forcibly encouraged to make restitution for their relative advantage. This is sometimes reflected even in attitudes towards advantage which can be neither helped nor shared, often described as the tall poppy syndrome (a recommendation to cut off the heads of tall poppies)[87] or a crab mentality (in reference to the habit of crabs in a bucket to pull back any crabs who attempt to escape). The Christian Bible has countless enumerations of this type of envy and remonstrations against it while the Hindu concept of karma usefully provides a justification for inequality and promise of eventual balance where none can be seen in current life.

Enforced equality is often seen in both fully egalitarian cultures and communities which are bonded by their relative inferior status, and there is considerable evidence that it may be an innate tendency. It is closely related to avoidance of unbalanced transactions which any advantage would necessarily incur and it is a natural force against the accumulation of power, or endosocialism. Although this feeling is more often described in terms of justice than envy, it is the same impulse to apply the group standards of justice to allocation of advantage. These two tendencies, to enforce egalitarianism and enforce the laws of endosocialism, are often combined. Groups seen as the negative image often refuse to let each other succeed but attribute credit to the endo-ideal instead of their peers. Women have historically been justly famous for this tendency, but it may be found in many disadvantaged communities as well. Envy may be considered an endosocial perversion of this innate drive towards balanced interactions. Instead of a drive towards equality or balance, endogroup justice is seen as the allocation of all advantage to the endo-ideal.

In a society filled with endoselves, any achievement or possession of another may give rise to envy. In a more bonded society, with a higher transcendental endogroup, achievement is met with approval as long as it is in recognition of an obedient reflector, not advancement to an endo-ideal.

Jealousy is felt within an endogroup if one member is closer to the endo-ideal than another. A person may be jealous of the achievements of their own spouse which threatens their position as the couple endo-ideal, they may be jealous of a their spouse's preference for a third party, or they may be jealous of another person's proximity to a nation-ideal such as a boss or celebrity. Jealousy is instigated by fear of a change in one's own endogroup status. Jealousy relates to one's own status relative to the group, as opposed to envy which relates to what is seen as any misplaced advantage. While envy can result in a longing for vengeance, jealousy may result in a competitive resolve to do better, as indicated by its Greek root *zēlos* which is also the root of zeal. It is not negative in this context, and is often attributed to god in Judaism and every god in many other cultures, such as that of the Greeks. Because it relates to endogroup relative standing, this is another exclusively endosocial emotion. The only similar exosocial emotion would be guilt in not having met one's own standards or ambition to improve.

Although jealousy is hopelessly conflated with violence, violence cannot be attributed directly to jealousy unless elimination of the threat will increase the jealous person's own standing. When jealousy is a result of an outside threat to a couple bond, it combines with either fear or anger to produce the usual violent responses to endogroup threats. If the threat is seen as removal of the endo-ideal's rightful property it may produce vengeful violence, as seen in the Bible's attitude towards women as the property of their husbands or various people as the property of god. The Old Testament condemned envy (wanting the property of another) but endorsed jealousy (wanting to preserve allegiance) as godlike, therefore sanctioned. This meant that men were not allowed to covet the property of another man but were allowed to exact vengeance if their 'property' such as wives or children strayed. If the threat to status causes the endo-ideal to experience shame, it may lead to punishment of the negative image to relieve the shame. In these situations jealousy is correlated with violence, it is not a cause of violence. The precursor to violence is the threat of a dissolution of the endogroup or the perceived insult to the endo-ideal. It would be more meaningful to isolate which of these three attitudes, the threat to the endogroup, the perceived property ownership, or shame, were actually behind specific acts of violence.

Jealousy in reflectors is caused by a desire for greater proximity to the endo-ideal, relative to another. Reflectors experience jealousy and pain along with anger directed towards their rival. This has often been used as a source of endo-ideal amusement in romantic and other relationships as the endo-ideal can torment rival reflectors to war with each other at no risk to themselves. Jealousy in an endo-ideal is caused by a perceived or dreaded change of allegiance by the reflector and is most often directed towards the object of possession. This jealousy is caused by a fear of weakening endo-ideal-reflector bonds within an endogroup. It results in rage which attempts to strengthen those bonds and prevent the escape of the other party. In death, the other party is still sublated to the killer, so it is often preferable to kill the other party than to let them escape the endogroup.

Pride, envy and jealousy are all the result of zero-sum or relative social attributes, where in order for one to rise, there must be a relative fall of others. All three can only exist within the relative state of the endogroup. Exosocial pride may be better understood as achievement euphoria.

Sorrow and joy

It saddened her that Luo insisted on holding on to her as if they had started to share some vital organs during their twenty years of marriage. She wondered if this was a sign of old age, of losing hope and the courage for changes. She herself could easily picture vanishing from their shared life, but then perhaps it was a sign of aging on her part, a desire for loneliness that would eventually make death a relief. - Yiyun Li, *Gold Boy, Emerald Girl*

Joy is the experience of euphoric energy obtained through euphoric conduits to sources such as nations, creation or discovery. Such joy may come from daily experience, as expressed in such concepts as *joie de vivre* in France or *pura vida* in Costa Rica. It may occur in a burst of expansion, such as during birth or death or other great exosocial expansion. It may also occur at a sudden discovery of a great euphoric source, such as experienced when falling in love or acquiring a new physical skill. For an endoself, who possesses no or few euphoric conduits, the closest feeling to joy is avarice, the desire of possession. The only euphoria they are able to experience is the secondary euphoria obtained through cruelty and destruction.

Sorrow is a result of euphoric depletion. This may occur due to the blockage of euphoric conduits, the unavailability of euphoric sources, the need for an increase in euphoric sources prior to exosocial expansion or the assignment of debt through guilt. There are three primary types of sorrow. One is *loss sorrow,* when euphoric sources are no longer available. Another is *expansion sorrow,* when exosocial expansion is forced, restricted or diverted. The last is *shame sorrow,* when exosocial freedom is lost due to the destruction of self by shame.

Sorrow is a state of grieving. It can occur upon bereavement, when one is deprived of a connection that brought them joy. In severe sorrow, the self can return to a catatonic state similar to that of a neglected child who has not yet formed a self. Sorrow can also be felt for the blockage of potential bonds. People grieve for the loss of opportunity to form bonds, such as those found in marriage, childbirth, travel or creation. Grief can be felt in the loss of freedom, such as freedom of movement or freedom to associate. A child who is prevented from playing with other children, a painter struck by blindness or anyone imprisoned may feel such grief. Sadness in the form of a general melancholy may precede periods of necessary expansion in life, such as adolescense or middle or old age.This melancholy precedes, and may initiate, the energy required for subsequent expansion.

Finally, grief can be felt at a loss of self, commonly depicted as a loss of innocence. This occurs when the self endures some traumatic event that causes them to lose dignity and trust and the ability to freely seek out exosocial attachment. Events such as rape or other attack, loss of home, loss of family members through death or abandonment, or extreme communal shunning can contribute to such a change in self. This grief can mark a transition from an exosocial existence to a negative image role and accompanies an extreme character transition. It can be seen as a permanent change and the loss of the ability to be happy. This is the sorrow that accompanies shame and it follows guilt transference. The pain brought by shame appears to be the result of a blockage of euphoric conduits. This sorrow is the last gift of a negative image, as it provides them with the motivation to expand which a reflector and endo-ideal lack. The motivation to expand is often expressed as hope and it is usually represented as the last gift of the desperate.

A person with a refracted core may be particularly affected by the loss of their endo-ideal as this person occupies their core self. In such cases, long-term dissociation and memory loss and a feeling of being not present, or nothing being real, are common. In some cultures, this feeling is externally encouraged as mourners are expected to live greatly restricted lives on the death of their endo-ideal, such as the three year mourning period for parents in Confucian filiality, or cease living entirely as seen in several traditions of suicides upon the death of a husband or master. These customs may be demands of proof that a person was properly sublated to the point of refraction, or perhaps they are evidence that such refraction was common. In other cultures, dissociation is considered abnormal or is unrecognized, but it is no less present. If the mourner is unable to develop a core self, through transference or growth, they may feel such emptiness for the rest of their lives.

Upon the death of a loved one, a primary caregiver may feel intense euphoria. This is not simply 'relief' as it is often described. This can be an effect of the euphoria they were producing and transferring to their suffering loved one in altruistic interactions, which is now kept by themselves. Following the birth of an infant, the mother may feel the typical, post-natal, euphoric surge even when the infant has died. These temporary surges of well-being may add to guilt and do not help with grief in the long term as they do not establish any new euphoric conduits. Any euphoria is an aid to health and should be encouraged, but these people may find they need the most support after the community around them is expecting they will need less.

Anger is a natural result of grief which comes from the need to rebuild a membrane. This anger is often directed outwards, in a quest to remedy whatever caused the death of a loved one or the destruction or loss of another euphoric source. This is usually a very healthy and helpful step in rebuilding the self as it encourages a drive to expand outwards instead of building an endoself membrane. People who ignore their family and friends and pour their energy and time into work, creation or travel are also seeking euphoric conduits that provide greater replenishment, which they need. Alternatively, they may be attempting to strengthen their traumatized personal membrane. Everyday relationships are often too draining in a time of crisis and may need to be shut out for the person's self-protection.

Extreme isolation and refusal to participate in any euphoric interactions is the opposite reaction. This may be caused by residual guilt in a negative image. It may also be accompanied by increased self-destructive behaviour as punishment for that guilt. Those that fall into addiction or refuse to work or interact are often experiencing a negative image guilt response. Guilt may also be present in others who feel the person died when they still had unbalanced transactions outstanding. It is very common for a regret for not doing more, or a statement that they were just about to do more, to be the first response from a person hearing the news of someone's death. Typical after-death rituals give people the opportunity to balance outstanding debt. Guilt management is particularly important for a negative image who will often feel that they ought to have prevented a death or died instead, or both. A lack of ritual to manage guilt increases the likelihood that the sufferer will have to rely on self-destructive punishment instead.

In times of grief caused by the death of a loved one, ritual and community can be extremely important in associating the individual with a wider self and encouraging them to see their pain as shared by the wider group to lessen its trauma. Community and ritual also serve to create an immediate protective membrane, to occupy time until a dissociated person manages to find themselves again and to manage any residual guilt through ritualized procedures established for the purpose. They also maintain a caregiving relationship with the deceased through spiritual ritual, lessening the abruptness of a traumatic break. The industrialized erasure of such community and ritual works only for the endoself.

All sorrow causes pain which, in a healthy response, encourages further expansion in order to heal. A person who has lost a family member may be encouraged by this pain, accompanied by the release from the caregiver endogroup, to expand their creation and discovery circles. A person who has lost their long term spouse may turn intensely to spiritual connections. A person who has lost mobility may expand relationships, a person who has lost physical freedom through imprisonment may expand mental freedom and a person who has been deprived of the opportunity to play may expand their imagination. Sorrow, like all pain, is a signal to repair what is damaged. Ultimately, sorrow is the pain that dissolves endosocial membranes and encourages or forces wider exoocial expansion.

Sorrow and joy are two examples of emotions dulled to near extinction in societies which celebrate and idealize the endoself. Those who do still experience sorrow and joy are met in industrialized society with bemusement and offers of medication.

Love and hate

Love never dies a natural death. It dies because we don't know how to replenish its source. - Anais Nin, *The Four-Chambered Heart.*

Love is not, as so many authoritative endo-ideals would have it, the meeting of the Other and reflection or negation of Self. Instead, as poets and lovers themselves have insisted since the beginning of poets and lovers, it is the completion of self, or at least a large step in that direction. Love is the fulfillment of many euphoric conduits. The erasure of self and existential power struggle so insisted on by Hegelians is the hallmark of an abusive relationship. This may once have been the patriarchal standard for magical bonds of wedlock, but it has never had anything to do with love or romance.

Love is a desire to create or maintain euphoric bonds and hate is the need to block a potential or formerly euphoric bond. It is impossible to hate anyone who is not a part of one's social membrane, currently, recently or potentially. Exosocial people feel attraction to sources of euphoria and revulsion towards that which blocks or destroys access to euphoria but attraction and revulsion are not the same as love and hate. Both love and hate are intense responses to others which are dependent on some shared experience, even if only through propaganda. Often the most intense hate is produced in the same populations which formerly experienced the most intense love, such as in civil wars or familial breakups. Both hate and love and the lesser emotions around them are measures of social approval. Love softens personal or group membranes to create a shared self and then it forms a new membrane around this self. Hate destroys the membrane, with the accompanying rage and sorrow, and then builds another without the shunned person. Love establishes euphoric conduits and hate blocks them up again.

Love creates a membrane around those who love, making empathy and shared euphoria easier. If that membrane becomes impermeable, the relationship becomes an endogroup and a power struggle. In this case, love gives way to exploitation and dependence. This occurs along with ownership and all the other trappings of endogroups and is seen wherever these are imposed on families, nations, creation, discovery, spirituality or other euphoric sources.

In all cases, love has three stages: *attraction,* marked by excitement and intense curiosity, *connection,* marked by joy in experiencing another, and *expansion,* at which point the destruction of the new shared self would cause severe trauma. This process is the same for the creation of any euphoric conduits, not simply relationships between people.

In an endoself, love is replaced by lust. In their case, the three stages are changed to *lust,* manifesting as an intense desire for possession, *possession,* during which the endoself seeks outside reflection in the form of admiration of their new possession and lastly, *disillusionment*, boredom and punishment of the object which is blamed for the disappointment. Again, this cycle is the same for any possession including travel, home, religion, etc.

Love is an exosocial attachment. However, the fear associated with too focused or overwhelming an attachment with one source of euphoria can lead to the desire to turn an exosocial attachment, or love, into an endogroup where one possesses the other. If the lover feels they could not survive the loss of their beloved, they may seek to entrap the beloved and remove their free will. This may be through sublation of their self in an attempt to make an endo-ideal of their beloved, or through demands for reflection and transfers of guilt in an attempt to make themselves the endo-ideal. In this process, one or the other must become the negative image, and the endo-ideal will come to despise them while still draining them of the euphoria they were initially attracted to.

It is not possible to love as the endo-ideal because the endo-ideal turns others into objects as soon as they are attained. The person they strive for is not present in the object they subsequently possess. Like Midas, everything they touch is transformed, not into gold but into themselves. As Sartre lamented in Being and Nothingness, *"As soon as I throw myself toward the Other's facticity, as soon as I wish to push aside his acts and his functions so as to touch him in his flesh, I incarnate myself, for I can neither wish nor even conceive of the incarnation of the Other except in and by means of my own incarnation."*[88] Neither is it possible to love as the reflector or negative image, as their self is found in the endo-ideal.

Guilt transference, construction of an endoreality and shame are all signs that a power struggle is occurring. A healthy love is marked by joy, gratitude and altruism. Any joy in an exosocial interaction is a shared joy. Any healthy relationship maintains balance to avoid guilt, power and shame.

Any love which forms an endogroup becomes a power relation and loses the quality of love, which is the ability to establish healthy, balanced, euphoric conduits. The subsequent cruelty that begins in such a relationship may be, at least in part, caused by a craving for a more true connection, even if that connection is through fear and pain. To continue Sartre's explanation, *"I take and discover myself in the process of taking, but what I take in my hands is something else than what I wanted to take. I feel this and I suffer from it but without being capable of saying what I wanted to take; for along with my troubled disturbance the very comprehension of my desire escapes me. ... It is this situation which is at the origin of sadism."*

Sartre, echoing most fundamental thought of his time (and since), claimed that *"all of men's complex patterns of conduct toward one another are only enrichments of* [sadism, masochism and hate.]" and he described sadism as *"an effort to incarnate the Other through violence"*, and *"the appropriation and utilization of the Other"*. Such an outlook is not valid for anyone except an endoself, which Sartre embodied and from which perspective he claimed universal truths. It may be considered a valid statement for many in his condition, however, and what a sad, bitter condition it is.

Object desire is a perilous, deceptive and ultimately destructive force. As Sartre and others have pointed out, sadism and masochism are intrinsically related to subject-object desire and sublation. This is not love at all. It is predation. Those that desire an object become disappointed as the object loses its gloss. Those that establish euphoric bonds with another change their definition of desirability to coincide with the source. In this way, a beloved may be never more loved than when they lie on their deathbed, a shell of their former self. This would make them an object of horror and revulsion to one who loved them as an object.

The confusion of object-desire with love is a result of placing endoselves in the position to define reality. When surrounded by discussion of love, and in full ignorance of their own ignorance, they authoritatively defined a thing they had no experience of. As a result, love and predation have been inextricably entwined in the annals of psychology, law and other authoritative institutions. This definition of love has been used as an excuse for the predations of an endoself, including rape, torture, murder, isolation and sublation in all forms.

The terms *soul mate* or *destiny* are often used to describe an exosocial relationship in which it may be perceived, sometimes near instantly, that there is a euphoric connection between two people. This is very different from the subject-object attraction which is based on a worldly desire for a shiny object, often because its characteristics have been found to correspond to items on a list or because they attract external admiration. This is the difference between the electricity felt between two strangers who pass in a crowd and the criteria submitted to a matchmaker. This is not to say a match from a matchmaker cannot eventually produce euphoria and result in love, but, as the saying goes, the match starts lukewarm and builds to a boil as opposed to the physical attractions that start at a boil and often cool to lukewarm.

Hatred arises from a need to strengthen a protective membrane and is a sign of weakness. Greater strength has no need of hatred. The negative image or reflector in a power struggle may hate the endo-ideal, but the endo-ideal feels simply contempt for them. Behind all hatred is fear. The endo-ideal seldom experiences true hatred, but they do experience the vindictiveness required to inflict punishment. This is born of the righteousness which accompanies their position as judge and is object-cruelty, not hate. Hate would require recognition of their victim as a separate person.

Hatred can only produce its own euphoria through violence. Euphoria is increased by membrane strengthening during war, which is simulated in rituals like sports. Spontaneous outbreaks of fighting between sports fans or players increases this euphoria, as does winning. Violence is not an integral part of hatred and can lead to bonding through shared euphoria. Hatred encourages the type of violence that leads to sublation, rendering impotent those they fear.

Hatred rises from a need to protect a vulnerable self from forming a bond with another. It can protect those within an endogroup from weakening their membrane with exosocial ties. It can separate reflectors and negative images and ensure social punishment of the negative image by blocking empathy. It can also help save a reflector or negative image from a predatory endo-ideal. Hatred provides the motivation for endosocial membranes which anger is used to build. Hatred also provides the fear which demands sublation of the other.

Hatred of self accompanies shame. The hatred of all reflectors for the negative image, is born of a fear of becoming the negative image. This hatred appears among those who are in some danger of being cast as the negative image and is not usually seen in the endo-ideal. An exception is on the occasions when an endo-ideal is made to feel temporary shame and may feel in danger of being cast as the negative image. At these times, their hatred is very strong and very dangerous.

Hatred is a sign of weakness and manifests as fear, shame or anger. For an endoself, it does not appear at all as their hatred is replaced by contempt, object-cruelty, or rage. It is doubtful that hate is nearly as useful a term as it is credited with being. It does not appear to be an emotion in its own right. At best, it is a cognitive state. It is definitely not a useful term on which to base laws. Laws should discourage predation and sublation, which are the abuse of unequal force, not a poorly defined cognitive state. So-called hate speech should be recognized as curses, that speech which casts a person as a negative image and transfers guilt to them unjustly. It is very unlikely that institutions built by and for predation and sublation are going to criminalize these behaviours. It is even more doubtful that any third age legal systems are going to outlaw curses and casting.

Sympathy and empathy

What you do makes a difference, and you have to decide what kind of difference you want to make. - Jane Goodall.

Empathy is a result of shared interaction. Empathy has been extensively researched in biology and tied to a large array of neural circuits which may or may not be shared through mirror neurons or other means. For our purposes, it doesn't matter. Mirror neurons indicate the action-reaction quality of empathy. By whatever means an empathic conduit is created, it is evident that one exists. The so-called emotional contagion experienced by infants or mobs is a result of empathy.

Altruism results from empathy and creates a balanced interaction if the recipient responds with gratitude. Gratitude has been shown to increase the frequency of altruism[89] and to have positive impacts on mental health. Such altruistic exchange results in a euphoric transfer and strengthens an empathic conduit between the two parties. Since this results in self-expansion, the benefits of altruism are shared euphoria.

Sympathy is a result of cognitive imagination. Where there are no shared empathic conduits, people are encouraged to associate those they have empathy with to those in distress to create a cognitive connection. Sympathy is closely related to pity. It requires no empathic bonds, as it is a cognitive decision based on observed facts or endoreality, not an experienced emotion. Charity is a result of sympathy. Charity is an unbalanced transaction which produces guilt in the recipient. If this guilt is accepted, it makes the recipient a negative image. If it is transferred, it makes the giver a negative image. Charity does not establish any shared bonds or euphoric exchange. Charity is more likely to divide its participants through guilt and debt, which is why it is so often resented by both participants. Sympathy and pity are also often resented for the same reasons. A decrease in empathy for another person's pain if they are perceived to have been economically unfair has been evidenced, at least in men,[90] indicating the alienating effect of perceived indebtedness.

Sympathy and empathy are often conflated in both scientific and academic literature, and are difficult to separate by most definitions, but there is a need to clearly separate the responses which result from empathic experience and the responses which result from cognitive moral judgment. There have been attempts for several decades to effect this change, with inconsistent results. The empathic connection results in a wider experience of self while the moral judgment, especially if passed through a strong endofilter, will result in casting the recipient of sympathy as a negative image and assigning debt to them. The current trend to separating terms such as *affective–perceptual empathy* (empathy) and *cognitive–evaluative empathy* (sympathy) seems awkward and insufficient, especially since these are, both biologically and socially, very different processes[91]. Since there are two words and two definitions, they should be allocated usefully.

For instance, people displaying characteristics associated with the diagnoses of psychopathic and narcissistic disorders have low empathy (affective–perceptual empathy) but average sympathy (cognitive–evaluative empathy)[92] which, along with other research, supports the idea that their supposed impairment is simply an endosocial barrier. Further research that indicates supposed psychopaths can empathize when they consciously try to[93] also supports the idea that there is nothing abnormal about them other than endogroup boundaries.

It is also necessary to clearly separate altruism, which is a balanced exchange of assistance and gratitude and results in empathic connection, from charity, which creates debt and results in a power struggle over debt assignment. Altruism may also be strongly rejected if it is attempted across an endosocial barrier which the potential recipient wishes to maintain. This rejection may be through a repulsion of the altruistic gesture or an immediate reciprocal action to change the nature of the act into trade, which occurs across endosocial boundaries. Such rejection will result in endoself contagion through a blockage of all attempts to establish empathic conduits.

A nation is marked by empathy. There is no, or reduced, empathy outside endosocial barriers. Endogroups can be weakened or made exosocial by an establishment of empathy for outside groups. Advertisers seek to gain sympathy through an empathic chain. The first step to gaining sympathy from an endogroup is to encourage empathic connection. Sympathy can only be established within an endogroup so establishing shared identity is essential. People are encouraged to have sympathy for group A because they have empathy with group B and group B has empathy for group A. Organizations fundraising for women's cancer used these strategies with their campaigns depicting victims as somebody's *mother, sister, daughter* or *friend*. A similar principle is used by those who declare *I have a lesbian/Muslim/African friend* to establish links between individuals and show that the membrane between groups is unimportant, or at least permeable. These are all endosocial strategies, as exosocial empathy does not require a shared endogroup or an empathic chain.

Empathy is most highly developed in an exoself and extremely dulled in an endoself. Within an endogroup, all empathy is vectored towards the endo-ideal, making the endo-ideal very likely to lose their own empathic ability since their empathy is directed inwards.

Sympathy is the foundation of the NGO industry which is set up to moderate altruism and ensure an endogroup structure maintains the power relationship between the benefactor and recipient. In these structures, gratitude is expressed by the organization, not the recipient and is performative, in the form of a card, a plaque or other object signifying virtuous status. Not only does the structure of NGOs intercept the establishment of empathic conduits, it makes the recipients of aid be cast as the negative image in the eyes of both the giver and the NGO. This is evidenced by the ongoing, global pattern of dehumanization and abuse directed towards recipients of institutional aid. This is especially marked when contrasted with the shared bonds and mutual respect which usually result from altruism.

This negative image casting is often expressed by people who prefer donating to NGOs to *ensure it is used wisely* or *to prevent the recipient from buying drugs* or other such derogatory assumptions. These feelings persist even in the face of repeated instances of NGOs preying on recipients and themselves buying drugs and absconding with or wasting money and all the other things the negative image is accused of. This is a side effect of any endogroup, which is to say every organization. CEOs are always thought to be necessary to ensure that employees are not lazy, incompetent or criminal, despite well documented instances of wildly destructive and criminal behaviour by CEOs.

Altruism results in shared euphoria. Charity results in virtue assigned to the giver and shame assigned to the recipient, which is evidence that it is an endosocial transaction, not an exosocial interaction. This may result in a bond between the giver and NGO but it still casts the recipient as the negative image. It is the goal of the endogroup to cut off all external supplies of euphoria and prevent an individual self from forming by monopoly of human dignity and all individual credit. Co-option of altruism is a very important part of preventing any euphoric bonds from forming and preveting replenishment of the carefully destroyed negative image. It is also an important tool in ensuring that all transactions remain unbalanced.

Boredom and excitement

'Tis better far to wish in vain than not to have a wish. - Charles Lloyd

In *Stanzas to Ennui,* written in 993, Charles Lloyd calls ennui a *"soul destroying fiend"* that chiefly reigns over those exempted from *"life's external woes"*. He also compares the endless quest for relief to that of Tantalus and claims he would *"rather writhe in pangs than bear satiety's plethoric heir."* His sentiment anticipates findings of the last several decades that indicate the suffering of those in solitary confinement is both harder to bear and causes more long-term damage than physical torture.[94] It is interesting that Lloyd characterizes boredom as an affliction of those with the least want. While boredom is certainly suffered now by all income levels, it has not lost all association with the wealthy.

Of all the human behaviours or emotions that may have been pathologized, boredom is the only one that always signifies a harmful environment or a maladjusted self. This is an emotion which is never seen in a healthy exoself unless it is being forced to submit to a more powerful will. It is also an emotion which is chronic in an endoself. Boredom, like the endoself, has never been pathologized. This is likely because of its association with the endo-ideal whose characteristics are always used as the definition of normative and because every institution is designed to create and enforce an endoself. Boredom and totalitarianism are intrinsically connected. Boredom is also the most receptive state in which to induce object desire, the goal of all advertisers under industrial endo-idealism.

A study published in 2014[95] showed that 67% of men and 25% of women gave themselves a shock, which they had earlier indicated they would pay rather than receive again, rather than pass fifteen minutes simply thinking with no stimulation. One man administered 190 shocks to himself during the fifteen minute period. The stimulus to seeking sensation is boredom, and boredom is a sign of an endoself. Unfortunately, there are no associated personality profiles that would indicate a correlation between boredom and endoselves, but there is plenty of evidence in daily observation or in writings. Unsurprisingly, connections have been established suggesting that boredom, destruction and depression are linked and they are all characteristic of an endoself.

Boredom occurs when someone is near a euphoric interaction they cannot access. This is a chronic state in an endoself who can never access primary euphoria and must always crave secondary euphoria through object possession and destruction. Many people have described boredom as nothingness which occurs in the absence of constant novelty and stimulus. Nothingness is life inside an endosocial membrane which blocks all euphoric conduits. This is the existential boredom of the upper classes, or the idle people of any class today. In the place of an expansion drive, endoselves are left with extreme boredom and a craving for objects and novelty. Instead of connection to their objects, they destroy their objects in their search for euphoria. Like Tantalus, they can see but not experience the objects of their desire so they endure an interminable quest for novelty. In place of the euphoria they cannot obtain, they crave dopamine, adrenalin, or any stimulation that will take them out of their emptiness.

Boredom also occurs through the blocking of euphoric conduits caused by the occupation of those conduits by an external intercepting force. The drive to euphoric connection is intrinsic. This drive can be blocked by external pressure extracting euphoria from the euphoric interaction. Boredom occurs when our expansion is blocked or when we are forced to do something we do not wish to do. Boredom is the resistance to mental sublation. Boredom produces memory loss due to the foreign occupation of the mind. People describe bureaucracy as torture because it is. Bureaucracy is violence akin to imprisonment, a theft of life and free will. The most bored people are those at work or school and the wealthy. Students with excitement toward learning are put into an environment that provides external, distracting and extrinsic motivation. In their resistance to the external occupation of their minds, students become resistant to discovery itself.

Boredom is a sign of severe psychic distress.

Excitement is the anticipation of euphoria. In an exoself, that is a drive towards exosocial expansion in search of the primary euphoric sources of interaction, creation, discovery and more. An exoself is in a natural state of excitement every day in anticipation of primary euphoric interaction. In an endoself, excitement is a drive to possession and destruction in search of secondary euphoria. Excitement felt by a hypoglycaemic near sugar or an alcoholic near alcohol is the same as a destroyer near destruction or a sadist near pain and terror. If an endoself is excited, everyone ought to be on high alert to danger, as an endoself can only obtain secondary euphoria through the fear, pain and other stress responses of others.

Attraction and repulsion are reversed in the exoself and the endoself. That which attracts one, repels the other and vice versa. The problem with fighting for the universal right to the pursuit of happiness is that the happiness of an endoself and an exoself are in direct opposition to each other. The trials and tribulations that endoself figures such as Schopenhauer and his ilk railed against were other people who were unable to provide the secondary euphoria the endoself claims as their due. This is still evident today. Exosocial people fight for liberation, or freedom to develop healthy euphoric conduits. Endoselves fight for subordination, or the right to enforce reflection and sublation and prey on others.

Sex and death

I sometimes try to imagine what would have happened if we'd known the bonobo first and the chimpanzee only later - or not at all. - Frans de Waal, *Our Inner Ape*

To Freudians and many other psychologists, sociologists and students of power relations, sex is the defining foundation of human relationships and societal structure. This probably says more about those thinkers than it does about humanity or society. At the time during which the sexual theory-of-everything was being developed in Germany, sex there was the primary vehicle through which guilt was transferred. Earlier in Germany, the vehicle was religosity, in other places it was loyalty, today it is money and tomorrow it will perhaps be a social perception of beauty through plastic surgery. In much Freudian analysis, guilt is the key, not sex. Sex is, however, a powerful tool in social attraction and repulsion and endogroup formation, not to mention a major source of shared euphoria. Love, or Freud's obsession with sexual desire, is not an accurate descriptor of the overwhelming need for social inclusion and fear of shunning, but they are not completely unrelated either.

In a strictly physiological sense, sex is simply one of a variety of interpersonal and personal acts which can be used to create either exosocial or endosocial bonds. As a tool of power, it is no more or less effective than many other methods of establishing power, for example, the power to define, the power over life and death, or secrecy and privacy, the sharing of food or home and other resources or direct shunning and inclusion.

Endoselves are characterized as either very promiscuous or asexual. Sex for them appears to be less a personal need and means to acquire euphoria, and more of a tool to extract emotional response from others or as a tool of sublation. (While an endoself is often promiscuous or asexual, asexual and promiscuous people are not necessarily often endoselves.) For Lacan and others who see sex as a separator that drives people farther away from each other, they can be believed that this is the effect sex has for an endoself. It is well-established that oxytocin has the effect of increasing bonds between attached people and increasing hostility where there is an endosocial barrier. What the Lacanians were really revealing is their own condition as endoselves, thus unable to establish a connection with their sexual partners.

Oxytocin is produced by both stress and orgasm. The role of oxytocin in both increasing bonding within groups and hatred of those without seems to indicate a relation between oxytocin and strengthening of endosocial membranes. The use of rape as a tool of war throughout history illustrates this dual purpose. For an endoself, for whom everyone is an outsider, sex may simply reinforce their isolation and misanthropy, as many endoself theorists have assured us that it does.

Many Hollywood romantic comedies depict endoselves bouncing off of each other like billiard balls, and a conflict centred around the need of each to subjugate the other, illustrating the extreme lack of connection in sex between two endoselves.. The exosocial and wider endogroup connections are very evident in romantic movies from France, Morocco, Nigeria, Korea or most places outside Anglo / Germanic regions. There, the focus of romantic comedies is on food, friends, family, trust, secrecy, wider social conflict around shunning and inclusion and all the many circles of euphoric interactions which encompass a romantic relationship.

Sex may not be the defining foundation of society, but it is not simply a tennis match either. The sex drive of some couples is an attempt to create a caregiver endogroup as a refuge from the nation-self. Orgies often indulged in by strong endogroups are an attempt to strengthen the nation endogroup relative to this competing couple membrane. All-male militias and churches sometimes have bonding sex with each other and rape enemies, children or women as outsiders. Sex, celibacy and rape have all been used throughout history to expand or define group boundaries. But not only is sex not just tennis, even tennis is not just tennis. Both involve mastery over the bodies of self and others, endosocial competition or joining with another person, release of hormones for bonding or shunning, and euphoria.

Bodily contact, whether from assault and rape or games and sex, will weaken the personal membrane of the receiver. Only the latter will weaken the membrane of the initiator. Attacks on another person strengthen the membrane of the attacker. In this way, sexual assault and physical attacks create an endosocial membrane around the attacker and attacked and position the attacker as the endo-ideal. The role of all physical attack, but especially rape, in establishing subordination has been recognized throughout history. It is not accident that rape and other bodily assault is part of every prison, every war and every system of institutionalized subordination, it is by design.

Rape and torture, euphemistically depicted in authoritative literature as 'sexual abuse' when they relate to children, often result in a refracted core marked by extreme dissociation[96]. This is a possible result of rape creating a couple membrane before the child has created a personal membrane, when they are at an extreme power disadvantage. The prevalence of a history of child rape in people diagnosed with so-called personality disorders is common to the point that Freud originally thought that child rape caused all disorders. [97]

If sex is so powerful in the formation of group membranes, either through love or hate, it is extremely harmful to children who have yet to form their own membranes and are therefore at far greater risk of being trapped in endogroups and relying on drugs to make up their lack of a personal membrane or unable to escape a childhood marriage. Contrary to Freud's assertion that early access to sex was the key to the growth of narcissism in leader figures, it was more likely the early rape of the leader's compatriots that destroyed their own ability to lead. Taboos on touching the person of a ruler or future ruler support this outlook. And the rampant child rape common to cults provides plenty of evidence of this. It was more likely the early rape of the leader's compatriots that destroyed their own ability to lead. Taboos on touching the person of a ruler or future ruler support this outlook.

Both rape and child predation have been depicted by predators as a means to acquire secondary euphoria. If this is the case, then the sublation of others must produce euphoria, or a substitute for it. This would explain why all the endoself theorists who defined modern reality were unable to distinguish between sex and sublation. Every oppression may then be motivated by a similar need for secondary euphoria by the dominant person. Abuse is not limited to merely the act itself. Viewing of child torture media as a means of experiencing secondary euphoria is also widespread and growing. The viewing itself is an invasion of another person's privacy, dignity and integrity. It changes the child from an equal person, holding ownership and privacy of their own self, to an object to be possessed.

The chain reaction of child abuse, where the abused often become abusers, may indicate that those with damaged membranes are seeking to repair them by damaging others. It has long been recognized that schoolyard bullies are those who have suffered from low self esteem or loss of dignity and confidence. If what they have lost can be found in the assault and sublation of others, it again indicates that euphoria or a substitute for it is produced by sublation.

Sex or rape used for the purpose of sublation can be replaced by any denial of bodily autonomy and trauma. *Feeding* is one phenomenon in which men feed women to a state of extreme obesity, often to the acclaim of avid fans. This is a situation where the man has complete control over her body and life and she has male endo-ideal approval. The same phenomenon was evident in the anorexia epidemic of the 1980s, among people who would tell women they were far more beautiful if they were nearly dead or dying. It is also evident in industrial and state or other endogroups where people are told that they are brave or heroes for risking their lives for stupid reasons created by an endo-ideal.

The issue at stake is body ownership and the approval is the approval accorded to an obedient reflector that relinquishes body ownership to their endo-ideal. Such avid reflectors obtain their own euphoria in the process, but this euphoria only comes from one source, at the cost of their own will and autonomy. This type of obedience challenge is used by human traffickers as well. The people they capture are put through a series of challenges that either break them and lead to them accepting their negative image or reflector status to such an extent that they do not challenge their captivity, or they push them to escape, through attempted flight or suicide. If they stay, it will be in a state of will completely sublated to their captors. For those that become reflectors, they will carry out their endo-ideal's will with a single-minded focus of a self fully occupied or refracted and no longer capable of empathy outside their endo-ideal.

In many cultures, from early Germanic to Congolese, penetration of a man was considered to subjugate him, or magically transform him into a woman. Women were considered to be subjugated by nature, an opinion philosophers and scientists have pontificated about for centuries with long treatises on passive eggs and active sperm. Under male endo-idealism, women are divided into obedient reflectors and the negative image. This is acted out sexually in the well-known madonna – whore complex displayed by male endo-idealists individually and in wider society. Women are pitted against each other in two different roles, the reflector to create the man as endo-ideal and the negative image to absorb his guilt. It is no coincidence that these societies created 'legal marriage' for one type of woman and 'criminal prostitution' for the other and both are pitted against each other in a zero sum game for the approval of the male endo-ideal.

These are strictly male endo-idealist perspectives and experiences and they apply primarily in the case of an extreme endogroup which has a great need for reflection and validation of their endo-ideal. In other words, it is the perspective of the men who initially developed sexual psychology. This is the same structure whereby the corporate endo-ideal pits 'legal workers' against 'criminal' workers and convinces them that they are in a zero sum game for the employer's approval, or the same game played out by states, churches, or every other endogroup. The phenomenon is not sex, it is sublation.

There appear to be three primary powers attached to the cocktail of chemical reactions produced by sex.

- One, it can be used as a tool for exosocial joining, in creating strong euphoric and empathic bonds with another person. The *exosocial power* can heal personal trauma and contribute to the health of both or all partners.

- Two, it can be used to create an endosocial membrane, with the subjects joined within the membrane or divided by it. The *endosocial power* can bond people as one self or turn mild antipathy or apathy into disgust, hatred and enmity.
- Three, it can be used to sublate one self to another within an endogroup membrane. This *endogroup power* can cause extreme dissociation and trauma in the sublated and contribute to their loss of will and inability to escape from the bond. This is the power of the necromancer who gains the ability to control two bodies with one mind.

In none of these roles is sex the only tool available to achieve that end, but it is a powerful and effective tool, nevertheless. Like laughter, sex can be replaced with violence for every one of its social powers, but is appears to be far more powerful than violence in each function.

The death drive is a hypothesis described by Sabina Spielrein in her 1912 essay *"Destruction as the Cause of Coming Into Being"*. This hypothesis was eventually adopted and expanded on by Freud. This death drive is not the same as exosocial expansion which ultimately leaves the bodily host. Spielrein's theory is an attempt to explain the drive towards destruction and the attraction of filth, horror and taboo.

Freud wrote that *"The phenomenon of life could be explained from the concurrent or mutually opposing action of these two instincts."* [98] and *"besides the instinct to preserve living substance and to join into ever larger units there must exist another, contrary instinct seeking to dissolve those units and to bring them back to their primaeval, inorganic state."*[99] Freud's interpretation of the death drive does nothing to explain what he depicted as its externalization towards others as aggression nor why it should sometimes be, as he postulated, directed inwards as masochism. Neither do his convoluted depictions of inverted masochism and libido, which turn the death drive outwards, attempt any rational explanation of what purpose such drives and their inversions would serve since these later-added explanations put them in opposition with his original death drive.

Freud was originally trying to incorporate a thesis-antithesis-synthesis triad for these drives, in trendy accordance with the Hegelianism of the day. However, this need for a negative image for every positive image only appears when the self is defined as part of an endogroup with an endo-ideal and a negative image. The interaction-self (exoself) includes both action and reaction and requires no negative image or counter-force. Freud interpreted Spielrein's work as a death drive with a *"task of which is to lead organic life back into the inanimate state."*[100] It is not necessary to belabour all the arguments against Freud's death drive which have already filled volumes, but the most important for this discussion is that it is based on an impossibility.

Life cannot change its state and suddenly become inanimate. If it is animate, all it can do is leave the host and disperse, regardless of what anyone defines life as. Freud continually depicts his theory as neatly *"restoring an earlier state"*[101] or *"the expression of inertia or elasticity present in what is organic"* but life was never and could never be inert, and the earlier state of life was most certainly not death. Neither of his statements, *"The goal of all life is death"* or *"The inanimate was there before the animate"*[102] make any kind of sense (and the former didn't when Schopenhauer said it either). In the latter case, there is neither evidence that life was ever inanimate nor that it will ever become so. It would be a contradiction in terms if it did. This is, as usual, yet another problem that comes from equating self, life, consciousness and a bodily host, four entirely different things.

The death drive was also Freud's attempt to use Newton's first law of motion which states that, unless an unbalanced force is exerted, objects in motion will stay in motion and objects in inertia will remain inert. Life cannot suddenly or simultaneously reverse direction and combine the drive to self-formation with a drive to self-destruction. Freud postulated two separate drives, *"working against each other since the first origin of life"*[103] but the only reason two such opposing forces would be necessary is if life itself had dual goals.

If interpreted correctly, Newton's first law would mean that the life force of a newborn infant which is expanding outwards and establishing a wider self will continue doing so, forever, unless it meets with a greater opposing force. The only drive that would fulfill both self-formation and self-dispersal under Newton's first law is a drive towards exosocial expansion, which neatly follows the pattern of an ever-expanding universe. Likewise, the will that Schopenhauer feels is the missing element in Kant's thinking is not, as Schopenhauer believes, a fairly inexplicable and perverse will to live in face of certain death but a will towards exosocial expansion. The problem with conflating life and the body is that it requires the nature of life to fundamentally change or be defeated upon death when all it really has to do is leave the host and continue its expansive tendency.

The drive towards filth, death and destruction is in opposition to this expansion, or progress, and it is by no means a universal drive. It is restricted to those protecting endosocial membranes and it is a force in opposition to the exosocial expansive drive. The drive to greater expansion and more euphoric conduits is an existential threat to an endoself or endogroup. The so-called death drive is a means to block access to outside conduits and trap secondary euphoria. It is a drive to power, which is obtained through transactions of unequal force. A force results from the interaction of two or more objects. With no external interaction, there is no outward force, so a barrier to outside interaction will divert the expansive force and cause it to become an inward vector, directing all of its force towards the endo-ideal. As the endo-ideal is the object of greatest force, all power from every interaction will accrue to the endo-ideal.

The role of a so-called death instinct, which is really endogroup attraction, is to subvert and limit the outward expansion of others. The endogroup acts to bind expansive chaos into an impenetrable membrane which contains a 'natural order' of the endo-ideal, reflectors and a negative image. The endogroup is a picture of totalitarianism. The death drive is just the totalitarian self patrolling its borders, no more organic or inevitable than the Shepherd dogs that once patrolled Albania's Accursed Mountains or the land mines of the Western Sahara Berm. The force exerted by this membrane is evident in the strenuous counter force required for a reflector, much less a negative image, to break from this endogroup force and recreate an exosocial self. It is also evident in how much easier it is for those subjugated by an endogroup to move to another endogroup exerting its own force than it is for them to leave otherwise. The ability of endogroups to pit their relative power against each other and vie for the reflectors and negative image of the other is also a measure of their power.

In a meeting of two equally exosocial people with equal euphoric attraction, they will be in perfect balance. Since this seldom happens, and varies by both individual and event, a diverse and extensive number of interactions and conduits is required to maintain overall balance. As well, altruistic euphoria and gratitude provide a balance in voluntary interactions. In an endogroup, all individual force is directed within a limited group. An endoself within that group will create an unbalanced force in every transaction that will eventually begin to deplete the other members and establish the endoself as the endo-ideal, which is the primary reason endoselves are so often able to establish themselves as the endo-ideal. If we were to use Euclidean vectors to describe this force, all endogroups will eventually vector primarily or entirely towards the endo-ideal. This is the structure of power.

The so-called death drive can be described very easily by the opposition between the euphoric attraction which connects the exoself to wider euphoric conduits and the need of an endogroup to maintain an endosocial membrane and access secondary euphoria, both achieved through destruction of euphoric sources and conduits.

Life does not hold two contradictory or opposing forces. The only purpose of life is exosocial expansion and the only force of life facilitates this. The purpose of endosocialism is the accumulation of power and the force of endosocialism facilitates this. Power is not life, although they are not unrelated. Life is discussed in far more detail in *Abstracting Divinity*.

Damage and deviance

No man chooses evil because it is evil; he only mistakes it for happiness, the good he seeks. - Mary Wollstonecraft, *A Vindication of the Rights of Men*, 1780

Psychology and psychiatry, like all endosocial institutions, are in the business of creating a binary reality. They divide people into good and bad, normal and pathological, sane and delusional.

In order to measure deviance, it is necessary to establish a normative standard, which is always the endo-ideal. In universal reality, normal and abnormal do not exist as they are relative terms based on deviance from the endo-ideal. In universal reality, all behaviour is normal. There is nothing else it could possibly be. All behaviour is a response normal to the given personality and circumstance. Given the right conditions, large amounts of humanity will prey on each other and self-destruct and that is perfectly normal. Measuring deviance from the endo-ideal does not assist in any way in the search for causes of behaviour and neither does it assist in defining normative, or healthy responses. Measuring deviance is a method of creating endoreality, including creation of the endo-ideal and negative image. The definition of insanity is disagreeing with endoreality and the definition of criminality is acting against the laws of endoreality.

We cannot judge outcomes based on desirability, as many people can be found who view the destruction of humanity with great excitement and will fight any attempt to stop it. The behaviour of the endoself requires modification, not because it is abnormal or undesireable, but because it results in negative interactions which harm others. Psychologists labelled people as abnormal for functioning within a society which causes every single person to act in a way they say is pathological. It is the transactions of power that need to be diagnosed, not people.

Roles are unique to interactions. A person will often play a very different role in their family than they do at their work, or in their church as opposed to in their business, especially if these are separate endogroups. A person may also display more extreme characteristics in times of excitement or stress. A person who is a strong reflector may find an external endo-ideal in an ideology or in a romantic interest. One of many problems with classifying individuals as disordered is it ignores the diversity of relationships each individual maintains. People can be mass murderers outside their social group and perfectly gentle and law abiding within. Brutal slave owners and traffickers can be upstanding members of their own communities. Men can be cruel and hateful to women but kind and helpful to other men. World leaders can be civilized negotiators internationally and brutally repress dissent where they feel they have power or ownership of people. It is relationships which are disordered, not people. Since it is people who must be sorted according to the laws of endoreality, psychology created the mythical individual self to facilitate its binary reality.

Psychological terms such as *self-hate* and *self-aggrandizement* attempt to reconcile an endogroup into an autonomous individual. The terms depict all external hostility, adulation and persecution as projections of an individual self. Karen Horney's *real self, pseudoself,* and *idealized self,* like Freud's *ego, superego* and *id,* were seen by both as residing in one autonomous self. Psychoanalyst's neurotic types which tend towards *self aggrandizement* or *self effacement* are reconciled through a tedious process of fighting for the emergence of a 'real' self instead of a recognition of which circle of self they have attained, the degree of membrane permeability and strength and the presence of an internal or external ideal. Horney's *expansive* and *self-effacing* drives ignore that people are usually capable of both behaviours towards different targets. Inflation and deflation of self depends on euphoric transfer.

Horney conflates the reflector role with a strong caregiver-self, two conditions frequently, but not always, present in women of her era. The caregiver circle and reflector role do not have any real connection. A person may be the endo-ideal of their caregiver endogroup and demand reflection from others while acting as a reflector or negative image in the wider nation-self. The fact that a person may be cast as a negative image or reflector in their nation-self does not influence their level of tyranny in their caregiver-self, or if it does, it may be only in a roundabout fashion as frustration from the nation-self is carried over to added cruelty in the caregiver-self. That is not a contradiction since these are two separate endogroups, making up two separate selves.

Horney and others see it as a contradiction creating *neurosis* and detachment from the *real self*. Horney also sees reliance on external relationships to help a person survive extreme depletion as neurosis and apparently idealizes the endoself as healthy and normative. Horney, whose theories formed the basis for what came to be known as Maslow's hierarchy of needs, makes many easily disproven assertions, several of which are still apparent in that famous pyramid. These discrepancies, such as all the people like Van Gogh who would purchase paint before food, are, predictably, dismissed as insane.

Those dependent on endogroups are encouraged to develop their own endosocial barriers, an endoself, to allow independence from groups, but only to the level of authoritative endogroups. The same independence so prized in the first circles become maladaptation if the subject shows independence from state or educational authority.

It is not the faulty formation of self which creates what psychiatry calls delusions or grandiose self-assessment. It is the fact that an endosocial barrier stopped the exosocial expansion of the self. If that endosocial barrier occurred at the lifegiver or caregiver stage, then psychiatry categorizes this as a pathology. If development had continued to the nation-self, the delusions and grandiose exceptionalism would be applied to a national endo-ideal as state patriotism, class conceit, religious fervour or any other extreme group affiliation. At the authoritative level, psychiatry no longer pathologizes exceptional delusions, as psychiatrists are part of the authoritative endo-ideal and have many exceptional delusions at this level themselves. A sign of the growing power of a transcendental endogroup is that allegiance to lower endo-ideals and groups becomes classified as criminal or insane. Thus, when states gained power, family allegiances were classified as *mafia* or organized crime. Under the strengthening mono-empire, nationalism at state and religious levels is now considered *extremism*.

People the DSM classifies as disordered are often simply attached to endogroups that medical and legal authorities do not accept. Those diagnosed with Cluster B disorders do not respond to shunning and inclusion motivators of state-defined society because the state is not their dominant endogroup. They exploit others because guilt does not traverse endosocial barriers. People in prison are more often diagnosed antisocial but they may have very strong social bonds to those within prisons or other limited societies. Anti-social behaviour is defined as behaviour directed at the authoritative endo-ideal. Thus, a person who assassinates a state leader is classified as *insane* but one who kills a woman or child is classified as probably *in love*, or at least *sexually attracted*. In addition, a crime committed by a negative image is attributed to the entire negative image. The same assassination by a person from a negative image would be classified as *terrorism* or *organized crime*, but in the endo-ideal it is individualized as insanity, or deviance, to avoid tarnishing the entire endo-ideal with guilt.

The depiction of so-called sociopaths as abnormal is an incorrect and contextually blinded assessment. Sociopathic or anti-social behaviour is the behaviour many or most people adopt against those outside of their endogroup or towards their negative image, as Hannah Arendt famously pointed out in her comments about the *"banality of evil"*.[105] The only difference between *normal* people and those labelled as sociopaths is whether their chosen endogroup and endo-ideal correlates with the one that institutional power wishes them to have. Even people categorized with *antisocial personality disorder* can be perfectly loving towards their own birth family and sometimes even towards a spouse and children. Many other people classified as normal in their everyday lives become pathologically antisocial if they interact outside of their nation selves. Still others are classified as pathological simply because their nation-self correlates to a gang or other group instead of a state. Credit and blame allocation that is typically associated with severe mental disturbance may frequently be simply identification with a wider self.

A 2013 study showed that people labelled *"highly psychopathic"* by the researchers showed a typical response when imagining pain to themselves but not to others and may have shown enjoyment on the pain inflicted onto others.[106] This shows an endosocial boundary, not a defective response. Studies showing lack of emotional response in so-called psychopaths should be matched with the response of the average endostate citizen towards suffering outside their state or the response of the wealthy towards suffering of those with no money. Without establishing the endogroup of the authoritative control and the dominant endogroup of the diagnosed psychopath, these studies are missing an important variable.

Every state has an anti-social relationship with its lowest classes, including those in prisons. The tendency to use prisoners for psychopath testing, and failing to account for the fact that prisoners have, by definition, been shunned out of the society they are meant to have empathy with, is a major weakness. If the state shuns a group of people, it is perfectly normal behaviour for that group to behave with reciprocal or intensified hostility to the group they see representing or reflecting the state, particularly if they have managed to form an endogroup of their own. Groups the state refers to as criminal gangs are often simply external endogroups, treating outsiders as the state treats those outside their boundaries. Behaviour that is normal for a state endogroup is also normal at every other level of endogroup. As an extreme example, the only reason some people eat chickens and not people is because of the location of their endogroup membranes. For some, this also precludes eating their pets, but not for others.

The group defined in the *DSM V* as *Cluster B personality disorders* only differ from wider endogroups in which endogroup has developed the strongest membrane. What the DSM V calls *antisocial personality disorder,* defined as a person who disregards the rights of others, is largely typical of an endoself or a person with a different dominant endogroup than the diagnosing institution. *Histrionic personality disorder* denotes an endo-ideal that the diagnosing institution or general public does not recognize as their own. *Borderline personality disorder* is typical of an endoself in a reflector or negative image role. *Narcissistic personality disorder* is an endoself in a position as the endo-ideal at some level and is far more likely to be diagnosed as such if the level is below that of the diagnosing institution. Endo-ideals at a national level are very seldom criticized or diagnosed as abnormal for the same self-idealization or for conflating the entire state with themselves, because their endoreality is shared by those making the diagnosis. If an endo-ideal has attained a nation, discovery or creation level, such characteristics are often considered to indicate *genius,* not disorder.

Black and white or binary thinking is a result of an extremely impermeable membrane around one's individual or group self. Attributing all virtue to the endo-ideal and vilifying the negative image is normal endogroup behaviour, though extremes vary. The extreme alternating idealization and devaluation sometimes referred to as *splitting* and associated with various diagnosis, including what the DSM V calls *borderline personality disorder* and *narcissistic personality disorder* is the effect of shunning people in or out of an extreme endogroup. The reactions considered overly dramatic in an individual are considered normal when seen in national reactions to celebrity news. Overly dramatic reactions simply pinpoint the location of a person's dominant endo-ideal. Delusions of grandeur are simply strong identifications with euphoric connections expressed in the only terms possible within the individualizing nature of psychiatry. Most behaviour becomes much more predictable and logical if it is situated within the dominant endogroup and role and viewed according to exosocial or endosocial motivations.

The subjective endoreality which assigns virtue to the endo-ideal and guilt to the negative image leads to poor risk assessment in both, as the endo-ideal overestimates the positive and the negative image overestimates the negative. Emphasis on the positive leads to risk taking and magical thinking. Emphasis on the negative leads to existential crisis and depression. Endo-ideals emphasize the positive due to their endofilters and negative images emphasize the negative for the same reason. Studies have shown that trauma, which could have caused a person to be cast as the negative image, increases their negative or dissociated perception of events in the past[107]. If a change in role changes perception, an endofilter exists.

Personality disorders indicate a conflict between dominant and authoritative endorealities. This is apparent in the fact that the same symptoms which obviously fit a Cluster B disorder are rarely diagnosed, or at least rarely recognized as problems, in members of the authoritative endo-ideal even though they are very typical endo-ideal traits. Juvenile delinquency may have been a problem for an endoself who is not a nation-ideal but one who has attained that level may have had no problems with a wider society designed for them. An endoself who did not make it past lifegiver expansion may have no empathic bonds, while those in wider circles have limited ones. An endoself at a discovery or creation level may have great passion for their chosen activity and still be ruthless in its pursuit. The authoritative endogroup excuses anyone who is viciously cruel to only certain groups, such as poor people, women, prisoners or people on the other side of a state war. It declares that personality disorders, like terrorism, are only a problem when the authoritative endo-ideal are affected.

The biggest cause for the creation of endoselves is the institutional idealization of the endoself. All of the institutions of industrialized states are designed for an endoself and they all make exosocial interaction nearly impossible.

Academics and scientists have a history of conducting studies of only the United States or Europe, and formerly only men, and claiming universal truths based solely on their own endo-ideal. Since the endo-ideal are the personalities which Freud unhelpfully characterized as narcissists, it is no surprise that these character traits have been continually depicted as both normal and normative by the endo-ideals who define reality for societal institutions. Freud labelled *"absolutely self-sufficient narcissism"* as a normative standard for infants and one which people struggle to return to.[108] Kohut went much further and ordered mothers to mirror the good qualities of their children in a deliberate attempt to create narcissists which he considered the best model of development.[109] Most of the power pathologies have not benefited from the study restricted to men who display most of them. Normalized narcissism, or endo-idealism, and the deliberate development of endoselves, forced those societies under the influence of psychology to produce increasingly more child endo-ideals and endoselves.

Endosocial membranes do not typically bother the person or people inside them. In fact, the person possessing one sees that membrane as all that is protecting their self. It is the people outside of an endosocial membrane who are hurt, as well as the negative image. Endogroups also do not bother institutions promoting them. No state objects when a citizen volunteers to kill the negative image or people outside the state endogroup, and no church objects when their believers think themselves more virtuous by association than those outside.

The depiction of personality disorders such as narcissism and sociopathy as egosyntonic and difficult to correct, as the subjects are happy with themselves, could very well be related to this institutional approval of personality traits more common among the endo-ideals of authoritative society. Traits considered egodystonic, those that make the subject unhappy, are more common in the negative image where institutions and communities will quickly punish deviance, or simply existence. Even among populations such as those in prisons, antisocial character traits are still given leadership roles. A person with a personality depicted by psychiatrists as *hysteria* or *neurosis* was likely to be institutionalized and possibly experimented on with electric shocks, brainwashing, and hysterectomies. It is understandable that this would cause perception of those diagnosis as egodystonic and those traits which resulted in promotion to the top levels of academia, business and politics as egosyntonic. The most egodystonic disorders are depicted as those which seem to reflect the most fear of social shunning. What is egodystonic depends on the culture, but personality disorders are rarely examined in populations that deride exploitative behaviour and value humility.

Cluster C disorders are diagnosed in people who are exhausted and depleted by predators. Like Cluster B disorders, these are not real disorders. They are logical reactions to individual reality. Cluster C disorders are largely the result of the actuality or fear of shunning, assigned guilt and cognitive dissonance. Someone cast as the negative image is vulnerable to the so-called cluster C and A disorders.

Both handwashing and *obsessive compulsive* behaviours are associated with guilt[110] and have been since long before psychology decided to pathologize such behaviours. Excess guilt is a condition associated with any negative image and this behaviour can manifest chronically in someone cast as the negative image or episodically in endo-ideals confronted with a break in their protective endorealities. It is quite common for endo-ideals to manifest such behaviours, often to an extreme degree, when the repercussions of their guilt finally catch up to them, but their defences usually protect them from long term guilt behaviours. A criteria for diagnosis is that it must be a long term behaviour, which typically excludes the endo-ideal from diagnosis.

The DSM defines *Dependent personality disorder* as someone with excessive fear and anxiety, helpless, passive and dependent on others. In schools, industry and states, this is the ideal reflector, but it is suddenly pathologized at a caregiver level. *Avoidant personality disorder* or anxiety caused by social shunning is universal in the negative image and also in anyone with severe depletion due to environmental factors. Depleted resistance to stress triggers an overwhelming response to any stress, and social situations cause anxiety for anyone cast as the negative image due to the shame inherent in the role. Every single person in northern Canada and other isolated parts of the world would be classified with *Social anxiety disorder,* the lucratively renamed *shyness,* which also occurs more often in females than males for the same obvious reasons. Shyness, or being cast as the negative image, does lead to alcohol and marijuana dependence or overuse.[111] Both alcohol and marijuana seem to be drugs of choice for those with depleted membranes and may eventually turn them into endoselves.

In Asia, shy and inhibited behaviour is more approved of and leads to more leadership opportunities but in the U.S., where the assertive competitiveness of an endoself is more valued, shyness is considered disordered. Psychiatric institutions include disclaimers for cultural variations in diagnostic criteria, but the fact that these so-called disorders change by culture[112], or authoritative endogroup, means they are magical words with no meaning outside of endoreality. Their only purpose is to pathologize the negative image and idealize the endo-ideal.

The amount of scientific papers that casually ascribe motive to behaviour based on no evidence whatsoever is another indication of their purpose, as attributing guilt follows casting the negative image. The fact that those so-called disorders most often ascribed to the negative image are fed dangerous and damaging pharmaceuticals, while those associated with the endo-ideal are promoted and normalized and presented as incurable, is the punishment that follows guilt assignment. The closed and endosocial nature of science has a lot of issues at the best of times, but in the case of psychology, the entire structure is a magical fiction.

All of the Cluster A disorders depict a person in severe distress and the causes are as varied as childhood trauma to the early formation of self to an averse reaction to drugs. A lot of the symptoms are related to a reaction to being cast as the negative image but a lot of the symptoms bear no relation to each other and could arise from a great number of causes. Many are also typical of transcendental endogroups. Every state could be diagnosed as having *paranoid personality disorder*.

Schizoid personality disorder is simply a person trapped in their lifegiver self, one whose exosocial expansion has been blocked prior to the caregiver circle or who has received some trauma that caused them to regress to the lifegiver circle. Self development is pathologized when it stops at the lifegiver circle but not when it stops at any of the other circles as endogroups are designed to stop development at the other circles. A woman blocked from expansion past the caregiver circle or a man past the creation circle are usually awarded high social approval and are considered by psychology to be very well adapted. Such stunted growth meets with higher approval then the drive to continue expansion, which is usually considered a maladaptation. In fact, the diagnostic criteria of all personality disorders specifies life success as status, wealth and successful relationships, which translates to people stunted at those levels.

Schizotypal personality disorder relates to a cognitive break between authoritative endoreality and personal reality or dominant endoreality. As with the other DSM V disorders, it is meaningless to define the deviant without defining the control. Given the delusions typical of all authoritative endorealities, those that do not see the world through the authoritative endofilter may not be the ones suffering the greatest impairment. To return to the discussion on development in the third chapter, perhaps drugs or trauma damage the cognitive filter that creates an individual reality. The person is then viewing reality as it is without an individual filter, and it is thus difficult for the brain to process. It would make more sense that a cognitive filter is damaged than that people create entire realities out of an undefined 'imagination', which is no explanation at all. Cognitive dissonance between authoritative and dominant endogroups is known to produce great mental strain, and that strain is likely the cause of many adverse symptoms with the condition, as well as any strain resulting from a loss of filter.

What ought to be diagnosed long before an individual is their environment. There is a very large body of research connecting food and environmental factors to various behaviours, but still the victim is pathologized, not the substance. Even the most exosocial individuals may enter what psychologists call a dissociative state when under real or potential stress. The adrenalin or other fear reactions cause their exosocial membranes to become temporarily endosocial. People or animals with this reaction are exosocial when they feel safe, happy or healthy but become endosocial under duress. They are unable to seek or obtain comfort from social relationships when they need it most. In times of crisis, which are all times in dissociated, industrialized society, they must seek out endosocial relationships. Just a few factors outside the individual that need to be considered are below:

- Drugs (including pharmaceuticals), sugar, alcohol and other poor dietary factors.
- Water, air and emf pollution.
- No interaction with nature or healthy relationships.
- Surroundings of garbage, filth and destruction, an endoself utopia and exoself dystopia.
- Escalating anxiety from the overwhelming stress of day to day life,
- Constant exposure to violent endosocial media and depressing, futile news.
- Massive self-perpetuating industry of pathology, pharmaceuticals and self-help, all aimed at individuals and their mothers instead of societies and environments.
- Removal of agency and choice, constant instability, shock and isolation.
- Cognitive dissonance inducing, ever-changing, authoritative endoreality.
- Overwhelming guilt due to non-stop unbalanced transactions.
- Privacy violations causing the most extreme resistance to sublation.
- Boredom caused by blockage and interception of euphoric conduits.

An accurate assessment of mental distress causes and manifestations would lead to pathologizing entire states, which is something frowned upon by those authoritative states. Today, lifegivers and caregivers are facing overwhelming odds against raising strong adults, from the surrounding environmental stressors on both the caregivers and the children, the complete lack of any external welcoming society of support and the continued attacks on caregivers and caregiving. The environmental stressors also contribute to the creation of so-called natural causes, as stress is passed down in DNA and in maternal hormones. Disorder definitions are meaningless groupings of symptoms in search of a cause. Looking at these so-called disorders instead of the vast array of reasons for a person to be experiencing such crisis is akin to attempting to prevent death without ascertaining its cause. The only purpose served by pathologizing the individual is guilt transference from the industrial-scientific endo-ideal.

The personality disorders increasingly affecting the entire world are a varied collection of symptoms related to an inability to access primary euphoria. Treatment must therefore focus on establishing healthy euphoric conduits and removing unhealthy relationships, marked by sustained imbalance of power. Establishing neutral force relationships, such as those with discovery or creation, and restricting personal relationships to those which are determinedly exosocial is necessary. Long term rebuilding is helped by supportive relationships, new ways of establishing connections to euphoria through activity typically designated as 'hobbies' such as art, sport or gardening, or other exosocial creation, discovery or spirituality. The most important aspect of personal health is preservation of ownership over the inner circles of self, or privacy, a difficult challenge under global totalitarianism.

Every so-called personality disorder revolves around shunning and inclusion. What Freud considered the two great drives of sex and death are just manifestations of shunning and inclusion. Without mapping a person's endogroups, measuring the strength of each and ascertaining the role they play in each, and identifying the dominant endogroup and the authoritative endogroup, it is very difficult to interpret behaviour meaningfully.

Neuroscience has produced very interesting information on the brain and its development patterns and the hormonal responses associated with personality. Unfortunately, much of this work funded in neuroscience is tied to the disorder designations of psychiatry, which are arbitrary to the point of meaninglessness, and prone to ascribing motives with no basis or supporting evidence. It is straightforward to test any of the claims made in this book, including:

- the boundaries of a person's dominant endogroup
- the location of a person's endo-ideals
- the allocation of guilt
- the speed in which the shame response is eliminated by compensatory behaviour
- the method in which the shame response is deflected: laughter, anger or external guilt assignment
- boredom and excitement responses to primary euphoria and secondary euphoria
- the effect of magical words in attributing blame, authority or credit to the endo-ideal or the negative image
- the presence of endoreality or endofilters which interpret reality differently from universal reality and the correlation

of endofilters with external endo-ideals
- the nature of the substances referred to here as euphoria and secondary euphoria and the methods of obtaining or producing them
- The measure of hostility directed towards an amputated core, negative image or rival endogroup

Some studies exist which provide basic research in these directions, such as studies which map empathic response[113] and excitement in response to the distress of another, impaired perspective taking, risk assessment and more. What is primarily needed is the initial mapping of endogroups and roles in order to interpret these responses. Unfortunately, neuroscience, like every other science, is at the service of state and corporate coercion. Any results are therefore far more likely to be used to enforce allegiance to authoritative endogroups and sublation rather than healing and allowing exosocial expansion.

The basic tenets of exosocialism are:

1. Human behaviour naturally follows exosocial expansion.
2. Health is dependent on a strong, permeable, personal membrane and numerous, diverse euphoric conduits created through exosocial expansion.
3. Environmental and health hazards inhibit formation of euphoric conduits and causes development of an endoself, which leads to social problems including predatory behaviour.

4. Formation of an endogroup inhibits external empathic conduits and balanced interactions, and leads to social problems related to shunning and inclusion.
5. Strong endogroups enable guilt transference which result in displaced guilt symptoms in both the negative image and the endo-ideal.
6. Strong endogroups create cognitive dissonance between endoreality and universal reality which can cause severe stress.
7. Strong endogroups cause euphoric depletion of the negative image and, sometimes, the reflectors. In a revolutionary incident, this depletion can reverse onto the endo-ideal. Euphoric depletion is caused through chronic stress, fear, sorrow, instability, guilt, blocked or intercepted expansion and violations of privacy.

Personal distress should then be treated through the following means:

1. Look for the effects of environmental hazards which nearly every person in the world is suffering from.
2. Examine endogroups the person is a part of, identifying dominant and authoritative endogroups for possible cognitive dissonance and examining the roles the person occupies for guilt assignment and endogroup or negative image hostility. Look for refracted or amputated cores.
3. Examine the euphoric exchange of daily interactions looking for imbalance. Identify guilt, shame and euphoric depletion or predation, particularly of the

inner circle of self.

Despite the continual references in this book to endoselves and exoselves, there are no living people who display all of the characteristics of either, as to do so would be to be dead. These terms are used to describe interactions in which people display primarily exosocial or endoself characteristics. No person occupies the same role in all aspects of life. This means that no whole person can be pathologized or diagnosed as occupying any of these roles. Every person is a composite of both exosocial interactions and endosocial transactions in which they occupy a variety of roles. The unbalanced transactions need to be minimized and the balanced interactions need to be encouraged for individual and social well-being.

The sources of euphoria and circles of expansion attained are also extremely important and will be discussed in greater detail in *Abstracting Divinity*. As an example of aspects to examine:

- For each circle of expansion in the person's life, how much growth has occurred at that circle? Boredom and excitement responses are very good indicators of blocked expansion.
- How strong is the endogroup membrane at each circle, or does one exist?
- How dominant is each endogroup in their life? What role do they play in each group? Which roles do they attempt to recreate and at what levels?

- How balanced are the interactions or transactions of their everyday life, as a cumulative total? Do they feel and express gratitude and generosity? Upon receipt of a gift (including those they paid for with money), do they feel dissatisfied or shortchanged? Do they dislike or punish the giver?
- Do they experience jealousy, envy or pride?
- Are they bored? If so, is boredom chronic or limited to certain occupations, groups or circles of expansion?
- Do they have daily and hourly sources of euphoria they anticipate with excitement?
- Do they feel guilt, shame, fear or anger?
- What is the nature of the interactions which make them feel any of the above and what is the role they played in the interactions?
- If they are suffering from sorrow, which type is it? Are they seeking healing through strengthening their personal membrane and seeking further euphoric expansion? Are they self-punishing due to guilt? Are they immobilized by shame or a refracted core?

The answer to a life of unbalanced transactions is to balance them. If a person starts each day by buying a coffee, they should say thank you. If they start every day serving others, they should ask for gratitude and if it is not forthcoming, leave. The reason certain societies are so unhealthy is because even such small balanced interactions are impossible in endosocial culture. The entire culture is designed to prevent such balance and to follow the laws of endoreality in assigning guilt and gratitude. This is not an individual problem. It is the societies that need to be examined, diagnosed and modified. Even very small gestures, like those in places where everyone claps for a pilot upon landing a plane or everyone says thank you to the bus driver as they get off, or people bow to thank or apologize to others in passing, are far healthier than societies which permit no gratitude or contrition at all. Teaching people to keep their own guilt on their own plate, to credit and acknowledge the gifts of others with gratitude and to seek exosocial expansion far past the bounds of endosocial institutions is essential, but necessitates dismantling totalitarian institutions of endosocialism.

The science of sociopathy

A thing is not necessarily true because a man dies for it. - Oscar Wilde

Psychology is the science which defines insanity. Psychologists, or the authoritative endo-ideal, have defined the criminally insane as their negative image. More accurately, they defined their negative image as the criminally insane.

Many of the early neuroses of psychology and psychiatry sound a lot like pre-menstrual syndrome, post-partum depression, pregnancy mood swings or menopause. Many sound like a reaction to being a woman under male endo-idealism. Many others are simply not the Anglo / Germanic, male endo-ideal. Today, most or all disorders sound like the results of being trapped in a predatory, totalitarian, endosocial structure and put under continual stress. In the past few years, several studies[114] have continued to point out that the vast majority of research in psychology is still focused on "WEIRD" (western, educated, industrialized, rich and democratic)[115] societies, or a tiny minority of the world's population. That population is, naturally, the endo-ideal and overwhelmingly endoselves as well.

Disobedience in wives was pathologized in a number of ways and remedies involved torture as punishment disguised as 'cures'. Hysterectomies were popular because the uterus itself was pathologized and believed, since at least 400 BCE in the teachings of Hippocrates, to cause *hysteria,* now thinly disguised in the current DSM V as *histrionic*. In the first century CE Aretaeus described the uterus as: *"in a word, it is altogether erratic. It delights also in fragrant smells, and advances towards them; and it has an aversion to fetid smells, and flees from them; and, on the whole, the womb is like an animal within an animal."*[116] and from that, identified hysteria as a condition of being crazy because female.

In 1851, a U.S. physician invented *drapetomania,* the race equivalent of hysteria. This was a 'mental illness' attributed to slaves in the United States who ran away instead of being *"spell-bound, and cannot run away."*[117] which Cartwright asserted as the normative condition for slaves. The term spell-bound is not at all coincidental in portraying the *natural condition of bondage* which slaves, including women, were supposed to be held by. The cures for drapetomania involved whipping and removal of the two big toes. The far more widespread (and of much earlier origin than psychiatry) diagnosis of hysteria involved electroshocks and removal of the uterus. In both cases, the negative image was pathologized by their own enslavement. The inventor of drapetomania is now reviled as a *pseudoscientist* while the inventor of hysteria is heralded as *the father of medicine.* It is easy to recognize the early guilt transference and punishment of the negative image under the auspices of psychology.

Since then, psychiatry has been called *the father of genocide*[118] for its authoritative role in advocating genocide long before the second world war and enabling genocide during that war (and many others). Psychiatry has aided authoritarians by depicting not only resistance to enslavement, but any political disobedience or rejection of endoreality as mental illness.[119] The Nuremberg Trials convicted a number of psychiatrists for their role in enabling genocide. Future trials ought to convict far more for their role in developing torture programs for the CIA and every other totalitarian state, as well as methods of state and corporate coercion under totalitarianism. Military psychology is devoted to the manufacture of endoselves and the destruction of self in order to sublate others.

In a classic example of blaming the victim for doing what was done to them, medicine took authority from community healers and gave it to corporations to cover up real causes of illness and sell corporate cures. Psychologists created a vast library detailing the ways that mothers were not competent to raise children. They insisted that people needed psychologists to discover that all babies were cannibals and boys naturally wanted to rape their mothers and murder their fathers and if it seemed like they didn't, it is just because they were suppressing that urge and that was making them sick. Psychology diagnosed the 'moral hysteria' (the *women are insane* disorder) of parents who didn't want their children raped and criticized objections to paedosadism as a feminist attack on *"normative masculinity"*.[120] Psychology took the symptoms of reaction to corporate poison and blamed them on caregivers, vilifying mothers for personality disorders caused by exhausted adrenal glands, blood sugar instability and other reactions to a toxic, dissociated and totalitarian environment. Lastly, people diagnosed with personality disorders were converted into product for the psychology industry.

It seems incredible that humanity would put a group of people in charge of defining normative and deviant without any examination of the people doing the defining. Considering the widespread torture, genocide enabling, human experimentation, demonization, guilt transference, complete absence of empathy, using others for their own advancement, self-aggrandizement, pathological lying to the patients and the public and grandiose claims, if ever an institution could be described as sociopathic, psychiatry is it. It normalizes sublation and predation and pathologizes resistance to them. Perhaps this is not the most qualified institution to draw conclusions from studies on lack of empathy or endogroup solidarity, or to decide what personalities need to be designated as deviant in contrast to their endo-ideal. It is not difficult to see why psychiatry continues to produce findings reflecting an endoreality which is both incomprehensible and puerile to those outside and will continue to do so until open science is established.

The psychopath industry, an incredibly lucrative industry for psychiatry and entertainment alike, is itself a model of a highly dangerous endogroup. The authoritative endo-ideals create an ever-changing, ephemeral and unfalsifiable endoreality and demand reflection with a sense of urgency spurred on by the spectre of the twin negative images of madness and criminality. Any consistent criteria for diagnosis of the so-called psychopath would include probably everyone at the head of the psychopath industry and a great many of those who have made their mark in psychiatry or psychology. This is an industry built on fear and demonization of the other. It provides binary and absolute diagnosis where none is possible. It insists on the inherent, absolute and incurable inhumanity of the other, which they cannot possibly know. The psychopath industry conveniently focuses on the current primary enemies of the authoritative endo-ideals, unsublated endo-ideals of lower endogroups. Psychology has never failed to move with the times to pathologize the current enemies of their authoritative endo-ideal.

It is not at all difficult to see the root and body of all of psychiatry as sociopathic. It is very easy to diagnose the entire industry with any of the categories they have ever used to describe sociopathy, including Robert Hare's entire famous checklist. From the initial demonization of the most vulnerable to the vast history of sexual abuse and experimentation on vulnerable patients by therapists, examples of predation are endemic.

The methods which the industry uses to isolate the general public from all knowledge not sanctioned by the industry through virtuous claims of *protecting patient privacy* (or now, *national security*) conceal the harmful and atrocious practices. The insistence that they have a monopoly on defining an unfalsifiable reality and ascribing madness and inferiority to any who disagree clearly establish them as the institutional endo-ideal. The variable and relative nature of all of their authoritative knowledge excludes any of it from universal reality. In pursuit of their supposedly heroic goal of saving humanity from the inhuman other, they have followed such inhumane paths as torture, genocide and human experimentation, always maintaining their own exceptionalism. The negative image is made to pay for their own shunning and punishment in a final guilt reversal and carry the stigma and shame for what was committed against them.

It is also very easy to see that this behaviour is typical of any endo-ideal. All endo-ideals use the rest of their endogroup as their product, torment, torture and dehumanize their negative image, define endoreality, demand reflection, make grandiose claims and create fear of the other, everything the psychiatric industry has done. This is the same behaviour that the people diagnosed with the DSM-V cluster B disorders display. It is also the behaviour displayed by the endo-ideals of the wider scientific endogroup as well as states and supranational industries. Individuation allows psychiatry and the world which reflects them to pretend that only those endo-ideals who have not attained an authoritative level are pathological. Like the term *terrorist,* whose actions can only be distinguished from state militaries by the qualifier *non-state actor,* or the term *murder,* which can only be distinguished from state executions by the qualifier *unlawful,* the qualifiers serve to separate the endo-ideal from the negative image. The terms do not differentiate between identical actions, they merely accord status to the actors. This relativity is the definition of endoreality.

The difference between a so-called sociopath and a hero or a bureaucrat or a judge is simply an authoritative endogroup boundary. Psychology is a method of cleansing the authoritative endo-ideal of all guilt, casting all blame onto the negative image and punishing the victim. It is probably not coincidence that this science arose at the peak of the industrial endo-idealism which cast both women and nature as its negative image and caused widespread illness, dissociation and mental distress. Like British Petroleum dumping the even more harmful dispersants on top of their oil spills in a final guilt reversal and punishment of the ocean for their own guilt, industry is responding to people in crisis due to environmental stress by forcibly injecting even more harmful toxins into them.

This has nothing to do with healing or care. No one has to exert great marketing campaigns demonizing people in wheelchairs as a hidden enemy to the public to convince everyone that wheelchairs are necessary. It is only mental stress that is demonized to create an other that society will torment as a negative image to the profit of multiple industries. Given the tendency of the endo-ideal to assign guilt and credit along lines of power, it is typical that they would gravitate to a profession which allows them to pathologize and demonize their own behaviour in others.

Empathy is reduced in proportion to the exaggeration or manufacture of differences. Scientific categorization is an obsessive search for differences. If there is a coherent goal to social science, the goal appears to be the alienation of every society, or the manufacture of endoselves. This is a difference, but not an improvement, on monolithic endogroups. Such alienation is often presented as the reverse process of sublation but it is a continuation of sublation under a different endo-identity. The reverse process of sublation would be a dissolution of endogroups. Both psychology and sociology are in the business of creating the Other.

It has been the quest of the schools of psychiatry and psychology to categorize and differentiate characteristics and responses into lists of disorders and deviance. They create laundry lists of objectionable behaviour and symptoms, group them under umbrellas with little unifying factor and then create vague diagnostic guidelines around the presence of some arbitrary number of the symptoms on each list. These lists are used to separate the normal from the pathological, based on the subjective and often secretive, but very authoritative, assessment of those paid to assess. Illness diagnosis, especially mental illness, by symptoms instead of causes, creates groups of defective people instead of causes to be addressed. This leads to symptoms in search of a common cause, which is unproductive since the body and mind react to many environmental stressors in a similar manner and different bodies and minds have different reactions to the same stressors.

These arbitrary groupings of symptoms are stamped with labels which impart no understanding and depict symptoms as the result of individual characteristics. Diagnosis serves no purpose except as a license to pharmaceutical dispensers. The process of categorization is an exercise in corporate marketing. Patients are rarely told to eliminate sugar and other harmful foods or avoid water, air and emf pollution despite an incredible body of research confirming the personality altering affects of all of these environmental hazards. Indeed, those that point out such research are vilified as the negative image and it is the victim that is diagnosed, as *allergic* or *sensitive,* instead of the substance or pollution. It naturally follows that the person is treated (punished) not the substance or pollution. So-called personality disorders tend to centre around the social motivators of shunning and inclusion but they are almost exclusively examined as though each person was raised in a vacuum. At most, only the mother is blamed, ahead of obvious factors like dissociated, industrialized populations, physical illness caused by diet, pollution and other adverse corporate activity, and destruction of self through totalitarianism.

The idea that people respond differently to environmental stressors because they are *abnormal* is the most unscientific idea imaginable. Everyone is normal, and responding in a normal and predictable fashion to whatever conditions they are given to deal with. Blaming the subject for the observed reaction is completely anti-science. Differences in people and their environmental responses are based on differences in the relative health and strength of their various social membranes. It is not stress that inhibits expansion, it is the response to stress. These symptoms are not caused by stress alone but by the endosocial role people occupy during times of stress.

Diagnosis puts the blame and stigma for an illness on the person instead of the cause and allows claims that only some overly-sensitive (defective) people have adverse reactions, and it is their problem to resolve. The cause of the illness retains its *normal* standing. This is predictable since the causes are usually earning profit for corporate endo-ideals and the victims, according to the laws of endoreality, are the negative image. Like IQ in the last century, which was always tied to personal shortcomings, preferably attached to sex, race and class, illness today is a stigma of weakness in the victim. Courts which require the victims to prove (with no access to authoritative research facilities) exactly which corporation was responsible for their particular symptoms and medical resources which require victims to pay, not corporations, are evidence of who is assigned guilt. It is also evidenced in the fact that, even where people are entitled to health care, they are never deemed entitled to a healthy environment. The terms *sensitivities* and *allergies* both put the focus on the victim's reaction, not the initial fact that they were attacked by people poisoning their environment with toxic substances.

Finally, the categorization of people leads to the creation of endogroups with a *normal* endo-ideal and a dehumanized, *pathological*, negative image. People are encouraged to ignore their own, lived, experience in favour of the authoritative opinion of psychiatrists who tell them that their loved one is a different category of humanity, incurable, guilty, and primarily, *not like you and me*. In lieu of any exploration for behavioural causes, the victims of diagnosis have all manner of evil intent ascribed to them. Books with highly authoritative authors insist that they understand what each person is thinking and the motives behind their behaviour. *They study emotions! They don't feel a thing! They want to destroy you!* Not only could these reality-defining experts not possibly understand or have any evidence on which to base such conclusions on motivation, they dismiss every testimony of the diagnosed as *pathological lying*, a phrase which only means to disagree with the prevailing endoreality.

People certainly exist whose behaviour is cruel, destructive and destroying the earth and the lives of every living thing on it. It is not enough to simply depict these people as separate from us and incurable. It is not enough to simply rely on endoreality and a highly selective and inconsistent system of categorization created by an endo-ideal in order to designate a negative image, with no further explanation. The issue is not each individual stress response; it is the proliferation of stress. The people producing stress are the endoselves in search of secondary euphoria and guilt transference. Instead of addressing the behaviour of these people as the problem, medicine simply abstracts them into the unavoidable and normative with phrases such as *our modern way of life*. Further, the totalitarianism and industrialization that creates endoselves is marketed as necessary to protect us from those very endoselves it creates.

For years, institutional knowledge has sneered at the idea of a group self, in defiance of all observable reality and all prior belief in history. Institutional power validated the cocaine ramblings of a single-minded gynophobe to the level of a science in psychology and then medicalized this weakest of all sciences with psychiatry to further punish the negative image it identified. For years, these same authorities have refused to accord sociology any status beyond that of a quaint collator of legends and customs or a vehicle for the creation of endless new endogroups. Society is never diagnosed. When any evidence clearly illustrates that society is the root of every problem identified by psychology, it is greeted as a whiny excuse or an inevitable and irremediable struggle. If society is blamed at all, the guilt is placed on the head of society's scapegoat, the mother.

Endogroups clearly exist. Not only all historical knowledge, but all examination of power and dependency relationships in neuroscience confirms this. People within endogroups clearly act very differently than they do outside of endogroups, with the exception of endoselves, whose perspective is used to define authoritative endoreality.

It is time to examine the fact that psychology is endoreality, created by the endo-ideal to punish the negative image and exalt the endo-ideal as normative. The vast amount of mental struggles people are enduring are the result of environmental destruction, societal exploitation and the cognitive dissonance created by endoreality. Those that do not struggle, but instead prey on others, are a result of the institutional glorification and enforcement of the endoself and also environmental damage. This is a problem that psychology largely ignores, or attempts to normalize.

It is also time to acknowledge the role of the entire medical profession as executioner. Society, manifested in law, psychology and economics, passes judgment on its negative image by handing them guilt. That guilt manifests as illness, poverty, crime, misery and self-destructive behaviour from within and without the individual. Illness is then further punished in a final guilt reversal by the dehumanizing and dignity-destroying practices of the medical profession. Any patient is familiar with the negative image status they are accorded with each diagnosis. Treatment is the most oppressive institution in society, beyond even that handed out in prisons (which are, not coincidentally, also medicalized). This medicalization was introduced to all aspects of life where the negative image exists, in childbirth and female lives in general, in schools, in prisons and among elderly and poor people. Much of medicine is thinly disguised torture. Much of acknowledged state torture is medicine, performed under medical auspices. The victim is the lowest negative image that can absorb all of the guilt for industrial endo-idealism.

To present as the victim of the endo-ideal, through either corporate pollution and destruction or social policies, is to identify as the negative image and a candidate for punishment. This is why the endo-ideal refuse to defend against corporate destruction, even when that destruction costs them their own life and health. Both the medical and the technology industries are part of the vast and growing punishment industry which tortures the negative image to absolve the guilt of the predators. Both also transfer guilt to the negative image for their own destruction through reframing corporate pollution and destruction as individual illness and weakness. In some places, the victim is made to pay for their own punishment in the form of medical fees, to effect the final guilt reversal. No amount of regulation is ever going to curtail the punishment of a negative image for the guilt of the endo-ideal. The only solution is to repeal the laws of endoreality by dismantling and prevention of endogroups.

Psychiatry is a huge industry which serves the dark triad of the pharmaceutical industry, the state coercion industry and the corporate deception industry and silences the victims of environmental and social destruction. So far, the contributions of neuroscience have been about as reliable in establishing cause and affect between neurological findings and psychiatric diagnosis as phrenology. Even if neuroscience manages in the future to provide some factual underpinnings to psychiatry, the motivations are still, to use their own diagnosis, sociopathic. On the other hand, the findings of neuroscience correlate very well with the principles of exosocialism.

As anyone who has been near hospitals knows, the care industries are filled with kind and altruistic people who truly care about the vulnerable people they are working with and are trying to help them heal. As anyone who has been near hospitals also knows, the care industries are also filled with predatory endoselves who are there for the express purpose of causing pain and misery to their victims. This is not a reality that is limited to hospitals; it is true of every institutional care industry and it is a symptom of the power structure and the compulsion to punish the negative image as well as the proliferation of endoselves.

People who are suffering need community support and solidarity, not ostracization, labelling and isolation within the walls of predatory power structures. Cures need to be a result of open science and open community feedback, not dictated from the top to benefit profiting corporations with no community input possible outside of law courts. A power structure and industrialization of care was always going to result in predatory care industries. Identifying as the victim of an endogroup is presenting oneself for guilt reversal and punishment.

For a long time, people have been convinced to measure their social well-being by the state of the wealthy, or at least The Taxpayer. Every society ought to be measured by the treatment of those who are the most vulnerable. In endosocialism, the weakest are the point of social failure, just as in exosocialism, they are the point of social focus. In endosocialism, the weakest are the guilt sacrifice. In exosocialism, the weakest are an opportunity for altruism, to alleviate a shared pain.

Sociology has never gained the widespread acceptance of other sciences. The problem is not to be found with sociology, which is far closer to what science claims to be than something like theoretical physics or psychology. The problem is that sociology ought to be an examination of endoreality, and authoritative endogroups do not like having their endoreality examined.

Sociology ought to be the most important and critical area of study today. Society needs to be examined, at both a micro level, as the relationships of a caregiver circle, and a macro level, examining the nature of the totalitarian mono-empire. Examining our daily interactions and transactions and seeking to prevent imbalance and endgroups ought to be the first priority of the entire world right now.

Psychology does not have any basis for existence outside of its role in creating endoreality. This is very evident in the tendency of its practitioners to keep creating new branches of study which properly belong under biology or sociology. Psychology itself has no role outside of propagandist and executioner.

Sociology has been perverted into a tool of endoreality. The use of a Hegelian lens to manufacture endogroups does not constitute a science. Sociology needs, first of all, to escape the individualist idea of self, and second, to create a real science examining interactions and unbalanced transactions, as well as inhibition of expansion. Sociology must be, above all, a study of power, and power cannot be examined through an individualist lens.

Outside the walls

You think your pain and your heartbreak are unprecedented in the history of the world, but then you read. It was books that taught me that the things that tormented me most were the very things that connected me with all the people who were alive, who had ever been alive. - James Baldwin

In looking at the amount of force required to hold together the institutions of endosocial structure, it is evident that a far more powerful force must be opposing this structure, for it keeps winning. People have a natural tendency to create egalitarian communities and a natural tendency towards exosocial expansion. Both of these tendencies require extreme force to overcome so they must themselves be very strong forces. Totalitarianism is an effort to overcome these twin forces.

Life is an exosocial movement fighting for liberation, or the freedom to expand. Power is an endosocial group demanding reflection of endoreality, or the sublation of others. Living creatures were meant to be actions, not nouns.

The evolutionary purpose of an endogroup was power formation. The modern purpose of an endogroup is primarily debt management. It allows unbalanced transactions to bypass or deflect the guilt and shame response so that the chosen endo-ideal can accumulate all the power of the group with no inhibitions. The endogroup is a defensive structure which allows all power of the group to be focused in times of crisis. Endogroups were never meant to be a permanent state. Unfortunately, endosocialism is now a self-perpetuating structure which has shaped every aspect of modern lives and provided the foundations for all global institutions.

The natural inhibitions against power accumulation have been extremely dulled by the rise of the endoself as a normative model of social development. Both environmental stress and social engineering have contributed to this rise and inhibited the usual force of the exosocial drive in tearing down these power structures when they are no longer necessary. Once established in a permanent state, an endogroup acquires the nature of an insatiable ponzi scheme.

We are now at the peak aspect of the global power ponzi scheme and it is about to collapse. It is urgent that we examine both the structure of the endogroup and the nature of exosocialism. The law of the last circle (illustrated in *Autonomy, Diversity, Society*) shows us that the nature of endosocial populations causes them to attempt to fall back to the last real or imagined endogroup structure when the current one collapses. Since there is no transcendental endogroup possible over a global mono-empire, the only alternative to regression is advancement to exosocialism.

It is not just the endogroup but also the endoself that is in charge of every aspect of industrialized society. The impenetrable membrane and lust for possession and destruction of the endoself is nearly essential for any person who has climbed to the top of today's institutions of power. Even if endoselves are always around, due to poor health or whatever cause, there is a very big difference between an endoself living in a society which shuns their behaviour and rewards any attempt to change it and a society which celebrates, institutionally supports and strives to create endoselves and makes exosocial interactions illegal.

Endless volumes have been written in the last centuries describing every human interaction as a struggle of wills, a war, a master – slave relationship, or symbolic murder of one or both. These depictions have come from Hegel, Foucault, Freud, from biology, sociology, psychology from politics, architecture, economics, and from every other aspect of study from any discipline that has sought to understand or establish the dynamics of human interaction. As always, we reflect what our endo-ideals define us as. If we are to move out of a structure of warring endogroups and into a structure of exosocial collaboration, the first change must be in our thoughts and intentions. We need to redefine what is normative and to move past that so-called love which is really sublation and that so-called care which is really predation. We need to resist revolution and achieve liberation..

Endosocialism is the cause of all sustained human conflict. An empathic relationship precludes systemic violence. In exosocial interactions, we experience the pain we inflict, through guilt. There is a world outside Hegel and Kant and all of the subjects and objects and assertions and negations that followed them, a world beyond masters and slaves, winning and losing and good and evil, a world beyond yinyangism, Manicheism and heaven and hell. That world is just outside the bubbles most of humanity live in.

An endogroup cannot be removed by another endogroup. It can only be rebranded. An endogroup can only be removed by exosocial interactions which establish relationships through the group membrane until it dissolves. Endogroups are created by those with damaged personal membranes and no path to access primary euphoria. Secure, exosocial individuals are required to create an exosocial environment with strength and integrity.

There are many ways to remove an endo-ideal that are far more effective than assassination. One is by assigning them guilt and not allowing that guilt to be reclassified as a virtue. This has been the propaganda method used by several of the latest corporate coups in South America, including the most recent coups in Paraguay (2012), Brazil (2016), and Bolivia (2019). To remove all power, real guilt must be proven against all of those in power, which is not nearly as difficult as it sounds. Power is never benevolent and never inert. Where it exists in great excess, atrocities always exist in great excess as well. Another method is to usurp the right to define reality and refuse to reflect endoreality. This is an adherence to the provable facts in universal reality and a rejection of relative facts and magical words whose only meaning is a tool of endogroup shunning or inclusion. This is the opposite of not believing in anything or being flexible with ephemeral, changing reality. A third method is a refusal to reflect endo-identity which, as the endo-ideals correctly point out, is their *right to exist*, as an endo-ideal at any rate. This includes a refusal to grant relative judgment as dictated by the exceptional myth. Mass disobedience, or a refusal to accept their right to define law, including ownership, has been well recognized and not well enough used. Finally, and most importantly, recognition and blocking of those who police the laws of endoreality is required, at every level.

None of these tactics will matter as long as the subsequent structure is simply another revolutionary or transcendent endogroup, however. Dismantling power is an urgent necessity, but creating replacement structures is far more urgent. The rest of the books in this series are an attempt to examine the problems before us in our paths to build these structures and to suggest where we might look for solutions.

In the coming years, dismantling power will prove to be shockingly easy. The most difficult part will come in being ready for what comes next. Recognition of the law of the last circle, the swarm of migratory endo-ideals and targeted alienation are essential to avoid regression into previous tyrannies. Recognition of the methods of totalitarian coercion are necessary to resist the transcendental mono-empire. Most importantly, recognition of our drive towards exosocialism and the methods in which this is blocked is essential to our liberation. We cannot escape the walls we do not see.

Appendix A: Transcript of Whistleblowing Panel censored by Oxford Union

This is a transcript of what I said at a February 17, 2018 talk at the Oxford Union which is, to date, the only talk that has ever been censored by them, and was also subjected to a media blackout in the UK. It is very illustrative of what the Official Secrets Act of the UK and other state secrecy is actually protecting as well as how very easy it is to be censored by the self-proclaimed *"last bastion of free speech"*. This panel featured myself and David Shedd, the former director of the US Defense Intelligence Agency, who is also a former CIA operative and current private sector mercenary. It was censored before any widespread media coverage of Facebook and Cambridge Analytica collaboration, ICE concentration camps or Jeffrey Epstein. The transcript is of my parts only, to which I retain copyright and publish as open copyright CC BY 4.0, share and use in any way you wish. The rest of the book retains my usual copyright, CC BY-NC-SA 3.0.

Oxford Union: Introduce yourself

My name is Heather Marsh. I am an author and I write a great deal about mass collaboration and horizontal governance and I've worked for many years as an activist and journalist to amplify voices in urgent need of attention, primarily whistleblowers. I am also a software developer and I'm working on a project called Getgee which is a universal database commons that will help us share, audit and amplify open collaborative information, so that we can participate intelligently in our own governance.

My focus has always been human rights and horizontal governance. Of the human rights atrocities I have worked to expose, a very large number are associated with David Shedd and the organizations and allies he represents. As just one example, I fought for over a decade to achieve justice for my fellow Canadian, Omar Khadr who was abducted at 15 years old, subjected to the most horrific torture at the CIA black site Bagram, then trafficked and tortured for another decade at Guantanamo before enduring a show trial of invented court, invented evidence, invented experts and retroactively applied, invented crimes. The hell this Canadian child went through for 12 years was conducted by the organizations represented by David Shedd. It is deeply uncomfortable for me to be here today, on the same panel as someone whose work has established and worked to normalize ever-increasing drone murders, black site disappearances and torture and I hope it is uncomfortable for all of you as well, and for him. Beware of your contribution to the growing banality of evil lest you yourself become a cog in the machinery of terror.

I am here today because I want to talk about how our structures of power are evolving. There is probably only one thing I have in common with David Shedd and that is that we both want a world without whistleblowers. He wants to crush whistleblowers and I want a world where the caregivers of our communities and land hold institutional power, where everyone's voice is heard and those who terrorize us all with impunity lose the power to do so.

The opening was some generic question about whistleblowers.

If there is one thing I would like people to take home today it is the definition of whistleblower. There seems to have been an effort lately to equate whistleblowers solely with an elite, western, usually male leaking documents. A few days ago I read an article about a program for whistleblowers in the US intelligence agencies. It was a human resources program for employee grievances. The people they were calling whistleblowers were torturers at Bagram who didn't like having a female boss or assassins who felt overlooked for promotion. And then, there was a cover full of whistleblowers on TIME magazine this year, but they were called Silence Breakers! What is a Silence Breaker if not a whistle blower? You know, there are no female philosophers because a female philosopher is called a feminist. Apparently we have the same sort of thing happening here, there are no whistleblowers outside of this elite demographic because they are called activists or silence breakers or something.

I have worked with many whistleblowers over many years. I worked with Rohingya activists from 2012 on to help convince the world that they were in fact experiencing a genocide. I have worked with victims of trafficking networks and resource corporations and institutions like prisons and care facilities. Whistleblowers are people like the mothers of the Plaza de Mayo in Argentina who fought the silence of the dictatorship in defence of the disappeared, and all the movements like them that have followed in their steps, like Central America's Caravan of Missing Migrants, Nigeria's Bring Back Our Girls movement, the Missing and Murdered Indigenous Women movement in Canada, the Missing Students activists in Mexico and the people standing up against ICE pogroms in the United States right now. They include labour activists like Kim Jinsuk, a woman who in 2011 stayed up a crane for 309 days to protest the lack of labor rights in South Korea, and Hua Haifeng, who was arrested in China recently for exposing abuses against workers in the factories manufacturing Ivanka Trump's brand. They include Maria del Rosario Fuentes Rubio, who was murdered for her reporting on Mexican cartels in 2014 and Daphne Caruana Galizia, who was killed by a car bomb in Malta last October for her work exposing organized crime, They include the environment caregivers now being killed at a recorded rate of four a week and increasing. They include Helena Maleno who has been credited with saving the lives of at least 10,000 refugees in the Strait of Gibralter and is now facing imprisonment in

Morocco and your own MP Jo Cox who was murdered because of her work in caring for refugees.

Obviously we could do this for days. Whistleblowers come from absolutely every demographic but there is one group that is very over represented and that it is the caregivers of our communities and land standing against the impunity enjoyed by powerful criminals. The media coverage depicting whistleblowers as a fairly elite demographic of western male hackers leaking documents is a little disproportionate.

But those in power do understand where the threat to their impunity is coming from. China arrested five women in 2015 just for distributing pamphlets against sexual harassment. Canada openly identifies First Nations communities and environmentalists as target groups to be monitored for terrorist activity and it is obvious in the terrorist definitions of every country. The definition of terrorism in the five eyes is attempting to influence your community or government, which is also the definition of democracy. Participating in your own governance, alerting your neighbours to what is happening, is defined as terrorism. So this redefinition of whistleblowers as scary non-state actors and hostile intelligence services, this will be used against the women and men who are the community and land caregivers of every nation because these are the number one threat to the corporate mafia that wants immunity from prosecution for their crimes. As soon as laws against whistleblowers are passed they will be used against people accusing MPs of rape or people letting the public know that Trudeau has just turned more lakes into toxic waste dumps for mines or people boycotting Israel or the NRA. It is this groundswell of community and land caregivers, the rising up of 7 and a half billion people participating in their own governance, that are the real threat to corrupt power.

So we need to define whistleblowers properly or we are not going to come up with solutions that will actually meet their needs. A human resources program in the CIA will not help all these people. Even in the case of John Kirakiou, obviously he never should have been imprisoned for pointing out that there was torture at Guantanamo, but everyone in Guantanamo would have and did try to tell us the same thing. It is the people in Guantanamo and every other prison who we should never have allowed to be silenced in the first place and those are the voices we need to make sure we hear.

OU: What do you think the media is missing in their coverage of whistleblowers?

I remembered what I don't like about the media coverage of whistleblowers. I feel like it is covered in such a personality centred, celebrity focused way that it is like listening to people discussing Harry Styles' hair. There are important issues to be discussed in the structure of power that allows only some people's voices to be heard. How can we hear directly from voices which are being silenced? This is something I have been working on for years because it turns out, you can murder millions of people without leaving a paper trail or inspiring an insider whistleblower. How do we make sure we hear all voices? If mining corporations in the

Yasuni say indigenous people are just killing each other and it has nothing to do with them, who outside can prove that one way or another? With the Rohingya genocide, ironically the best documentation we could get was from Google maps, which showed villages which had been there earlier and now they were gone. I've thought a lot about different solutions for years, like uploading testimony in actionable affidavit format from places like Myanmar or UN peacekeeping camps or anywhere people are silenced and at risk. Like the current Oxfam story. That was absolutely no surprise to anyone who works in human rights, and it is certainly not just Oxfam either. You will find this everywhere you have this same structure of power and secrecy at the top and fear and silencing at the bottom. We've seen it in NGOs, militaries, UN peacekeepers over and over. This is why I am working on a universal database, to try to democratize this access to a megaphone and bring us information from everyone.

It is not new laws we need, we already have so many international laws protecting our human rights, our rights to freedom of expression, our right to knowledge, *our rights to not be tortured and murdered, our right to a fair trial,* and these are all being ignored. We don't need to create another witness protection program with the mafia in charge of it. It is our governance that needs to be revamped. We are still governed by a form of democracy created before women or children or indigenous people or labourers were considered persons or part of the demos and before any international networks existed below the level of trade empires.

It's been almost four hundred years since that awful Cambridge man argued in Patriarcha that an all powerful patriarchal system was the only legitimate form of governance and Robert Filmer was most decisively refuted by Oxford's own John Locke, who ought to be familiar to anyone from the United States as well, since he was fairly influential in creating the ideology they are supposed to be run by. I did think that western democracies were done with this debate. If you want to live under an all powerful patriarchal form of governance, you move to an absolute monarchy or a dictatorship, not a democracy. Patriarchy and democracy are incompatible. We settled this nearly four hundred years ago. And it is customary for those who uphold this absolute form of secretive tyrannical rule to call people like me anarchists, but if all anarchy means is there are no absolute rulers or centralized authority, then shouldn't that be a basic tenet of a democracy?

If you do want democracy, it's not just media that needs to be free. It's not even just speech. It is knowledge. An uninformed vote is a coerced vote. People without reliable information they can trust will follow ideologies and demagogues blindly and we are seeing more and more of that lately as our access to information and our trust in information is eroded. And when government is conducted in secrecy, the atrocities that have repeated throughout history will happen again, as they always do in the dark. We really don't need to keep proving this. So we don't need reactionaries trying to shore up some ancient flailing patriarchy with increasing tyranny and secrecy. We don't need revolutionaries knocking off figureheads and installing their own messiahs onto the same structure. We need to build a democracy that is right for today, that includes everyone and resists tyranny, and that means democratic access to knowledge and participatory governance.

[At some point another panelist said they liked Obama and I said Obama had paved the road Trump was driving on and pointed out Obama's intention was not to close Guantanamo but to bring it onto US soil – where ICE detention centres continue to proliferate.]

OU: What do you think motivates whistleblowers to take these risks and why don't they go through proper channels? I know what you are probably going to say …

Well yes, because the majority of the whistleblowers I deal with don't have proper channels and they aren't given any choice over the situation they are in. That is the whole point, they don't have institutional power and we need institutional power for community and land caregivers and an end to the secrecy and impunity at the top. Because we are told that we need these structures of absolute power and secrecy for our safety, but intelligence agencies are not competent to protect you from ISIS or anyone else. The heads of most of the top intelligence agencies in the US were compromised recently by a 15 year old British boy called Crackas with attitude and he wasn't hacking, he just guessed his way in. An Australian student just noticed the US military was revealing all their military locations in Syria through the Fitbit app. Australian MP's just sold a load of Top Secret documents in an old filing cabinet. There are homemade drones taking out military planes that cost more than your health care. They are not competent to keep you safe, but even if they were competent, our safety is not their priority.

I remember in one of the mass shootings in the US, this one involved really tiny kids, and there were two things that really stood out for me about this case. One, the mother was completely blamed for her son's actions even though she was his first victim. President Obama and the media both left her name off the victim lists as if she was a perpetrator or a non-human. The other thing that struck me was that she was entirely blamed – but she had no community support she could have relied on. This was a single woman, living with an obviously violent and very disturbed adult son, and she had absolutely nowhere to turn for help. How is she supposed to be responsible for something she has no power to stop? And we've just seen the same thing happen again in Florida, the students and teachers and community were blamed for not doing enough but they did everything in their power and they were ignored because the politicians are not listening to them. Look at the #ArmMeWith hashtag on social media this week, teachers are asking for books, time, resources, mental health care, a decent adult to child ratio – they are saying they don't need guns, they need the resources to build community. And the US government is offering guns because that is profit for the only nation they care about, which is the weapons manufacturers and the NRA.

Some people have been really worried in past years about terrorists entering into Europe with refugees and yes, of course, they have. Not nearly as many as some people would like you to believe, because we all have our own homegrown terrorists now, but yes, some have come through camps, and the people in refugee camps will tell you who those people are. Or online communities will tell you. In Canada, we had a man a couple years ago who used to torture kittens to death and upload the videos online. He was reported by most people who saw the videos and they were ignored. Then he went on a gore site – you would think if we have some patriarchal power trying to keep us all safe they must be monitoring gore sites, right? – and he advertised an upcoming murder. He was reported, and the reports were ignored. Then he horrifically murdered someone and uploaded that video. He was reported by so many people. One retired police officer in the US reported him to the RCMP, the FBI and his local sheriff. Everyone ignored all the reports. He took the body out of his own apartment, past the CCTV cameras on his building and street, and put it in a dumpster. Then he took his biometric, smart, Canadian passport, under his own name, which was now all over the international news and on an Interpol warrant, and he boarded an international flight from Canada to France and then to Germany, where he sat in a cyber cafe reading articles about himself until finally a man in the cafe went out and got a police officer to come in and arrest him. Is this blinding incompetence or is our safety maybe not really a great concern for intelligence agencies?

The answer of course is both. They are not competent to keep you safe, but also they aren't listening. The mothers, the caregivers, the schools, the people online, the people in refugee camps, these people are all ignored. They are listening to corporations like Areva or Shell. Boko Haram took root initially in an area completely overwhelmed by the corruption of Goodluck Jonathan's government and the devastation brought by Shell and other oil companies. Areas like Mali and Niger were equally devastated by France's Areva corporation, among others,. The people living on that land were being murdered and left with no means of survival by criminal corporations and complicit government. Again, the lack of power and the extreme abuse of community and land caregivers creates vulnerability to the growth of terrorism. And it is no secret to the intelligence communities that this is the trigger. The minute you hear protests start against Areva, you also start hearing France and the United States talking about growing extremist threat because they know very well that extremism follows backing people into a corner with no way to turn. So again, the solution is to empower the caregivers, listen to them, and end impunity for criminal corporations. If you know corporate policies are going to cause the growth of ideological extremism, maybe change corporate policies before that happens. Protection available only to the highest bidders is not security. Security is strong involved and supportive communities networked with other communities.

Response to David Shedd responding to above by saying *"our men and women in uniform"* are heroes, invincible, have so much data, etc., etc.

I think if we are going to talk about national security on this panel, we need some context. David Shedd belonged to the most powerful, well-funded, weaponized, international, organized crime syndicate the world has ever seen. Not even counting the other organizations he is affiliated with or those he calls his allies – just looking at the CIA by itself – they are in the business of assassinations, they manage black sites for torture, they work with with local mafias, cartels and militias all over the world, they run operations trafficking weapons, drugs and people all over the world, they have ongoing programs of human experimentation … these are just a few of the things the CIA itself has done, not counting their network of allies. They are part of a vast criminal network that is now planning even greater expansion, more torture, far more disappearances, far more murder. So when these men talk about whistleblowers threatening national security, we need to ask three obvious questions: what is security to them, who is their nation and who are the whistleblowers?

So given that we are dealing with criminals and members of criminal organizations, what they mean by security is immunity from criminal prosecution. And we have seen that. They do not keep us safe, we have plenty of evidence of that, but they certainly do keep themselves safe. The US military bombed an MSF hospital. Can we investigate? No we cannot, they have bulldozed the evidence. They "tortured some folks" and they plan on torturing a lot more, but that's classified. Jeffrey Epstein is a man in the United States known to have raped and trafficked dozens or hundreds or who knows how many children. The US Attorney General at the time, Alberto Gonzales, said he would have instructed the US Justice Department to "pursue justice without making a political mess". Epstein's little black book contains people like Donald Trump, Bill Clinton, Prince

Andrew. There is only one way to interpret that directive and that is impunity for anyone above a certain social strata or anyone with blackmail on them. The Pentagon, since 2010, has refused to investigate, at that time it was over 1700 cases, of child abuse media they have found on Pentagon computers. The people in the US are finally starting to talk about all the taxpayer funded NDA's that protect people in congress against reports of rape and sexual assault. California alone has reportedly paid more than $25 million in the last three years to buy criminal impunity for their politicians. In the UK, you have your own child rape inquiry where UK police have spoken many times of investigations which have a strata they can't go above – where those above that strata are referred to as the Untouchables, protected by the Official Secrets Act and many other layers of secrecy. Your former Oxford Union president and UK Prime Minister, Ted Heath, how many people came forward and said they were his victims as children, but there was never an investigation during his lifetime.

So security for them means immunity from criminal prosecution, not just for their actions against so-called enemies but against anyone. The current CIA head talks about a bureaucracy that slows down the CIA – that bureaucracy is our human rights and that is how they see our lives – as bureaucracy. If they kill too many of us at once they have to fill out a form. And that slows them down. Pompeo wants 'agile' assassins. He wants killers who 'fail fast and break things', as if they were writing stupid apps instead of murdering children. He wants 'disruptive' terrorism. And their security is the freedom to do this with impunity and in secrecy.

And who is this nation they want security for? The US were supposedly enemies with Syria and allies with Canada when they were abducting Canadians to be tortured in Assad's prisons. Their allegiances change at the drop of a hat and they all have each other's secrets anyway. That is the whole point of their industry. The entire supranational intelligence community has access to each other's secrets – they need security from the rest of us finding out. And their nation is anyone with enough money to pay them, corporations or states. You had Erik Prince speaking here a while back, the crown prince of mercenary contractors. He made his fortune at the top ranks of US military and intelligence and then contracted all that information to supposedly US enemy China. I believe David Shedd is also now in international private practice. Their nations are whoever can pay. We didn't really need the US Patriot Act to tell us our intelligence agencies may be allies but the people in our states are certainly not their allies.

This is not national security. It is certainly not security for my nation. My nation consists of the caregivers of communities and the environment all over the world. They aren't spying on corporations and telling communities what corporations are up to, they are spying on communities and selling that information to corporations. The victims of Jeffrey Epstein, all the victims whose abusers are protected by official secrets and taxpayer funded NDA's, none of these victims are part of their nation. Their nation is the international intelligence community and the politicians and corporations who can afford to pay them. This is not national security. It is a mafia protection racket available to the highest bidder.

Response by David Shedd.

HM: Why are you not doing anything about ICE internment camps in the United States if you care so much for latin americans?

DS: What camps???

HM: Maybe you should read the news.

[Some more back and forth about ICE where I discussed their access to intelligence data and potential to become an intelligence agency and Shedd denied everything and rolled his eyes at the audience. After the panel, the other panelists left and the audience stayed and asked a lot of questions about ICE. I explained that they were comparable to the Gestapo and some of their activities at that point (February, 2018).]

DS: Our brave men and women ....

HM: Torturers.

DS: Torture??!? What torture???

HM: Have you not read the Torture Report? Obama declassified part of it, didn't you know?

DS: Stop. Our brave men and women devoting their lives ...

HM: Torturing people.

DS: I asked you to stop.

HM: I asked you for twelve years to stop torturing my friend and you didn't stop.

THE END

Note: There was a meet and greet before the panel. David Shedd outlined work he was now doing in South America to "ensure compliance" with banking regulations. I asked: "Is that meant to ensure the United States has a monopoly in money laundering?" and he said he didn't know. Shedd also said he works with a charity to stop trafficking of women and children in South America, overlooking the obvious first step of getting the CIA and its contractors to stop trafficking women in children in South America, and he deplored that Russia was beating the US to the destruction of the Arctic.

Appendix B: A telenovela of endogroup roles

While it is always relationships that ought to be examined, not people, the exaggerated characters and situations of a telenovela create social situations rich with endosocial cliche. All romance and action stories tend to use highly endosocial situations and stories. The obvious drama potential makes them entertaining, but it is troubling that we have so few examples of exosocial behaviour, either in our entertainment or our histories.

In any case, here is an analysis of the fictional characters of a popular U.S. sitcom (based on a Venezuelan telenovela) and the endogroup roles they play. Feel free to disagree and examine the characters and plot through your own ideas of their motivations, but hopefully this fictional example will help clarify some of the concepts. Complete with spoilers, here is an analysis of the characters in *Jane the Virgin* based primarily on the first season. It is probably no surprise that no healthy relationships exist in a telenovela but (with the exception of Petra's relationships) few deserve the label endogroups because the participants are somewhat free to develop. They all fall very short of being exosocial, however. An interesting aspect of nearly all Hollywood entertainment is that we are encouraged to empathize with the endo-ideal or endoselves and feel contempt or anger at the negative images. Cultural variations on this in the international film industry are interesting to note.

Alba is an endo-ideal, firmly ensconced in her caregiver group. She was a spoiled and wealthy girl who was also spoiled by her husband. They moved to the US because she wanted to escape consequences of guilt and he worked very hard to create a nice life. She professes a great deal of virtue in herself, including that of the perfect mother. She tells Jane that as her blood, she could never do anything unforgivable, but she refuses to forgive her daughter Xo, regularly. Alba tries to trap both Xo and Jane in the caregiver circle by presenting waiting (living with her) as the virtuous choice. She also supports the endo-ideal Rogelio ahead of her daughter and Rafael over her grand daughter, in deference to a transcendental male endo-idealism. She has no interests outside her family endogroup where she is the endo-ideal. She has ongoing guilt for 'slutty' behaviour that she continually projects onto her daughter who enacts the negative image slut and Jane who enacts her virginal reflector.

Xomara is a negative image at the caregiver level and she would like to be an endo-ideal at the creation level. She is perpetually wrong in the eyes of her mother and daughter who define what is right. She never acts in her own best interest. She pursues rejection in the music industry instead of success by growing her dance school. She never does anything on her own but acts as the reflector for Jane, Alba and Rogelio. Salvation is a man or fame at a level that even she will not be able to deny her own self-worth (she hopes). She accepts the blame for wanting an abortion if Alba hadn't made her have the baby, in a guilt reversal enacted by Jane, encouraged by Alba. She also absorbs guilt over Jane for Rogelio who transfers the guilt for abandoning her while she was pregnant to her. She volunteers to take the guilt for Rogelio when he fires his mother. He accuses her of depriving him through her 'choice' to raise Jane alone and also tells his mother that it was Xo's choice that he not be a part of Jane's life.

Xo obediently enacts the negative image slut her mother casts her as, including telling her mother that Jane's father was a one night stand whose name she didn't remember. The idea of getting a house by herself apparently does not occur to her. She dumps the relationship with a nice football player who respects her personal boundaries in favour of the endo-ideal Rogelio who violates all of her personal boundaries, such as for privacy in her home or her romantic life. Rogelio puts her in a constant reflector-negative image struggle with his mother, just as Alba put her in the same contest with Jane . The only non-family woman in her life is someone she calls "slutty Chrystal" in an attempt to further transfer the guilt her mother transferred to her. She appears always in a reflector-negative image contest with other women. She is an example of a reflector-negative image who can only transfer allegience, as she transferred her endo-ideal from her mother to Jane when Jane was born.

Xo: *You said you'd respect my privacy.*
Rogelio: *No, Alba said she would. I have no respect for your privacy. I need to know.*

Jane is an endo-ideal at the caregiver level and shows strong endoself characteristics. She has been defining right and wrong since she could talk. Her mother is both her reflector and her negative image that she screams at and accuses of horrible things whenever she feels a need for a euphoric boost or guilt reversal. Xo seems to spend much of her time scared of Jane or anticipating abuse from her. Her relationship to her abuela is an example of what happens to the traditional rolling tyranny of filiality when it collides with a child-ideal society and endo-ideals produce even stronger endo-ideals or endoselves by vilifying those outside their circle.

Jane is never wrong. She treats her mother like crap and is never very nice, considerate or grateful to her friends either. She lectures everyone around her by accusing them of her own shortcomings such as overreacting to the slightest setback. She torments anyone who enters into a relationship with her by dominating every decision and ordering their lives to revolve around her. She shows a complete lack of empathy or sympathy towards Rafael's ordeal with the hotel, his father's murder or his mother. She also calls other women *bitch* a lot.

People apologize to Jane profusely, in nearly every episode, and she never forgives them, just tries to extract more humiliation from them. When she humiliates Rafael after his proposal (which she effectively ordered as a condition to sharing a place) it was presented as his fault. Guilt is assigned to others in nearly every interaction and it never attaches to her (even when she runs around saying she feels guilty it is drama to attract attention and induce more guilt in the others). When she refuses to have sex with Michael because she was lusting after Rafael (after using the event to make stress and work for everyone around her) she assigns the blame for her refusal to Alba. Even her nasty manipulativeness in ordering Rafael to manipulate Petra into imprisoning her own mother is justified with a guilt curse *"Petra is evil!"* and blamed on an idea from a *"mean girl"* because Jane can never be depicted as a mean girl herself.

She has no respect for boundaries with people she is involved with, personal or professional. As soon as she met Petra, she broke into her suite (and presented that as a virtue of being a concerned mother and used it to accuse Petra of not being a good enough potential mother) and manipulated Petra into giving her a night in the presidential suite. As soon as she decided to keep the baby, she ordered Rafael to hire her mother to sing at the hotel. She betrays the most intimate events between her and her boyfriends to everyone she knows as though no one else has ownership of their privacy. Even a casual acquaintance at her university was easily able to get enough gossip about Rafael's family from her to write a feature article. She uses both Rafael and Michael professionally, bribing just-met acquaintances with offers of a free suite at the hotel and asking Michael to personally persecute Magda, with a complete lack of gratitude. She interrupts both at work regularly and discourages or ignores their professional ambitions. She also uses the hotel without asking Rafael and sabotages him in season 2, booking her untalented neighbours to play for 2 weeks at the hotel. She uses Fabian for access to his horses.

Her rather confusing (because I decided it and I like plans but I will pretend to change my mind regularly and then change it back again in the middle of the event) desire to wait for sex is the only view that is considered throughout her changes of mind. She keeps her boyfriends attached by writing them porn and bringing them to the edge of sexual satisfaction but never granting it, which is not only quite a power play but also casts her as religiously virtuous and the person she is tormenting as religiously sinful (lustful). They are perpetually the antagonist to her protagonist struggle.

Her hesitation to advance out of the caregiver level and pursue writing is an unwillingness to accept less than endo-ideal status. In both university and work she recreates the caregiver demands for exceptional service and care from everyone around her and uses sexual (caregiver) relationships to facilitate that. Her expectation of being above the the rules that apply to everyone else are evident in her indignation at not being able to choose her school placement and in her contemptuous "I've been a little busy!" when demanding entrance into a grad program past the date. She also has no boundaries with the department head, filling his messages and wanting to do it again immediately after his email-only rule.

Her decisions are not subject to any of the rules she creates for others. She says she can't give the baby to Rafael if he is divorced but doesn't think the baby will mind her giving up all custody for no real reason (and blaming it on Michael) and she also doesn't consider the baby's former need for two parents when she decides to take full custody to spite Rafael (either time).

She is extremely vindictive and spiteful. When Rafael tries to leave she threatens to take full custody of the baby. She also 'accidentally' ruins Rafael's chance for a liquor license which he needs to provide for the baby, thus following the endo-ideal's standard modus operandi of punishing the giver for the gift. (Yes, she got it back, but now he is in her debt and she greatly added to his stress.) She tells Michael she is having fantasies about Rafael to torment him and cause everyone stress about the wedding, blames it on the priest and puts all the guilt on Michael for being mean to her about it. This, combined with her bad personal hygiene in season 2, both while camping and post partum, shows strong endoself tendencies. Aside from writing, which is a way she manipulates her boyfriends through porn, she does not seem to have any primary euphoria sources and instead entertains herself through dominating everyone's lives and causing them stress and pain.

Jane is more attracted to Rafael because he is a true negative image, whereas Michael is simply a reflector who still has some pride. Michael makes clear that he won't wait forever, Rafael has no such dignity. She doesn't seem to have asked Rafael's opinion about any of the baby's first names, which are all after men on her side and she has priority with the last name as well. Her best friend Lina is another negative image. We know she maintains her role as endo-ideal in her relationship with her son because we are told that she uses the trauma of his abduction against him to increase his guilt when he is 16. (If she was a negative image, she would still be apologizing to him for it.)

Rogelio is an endo-ideal at the caregiver, national and creative levels. Rogelio is very spoiled by his mother, his first reflector, who ensures that all of his love interests are his negative images. In fact, he attracts negative images, probably through his over-the-top promises of extraordinary romance which the starved negative images require to balance themselves. His love interest Darci is a negative image as well, as she dated two endo-ideals and said "I'm miserable. But here's a silver lining... now I'm famous, and fame, it really does a great job of masking that empty feeling. "As Rogelio casually degrades his love interests and violates their personal boundaries, and they self-sabotage to ensure they are despised by him, he returns to his mother for reflection. Creatively, he uses his agent as his negative image and basks in the reflection of his audience. He struggles with Jane's complete refusal to be manipulated by him. Unlike Jane or Magda, Rogelio is an endo-ideal with almost no endoself characteristics. He obtains his euphoria from primary sources such as beauty, creation and relationships, not cruelty and destruction.

"If you take a selfie and no one sees it do you even exist?

Emilio is a reflector and negative image at the caregiver level and probably an endo-ideal at the creation level. Emilio is both a reflector and negative image to everyone in his family. His wife Rose, who wishes to use him and eventually murders him, his daughter Luisa who cares so little about him she runs off with his murderer, his second wife, Elena, who left him and probably his first wife, Mia, who (presumably involuntarily) abandoned him and Luisa. His endo-ideal is Luisa. He and Rafael compete for the reflector role (Rose, Luisa and Jane all pit them against each other).

Rafael is a negative image at the caregiver level, which is his dominant circle. It is unclear what his roles are in other circles. Rafael does not enter relationships with women but with their ex-spouses. He is in a constant rivalry for the position of reflector as opposed to negative image, a rivalry he has been in since it started with his father. When he is rejected by women he feels all the shame of the negative image position which he probably was cast into by the abandonment by his mother. He has been involved with both a negative image (Petra) and an endo-ideal (Jane) and he treated each according to her role. It is possible his attraction for negative image Petra, which occurred when he was acting as a rich, drunk, playboy, was as a negative image to his temporary role playing as an endo-ideal. His transformation to endo-ideal could have been aided with the membrane-repairing effects of alcohol. This attraction ended abruptly after his conversation with his endo-ideal sister Luisa, who convinced him to reform (accept guilt, thereby transforming back into a negative image). It temporarily reappeared as Petra began gaining strength as an endo-ideal through her work with the hotel and at the school. His first endo-ideal was his mother. When he found out how awful she was he transferred allegiance to his father (as he explained in episode 22) and then he lost his loyalty to his father and determination to continue his father's legacy when he transferred to Jane. Rafael gets along wonderfully with endo-ideal Alba and has conflict with fellow negative image Xo.

Please, I don't have anyone else on my side. You have your mom, and your grandma, and your dad, I used to have Luisa but not anymore. I know what it's like to feel abandoned

Petra is a negative image at the caregiver level and an endo-ideal at the creation level. As constantly reinforced by her mother and every man in her life. Petra acts out her negative image role as a shallow and manipulating person and attaches to people who can be counted on to treat her horribly. Every person she is attracted to is an endo-ideal, at least towards her. She only falls in love with people who are unattainable. Like Xo and Darci, Petra seeks fame and power to help fill the giant void where her self-esteem ought to be. All seek acceptance at the creation level to compensate for their shortfalls at the caregiver level. Petra establishes herself as an endo-ideal at the creation level by firing the first person she encounters when she is gifted shares in the hotel. She also acts to protect her mother as endo-ideal. Her relationship with Milos, who gifts her hotels, co-owned by him, and makes Ivan lie to the police for her when he is not throwing acid at her mother and stalking her internationally, is about as endosocial as it can get. Her first endo-ideal is her mother and then she transfers to Rafael (and has her mother turn herself in). Every man she is attracted to is abusive towards her. Two or three try to kill her while others sabotage her and none have any respect for her.

Wow. Just handing over that ring makes me feel like a weight has been lifted.

Luisa is an endoself and an endo-ideal at the caregiver level. She refuses to advance as shown by her extreme incompetence at the creation level in her profession as a doctor. Luisa may have been cast as a negative image by the abandonment by her mother, but alcohol helped her to achieve her endo-ideal status. She is reflected by everyone around her, from her father, Emilio, to her brother, Rafael, to her lover, Rose. Her casual cruelty is evident everywhere, most notably in that 'accident' that almost destroyed her brother's only chance to have a child. Endoselves always have such 'accidents', particularly to punish someone they owe a huge debt, such as the one she owed Rafael for cosigning her insurance with the hotel, and they prefer to use a person's gift to punish them. She also then claims to be more virtuous than her father or Rafael because she cares less than they do about the money she lost them. She displays the same cruelty to Rose when she threatens to destroy her marriage and again uses the classic guilt reversal by saying she has learned from her shaman to be so honest. While her travel to Peru might have indicated an advancement to a discovery level, the fact that she went there to cause anxiety to her family and she acted there as a needy child receiving reflection (and drugs) from a shaman shows she was still acting at a caregiver level.

Luisa: How could you lie to me about something like that?
Rafael: You were dating the woman that killed our father and kidnapped my son.
Luisa: And that was bad, but it was in the past. She wanted to change.

Michael is a reflector at both caregiver and national levels. His relationship with two endo-ideals, Rogelio and Jane, indicate his comfort with the reflector role. His profession as a cop and his willingness to share credit with his colleague for his ideas suggest he continued in this role at the national level.

Magda is an endoself and an endo-ideal at the caregiver-level. She lies like a rug, torments her daughter, controls her daughter's relationships, tells her constantly that Rafael doesn't love her, and made her endure years of futile hard labour looking after an invalid mother – who wasn't actually an invalid. Not above a little murder if she can get away with it and will instantly flip the story to be Petra's fault. Petra instantly internalizes the guilt for an attempted murder and a real murder, neither of which she was even present for, like a good little negative image. Magda says she chose one identical twin over the other because she was 'prettier', indicating she sees her daughters as object possessions.

Rose is a negative image at the caregiver level. Endo-ideal at the creation level. While obviously an endo-ideal at a creation level, Rose may be a negative image at the caregiver level because she seems genuinely in love with Luisa, an endo-ideal. The self-sabotage inherent in a relationship which could have risked her marriage is also behaviour indicating a negative image.

Elena, Rafael's mother, is an endoself and an endo-ideal at the caregiver and creation level: Not only did she abandon her son, she deflected the blame for her absence onto the dead father who raised him, wrote her letters about him and gave her ten million dollars. As always, the endo-ideal will punish whoever they owe gratitude to and they prefer to use the gift to punish the benefactor.

It is not a coincidence that two of the negative images in this story got cancer, one was infertile, one suffered several attempted murders and even reflector Michael died after he lost his job and was fully sublated into a negative image at the caregiver level. There are no accidents and punishment follows guilt. Not one endo-ideal in the show suffered personally at all. Power has well-known life extending side effects as it sucks the life from the negative image. Okay, this analysis is based on fiction, but it's still true!

Key concepts

The law of uninhibited expansion: When an exosocial person is unable to form euphoric conduits at any level of expansion, they are uninhibited from forming them at a further level of expansion and experience an increased drive to do so.

The law of endoreality: All virtue, ownership, credit and victimhood are assigned to the endo-ideal and all vice, guilt and punishment are assigned to the negative image, by all committed members of the endogroup.

The law of the last circle: When an endogroup collapses with no transcendental endogroup incorporating it, the committed people within it will revert to their last real or imagined endogroup loyalties.

The law of authority: Authoritative endogroups are those with the institutional power to enforce their endoreality. Anyone opposing authoritative endoreality is declared criminal or insane as they define reality and law.

The law of power: Power is a result of actions of unequal force. The structure of power is created by endogroups allowing only involuntary interactions of unequal force.

The law of inhibited expansion: Endogroups are formed and strengthened by intercepting and removing all external euphoric conduits in order to redirect all euphoric interactions to the endo-ideal.

The law of transcendence: With no egalitarian counter force, endogroups will be continually sublated to larger, transcendental endogroups, At each level of transcendence, endogroups become larger and endo-ideals more powerful. Each level of transcendence is at the service of the higher group.

The law of diverted exosocial expansion: As all exosocial expansion in an endogroup is diverted into a force towards transcendence, this creates a voracious centripetal force driving a ponzi scheme of power.

The law of balanced interactions: All interactions must be eventually balanced or they will result in guilt which will be punished by shame and shunning. Small amounts of imbalance are a sign of a wish to continue a relationship, as they provide a need to continue interacting.

The law of guilt transference. Guilt can be transferred from the person who incurred the debt by a variety of means.

The law of reversed accounting: Guilt transference will create escalating abuse as every wrong committed by the abuser will be added to the debt owed by the victim, resulting in victims continually and increasingly punished for their own victimhood.

The law of unredeemed credit: Those who feel they have accumulated credit, including the endo-ideal, due to reversed accounting, will be greatly attracted to opportunities to redeem that credit through unbalanced interactions benefiting themselves or punishment of others.

The law of debt: Those who have accepted debt or guilt will be compelled to atone for the imbalance through unbalanced interactions benefiting others or self-punishment.

The reflector-negative image struggle: Commonly called 'competition', the reflector-negative image struggle is the primary struggle within an endogroup. It pits the obedient reflectors against the ostracized negative image in a zero-sum struggle for the approval of the endo-ideal. It occupies all force that may otherwise be directed towards the endo-ideal.

The revolution or liberation choice of the negative image: Identity and victimhood may be used to create a revolutionary endogroup or guilt and sorrow may be used for exosocial expansion and liberation.

The gifts of the negative image: Identity, victimhood, guilt and sorrow.

The eight steps of negative image creation and punishment: identification, melding, threat assignment, guilt assignment, curse, shunning, punishment and final guilt reversal.

Glossary

The following is a glossary of what I personally mean when I say these words. This is not an attempt to impose my definitions as the correct ones or an invitation to debate the definitions. It is only meant to apply to anything I say or write. As language is meant to be a shortcut to communication I try not to spend too much time discussing definitions. These books use definitions from universal reality unless otherwise noted. Terms using endoreality definitions are often denoted by single quotes.

Alienation: 1. The process by which many smaller endogroups are created within a wider endogroup. This can happen organically as a wider endogroup dissolves or weakens and it is also a political strategy used to weaken rival endogroups. 2. The separation of a part of the self, such as seen in those with refracted or amputated cores. 3. Separation created between two or more endogroups.

Altruism: An exosocial act of assistance to another in order to create egalitarian balance. If altruism is balanced with gratitude and approval it will establish a euphoric bond.

America: Two continents and 35 countries.

American: Residents of any part of America.

Amputated core: The alienation of a person's core self to cause the person's own core to be seen as an enemy outsider.

Anarchy: Society free of subordination to endogroups at any level. An exosocial society.

Anger: Anger can be *defensive, dominant* or *predatory*. Defensive anger protects a euphoric source or membrane. Defensive anger is against external threat and can be experienced by anyone. Dominant anger occurs within an endogroup and is used to sublate another. Predatory anger is a mark of an endoself and is used to obtain secondary euphoria through the stress response of another.

Anglo / Germanic: Living in states that speak primarily English and heavily adopt Anglo culture or are part of Germanic-speaking Europe. Specifically, anyone living in Austria, Belgium, Denmark, Finland, Germany, UK, Netherlands, Norway, Sweden, Iceland, Ireland, Liechtenstein, Luxembourg, Switzerland, United Kingdom, United States, Australia, New Zealand, Canada and South Africa. Notable for an industrial-scientific endo-idealism that took early precedence over the various church, filial or other endo-idealisms elsewhere. Recently, this group were the global endo-ideal through transcendental industrial-scientific endo-idealism. Currently being replaced by the mono-empire.

Anonymous: A stigmergic method of collaboration and the people who use it.

Approval theory of value: The value of goods is based on the amount of social approval they represent.

Approval economy: Economy based on societal approval and acceptance.

Authoritative endogroup: The endogroup with the coercive force available to enable them to define reality and law.

Auto-coercion: Transparent, consensual coercion a society applies onto itself.
Auto-objects: People objectified by themselves who thereby become subjects with the power to objectify others.

Autogenocide: Genocide instigated remotely, usually though media incited sectarianism or trade of drugs or weapons to the targeted population, but performed by the population on itself.

Autonomy: 1. Freedom from involuntary, unbalanced interactions created through possession of a healthy personal membrane and network of primary euphoric sources and conduits. 2. The right to governance by user group including governance of self for those things which impact only self.

Billion: A billion is a million million (bi + million), but the U.S. changed it to mean a thousand million so that they could have 'billionaires', a classic example of reality manipulation to serve an exceptional myth and magical words subject to the whim of the endo-ideal used to create endo-identity.

Binding Chaos: 1. The natural method of using extrapolation, experience and experimentation to bind chaotic input into meaningful packets of information as our brains are designed to do. 2. The use of extreme coercive force to prevent chaotic systems from living, evolving or creating change. 3. The transition from primordial chaos to today's segregated and isolated world. 4. Endosocialism.

Boredom: A sign of severe psychic distress which occurs when someone is offered a euphoric interaction which they cannot access or a third party is attempting to intercept a euphoric interaction. This is the chronic condition of an endoself.

Butterfly: An idea which can cause a hurricane of change. Reference to the butterfly effect.

Caregiver: A person whose work involves the care of other people, animals, communities or ecosystems.

Caregiver-self: A circle of expansion which includes or replicates those relationships first formed by a baby or small child with their home and caregivers, particularly if that circle has created an endogroup.

Centripetal force: Acts on unequal populations in forced transactions to create ponzi schemes of celebrity, wealth and power and endogroups. Slight advantages become huge by the requirement that everyone support those with resources or power in order to benefit. Creates and upholds endogroups.

Centrifugal force: Egalitarian force created in opposition to ponzi schemes which serves to either strengthen the existing ponzi scheme by increasing the defending force or collapse it.

Censorship by noise: Using celebrity or official status to amplify certain voices or opinions to the disadvantage of others who may have better or opposing information. Using astroturfing spam for the same purpose.

Charity: An endosocial act of giving which results in establishing the giver as the endo-ideal and the receiver as the negative image. This differs from altruism in the fact that no euphoric conduit is established and debt and guilt are incurred by the receiver, along with a negative image status.

Class: A societal construct (endoreality) resulting from classification of people relative to the endo-ideal. Modern usage is usually related to wealth endo-idealism.

Cognitive dissonance: Distress caused by a conflict between dominant and authoritative endoreality or universal reality and endoreality.

Commoner: A stable majority created to uphold the status quo, or overthrow it during times of revolution. Societal structures are designed for the comfort and coercion of commoners. Mass acceptance of this role creates a solid block of uniform opinions which can be used to create and uphold oligarchy and ostracize witches and wretches. Reflector at a state level or higher.

Community: A group affiliated around allocation of common resources. Communities may be societies, where allocation is through social relationships, or trade economies, where allocation is through trade.

Consciousness: A subset of reality filtered through empathic networks and sometimes subjected to the laws of endoreality through an endofilter.

Concentric circle: Peer promoted voices or ideas in a transparent, permeable structure where those at the centre receive the most amplification and ideas are audited and taught to the outer circles by knowledge bridges.

Corporate feminism: Feminism which emanated from the United States in the 1960s and was heavily guided by both the CIA and corporate interests. It created an endogroup out of an exosocial struggle for liberation.

Creation-self: A circle of expansion which includes those relationships related to creation. Often trapped into a career endogroup.

Creation euphoria: can be imparted through a euphoric object.

Culture: The euphoric conduits to divinity unique to a nation. Includes dancing, songs, art, spirituality, some aspects of creation, rituals, and euphoric objects. Does not include the endosocial trappings often associated with it such as exceptional myth and endo-ideal.

Currency: Abstract, dissociated approval which allows access to all benefits of society without contribution, membership or acceptance of the society's values or norms. Endosocial token to replace gratitude and approval and replace exosocial interactions with endosocial transactions.

Death Eaters: Members of a society where the norms or culture are driven by sadism. The agony of others is not a side effect of their actions but a goal. Death eaters are distinct from those with an individual personality disorder in that their society's norms, structure and actions are all constructed to feed their sadism. An endogroup supporting endoselves.

Democracy: Governance by representative or direct voting systems.

Demographics: Objectification and alienation of people through further division of the already objectified populations, usually in an attempt to create new endogroup identities.

Dignity: Preservation of ownership over one's own inner circles of self. This ownership creates personal integrity and strength.

Disciplinary spaces: Michel Foucault's idea of disciplinary spaces included state institutions such as hospitals, schools, factories and military barracks. I expand his definition to homes for women who are economically, legally or otherwise tied to them and states or regions where borders lock some populations away from means of survival and create a global surveillance system.

Discovery-self: A circle of expansion which contains those relationships unique to discovery. Often trapped into an academic endogroup.

Dissociation: 1. Separation of individuals from the dependency relationships which make up society. 2. Separation of self in the case of refracted or amputated cores.

Diversity: There is diversity between every two humans. In endoreality, this term is used to create endo-identities, which is the opposite of diversity. The word should be replaced with anti-endo-idealism to indicate that a thing is not restricted to the endo-ideal. A better path would be to simply point out endo-idealism and leave anti-endo-idealism as the default state.

Divinity: The source of euphoria. Possibly also Jung's collective unconscious and the source of Kant's synthetic a priori knowledge.

Divinity-self: the self created by euphoric interactions with divinity. These can include spiritual sources but can also be found in everyday euphoric sources, whether or not the subject experiences them as spiritual.

Divination: The deliberate acquisition of divine knowledge through skill, following a methodology. Some rationalism and even some science falls under this category.

Dominant endogroup: The endogroup which has the subject person or population most immersed in its endoreality or most sublated to it.

Economy: Resource allocation.

Emotion: Response to anticipation or experience of access to euphoria or anticipation or experience of an attack on a euphoric source.

Empathic bond: An empathic conduit that is strong and somewhat permanent.

Empathic conduit: The means by which emotion can be shared or jointly experienced between two sources.

Empathy: The ability to share the experience of an emotion with another through empathic conduits.

Endo-exceptionalism: Adherence to the exceptional myth of an endogroup.

Endo-ideal: The idealized self of an endogroup, embodying all virtue, ownership, victimhood and credit.

Endo-idealism: Adherence to the laws of endoreality which attribute all virtue, ownership, victimhood and credit to the endo-ideal and all vice, guilt and punishment to the negative image.

Endo-identity: A magical word used to set an endogroup off as exceptional and create difference where none exists.

Endofilter: A cognitive filter which causes the subject to filter all information from universal reality according to the laws of endoreality.

Endogroup: A group of affiliated people who use inclusion and shunning to define their society and are bound by an endosocial membrane. An endogroup may be temporally unlimited to allow ownership and appropriation of property, culture, achievements and victimhood from generations past.

Endoreality: A reality which exists only within an endogroup and is created with the laws of endoreality. Endoreality is filled with magical words which impart no meaning but serve to cast people as the negative image or endo-ideal. Endoreality is relative and has no meaning outside the perspective of the endo-ideal or endoself. Endoreality can change at the whim of an endo-ideal.

Endoself: Predator who can only exist, or prefers to exist, through acquisition of secondary euphoria.

Endoself contagion: The process by which exosocial interactions are blocked and discouraged in a population of endoselves, leading exosocial people to develop endoself behaviours through necessity.

Endosocial: Existing within the confines of an endogroup or endoself or according to the laws of endoreality.

Endosocial membrane: A membrane which blocks empathic and euphoric conduits and thereby creates endoselves and endogroups.

Endosocial martyrdom: Euphoria is forcibly taken from the endo-ideal to the masses

Endosocial tyranny: Euphoria is forcibly taken from the masses to the endo-ideal

Endosocialism: Belief that societies ought to be ordered within endogroup power structures.

Envy: Envy is the sense of injustice felt by members of an endogroup if external acclaim or a coveted item is held by someone outside the endogroup or its endo-ideal.

Epistemic community: A way to provide elite expertise for projects without relinquishing control to an elite oligarchy. People or ideas are peer promoted from within the user group and communities remain transparent and permeable to everyone. Acceptance or rejection of ideas is always up to the user group to avoid an unassailable oligarchy. Typically organized in transparent, permeable concentric circles.

Equality: An observably false idea that all people are equal used to justify imposing involuntary transactions of unequal force on diverse populations and preventing equivalence. Results in power accumulation.

Equivalence: The idea that all members of a society are entitled to equivalent benefit from the society and no one should be valued by standards of achievement which others have greater ability to attain. No one should be forced or coerced to strive for goals they do not choose or prevented from striving for those they do. No contribution to society is inherently of greater value than another although the degree of effort may be. Exosocialism.

Euphoria: Joy which contributes to well-being and self-esteem. May be acquired through euphoric conduits to primary euphoric sources.

Euphoric bond: A euphoric conduit that is strong and somewhat permanent.

Euphoric conduit: A path or method allowing the transfer of euphoria from one primary source to another.

Euphoric object: An object which contains euphoria from its creator or previous or current owners.

Exceptional lives: Lives which are given far more value by media and society due to endo-ideal status.

Exceptional myth: Exceptional myths encourage both unjustified glorification of the group and its endo-ideal and unjustified demonization of the negative images as well as other endogroups and their endo-ideals. The five primary types of exceptional myths address *creation, leaders, superiority, persecution* and *destiny*. A purely magical creation, like the endo-identity; its purpose is its function, not its meaning.

Excitement: The anticipation of primary or secondary euphoria.

Exogroup: This does not exist as an exogroup is simply a cluster of actions.

Exoself: A person with no, or very few, endosocial attachments and a large exosocial network.

Exosocial: Pertaining to exosocial expansion.

Exosocial expansion: Uninhibited expansion of self through continual establishment of euphoric conduits through relationships, discovery, creation, spirituality, etc.

Exosocial networks: Created by conduits between primary sources of euphoria to allow balanced euphoric interactions.

Exosocialism: Belief in the universal freedom to uninhibited exosocial expansion.

Extranational: Existing outside national or state structures.

Face: An integral part of a person, signifying a healthy personal membrane, free of debt and able to establish balanced euphoric interactions.

Fear: Fear is anticipation of an attack on a euphoric source. In a primarily exosocial person, the feared attack is on a euphoric conduit. In a primarily endosocial person, the feared attack is on an endogroup.

Feminism: The belief in the liberation of women to fulfill their full potential through uninhibited exosocial expansion. As Sylvia Federici and others have pointed out, the word feminism is a poor substitute for the concept of women's liberation. Removal of male and other types of endo-idealism would be much more helpful in achieving liberation than establishment of endogroup feminism.

First age of nations: A great variety of autonomous and complete societies, occasionally networked and sharing or trading with each other, which people lived in for hundreds of thousands of years.

Forbidden chamber: A construction which conceals secrets of the guilt of the powerful and forbids access to effect the endoreality law that knowledge of endo-ideal guilt is a greater guilt than the original crime.

Fourth age of nations: A potential society we could develop, more diverse, flexible and mutually supportive than the first tribal one and more rewarding and globally beneficial than the third parasitical, supranational one. A new framework must meet both our social needs and our need to develop to our full potential, ensure local autonomy but protect global commons, and put social responsibility back in communities but provide a global safety net for those shunned or harmed locally. This age would hopefully finally provide us with a balance between autonomy, diversity and society through exosocialism.

Fraternity: Decentralized patriarchy resulting from politics which espoused Liberty, Equality, Fraternity. Fraternity as a goal is not suitable to global collaboration as it implies both equality and unanimity of principles. It has resulted in a fraternity of endo-ideals aligned under endosocialism. They still claim the right to control the lives of other people and occupy the top strata of society like patriarchy but now they bear no responsibility for governance or any participation in society.

Gender: A social construct (endoreality) created in order to impose power relations based on sex with a male endo-ideal and a female negative image.

Genocide: The murder of a nation-self.

Gift: Goods or services allocated to a person who is not automatically entitled to a share by social norms, or goods or services one is not automatically entitled to by social norms, such as personal or rare property. Gifts are not an entitlement and frequently carry expectations such as eventual reciprocity or future friendship.

Governance: 1. Enforced subordination to an endo-ideal and enforced membership in an endogroup. 2. Caretaker responsibility of the user group.

Gratitude: A feeling of well-being and admiration directed towards the provider in an altruistic interaction.

Guilt: Acknowledgement of an unbalanced transaction resulting in debt to the guilty party. Guilt is transferable.

Gynophobia: Terror of women, the fear of becoming or being cast as a woman (the negative image), or a fear of the loss of patriarchal power or male endo-idealism. Particularly prevalent in those with an amputated core.

Hate: Hate is the need to block a potential or formerly euphoric bond.

Holosocial: A social group which includes everyone. May be exosocial but may also refer to endosocialism under a global mono-empire.

Homo economicus: The endo-ideal of classical economists. A pure endoself with no goals outside of the exploitation of others for personal power accumulation.

Honour: Hierarchical approval awarded from the endo-ideal, signifying the condition of not being the negative image.

Hostile seductive coercion: A force of seductive coercion from outside the society with interests in opposition to those of the society.

Idea based collaboration: collaboration that develops or verifies an idea or information.

Idol: object of euphoric storage for an endogroup.

Ideologues: Members of endogroups with an exceptional myth based on ideas attributed to them.

Independence: The state of living free from dependencies. This is impossible in reality but can be simulated by the use of currency to abstract human dependency.

Inhumanity: A failure to recognize people outside your personal endosocial group as human, indicated by a lack of empathy and marked by a denial of their needs to live dignified lives.

Integrity: Strength of personal membrane and exosocial network.

Interaction: Mutual empathic or euphoric transfer through action and reaction. If these interactions are not balanced, through reciprocity, gratitude, reparations, or other methods, they will result in a power transfer which will create an endosocial relationship of power or separation.

Iron law of oligarchy: Theory of Robert Michels, "Who says organization, says oligarchy". This theory says that oligarchy is inevitable and it is used as a justification for fascism. Oligarchy is inevitable under endosocialism but not through exosocialism.

Jealousy: Fear of a negative change to one's own endogroup status due to the relative rise of another.

Joy: The experience of euphoric energy obtained through euphoric conduits to primary sources such as nations, creation or discovery. An endoself may feel excitement, but never joy.

Knowledge bridge: People who help disseminate information from an expert to a novice level of understanding and collectively audit what the epistemic community is doing. Besides being essential for education and auditing, this is important to avoid demagogues who have the ability and time to develop mass appeal but are not the source of expertise. Epistemic communities and knowledge bridges allow elite expertise a direct path of communication to the entire user group and provide a path for anyone in the user group to achieve elite ebxpertise if they wish.

Laughter: Laughter is a reaction to the experience of euphoria or awareness of endoreality. The seven types of laughter are experience of euphoria, self affirmation, self destruction, social affirmation, social exclusion, endogroup domination and endogroup submission.

Laws: Coercive strictures which reflect the laws of endoreality.

Liberation: Freedom to continue exosocial expansion.

Libertarian: Desirous of liberty, as the freedom to do anything one desires, without social responsibility. Very popular ideology among endoselves.

Liberty: Coercion, responsibility and dependency are part of all human existence. The endosocial illusion of liberty for a few is created through dissociation, enabled by the trade economy. Exosocial liberty is freedom from involuntary transactions of unequal force and freedom to continue exosocial expansion.

Life: A force facilitating exosocial expansion.

Lifegiver: A woman who has given birth.

Lifegiver-self: The initial self created between a lifegiver and an infant.

Love: Love is a desire to create or maintain euphoric bonds. Love has three stages: *attraction*, marked by excitement and intense curiosity, *connection*, marked by joy in experiencing another, and *expansion*, at which point the destruction of the new shared self would cause severe trauma.

Lust: Avarice, or a desire for possession. In lust, the three stages are changed to *lust*, manifesting as an intense desire for possession, *possession*, during which the endoself seeks outside reflection in the form of admiration of their new possession and lastly, *disillusionment*, boredom and punishment of the object which is blamed for the disappointment.

Magic: 1. The ability to create or access a reality different from universal reality, used in both divination and in creation of endorealities. 2. The process of causing ideas or people to be shunned or accepted through the creation of endogroups, endo-ideals and negative images. 3. The transfer of guilt, especially through the use of magic words and ritual. There are several other types of magic but these are the primary meanings I refer to.

Magic words: Words whose usage is unrelated to their meaning in universal reality. Words used solely for the purpose of magic, such as creating an endogroup or casting information as authoritative or not based on association with the endo-ideal or negative image.

Masculinist: Male endo-idealist.

Masculinist theory: theory based on research that only includes men or is presented from an exclusively male point of view or which sets the experience of men as the normative standard.

Megaphone: A platform able to reach a large number of people.

Migratory endo-ideals: When a transcendental endogroup has an overpopulated group of endo-ideals, or they are under pressure, they will begin to swarm by creating a multitude of smaller endogroups at lower levels. This results in alienated societies and in the colonization of negative image groups both within and without the original endogroup.

Mono-empire: The transcendental global empire of the third age of nations.

Nation: Layered and overlapping societies gathered for community, cooperation and sharing, and existing across borders and generations. Nations may include sacred objects, rites, land and culture.

Nation-self: A circle of expansion which contains those relationships unique to a nation. Often trapped into a state endogroup.

Negative image: An endogroup role which causes a person to adopt the perspective of an external endo-ideal and uphold the laws of endoreality. Seen as the inverse of the endo-ideal. Embodies all vice, guilt and shame assignment within the endogroup.

Neo-necromancer: The powerful of the third age who seek to control populations through occupation of their most intimate circle of self, that containing control over the body, mind, self and life.

Outgroup: A population not included in, or shunned by, an endogroup. This does not include the negative image which is within the endogroup.

Paedosadist: There is no such thing as a sexual orientation called paedophilia. A sexual orientation, or sex, requires consenting partners. It is not sex if some of those involved are called victims, that is rape. Someone attracted to rape has sexual sadism disorder or paraphilic coercive disorder. Someone attracted to the rape of children is a paedosadist. A paedosadist who acts on their impulses is a criminal paedosadist and one who does not is a non-offending paedosadist.

Parasites: Those who obtain secondary euphoria by intercepting interactions between two primary sources.

Passive genocide: The denial of life essentials to populations where people will die without access to them.

Patriarchy: A form of male and filial endo-idealism with a hierarchical social structure and a paternal elder as each familial endo-ideal.

Pedosadist: US spelling, see paedosadist definition.

Personal membrane: A strong and permeable inner circle of self which controls intimacy and permits the establishment of euphoric and empathic conduits.

Photoshop: Remove aspects of a story which the writer does not deem relevant or agree with and leave only those which support the writer's bias.

Ponzi scheme: 1. A pyramid scheme algorithm which requires those at the bottom to support those at the top in order to benefit. This type of scheme never benefits more than a few. 2. Societal structure in which everyone tries to acquire celebrity, wealth and power, creating a centripetal force that holds oligarchs in place. Egalitarian systems imposed on unequal populations tend to ponzi.

Population: The people objectified and owned by the endo-ideals of an endogroup.

Power: 1. Power is energy acquired from unequal force which can only be achieved through transactions. There is no idle or inert power and there is no benevolent power. 2. Social approval that causes others to identify with and emulate the powerful ahead of themselves or others. This power can be used to realize one's own will or include or shun the will or person of others and it can also be used to accumulate wealth, celebrity, credit or any other offering that the social group brings. Once power is established, it provides the unequal force which can be used to turn every interaction into a transaction in which the powerful gain more power.

Predation: Obtaining secondary euphoria through involuntary transactions of unequal force.

Predators: Those who obtain secondary euphoria from others through stress, pain, obstruction and destruction. Endoselves.

Prey: Those with damaged personal membranes and euphoric depletion or those with expanded euphoria and no method of protecting themselves from predatory or egalitarian forces.

Pride: An endo-ideal emotion, a surge of power and affirmation of their endo-ideal status.

Primary euphoria: Euphoria obtained through direct, personal interactions with other living thngs, nations, including cultural experiences, euphoric objects, discovery, creation or spirituality.

Privacy: Privacy is ownership of an individual membrane and control over one's own circles of intimacy and the ability to establish one's own boundaries of intimacy. Privacy is sovereignty over the most intimate circle of self. It includes control over the body, the mind, the self and life.

Pure nationalists: Those that try to create endo-identities and exceptional myths around nations.

Race: A social construct (endoreality) created in order to impose power relations by arbitrary classifications according to real or imagined heredity.

Reaction: A movement demanding change back to a time when a larger portion of the people at the top of the ponzi scheme of power benefited from it. Reactionaries have no interest in changing underlying principles or helping those at the bottom except with promises of reforms trickling down. Reforms in a ponzi scheme will never trickle down as what feeds the top, bleeds the bottom.

Ren: Confucian term once translated as manliness, which is, in the old sense of the word man, humanity. Described most clearly in *The Analects* where it mentions equitable relationships and healthy self-valuation. A term that may be somewhat equivalent to face or personal membrane.

Reflection: The process whereby the empathic conduits of a person are all directed to an external endo-ideal and they act as an obedient enforcer of the laws of endoreality for that endo-ideal.

Reflector: An endogroup role which causes a person to adopt the perspective of an external endo-ideal and uphold the laws of endoreality. Seen as obedient and selfless and so avoids the guilt and shame assignment of the negative image.

Refraction: The process whereby a person's core self is occupied by an external self and they give up all autonomy and will to the occupying endo-ideal. Extreme dissociation can result from refraction.

Resistance: Building new systems and exosocial networks and defending them against oppressive coercion. Removing power from those at the top of the ponzi scheme by removal of reflection of endoreality. Removing institutional power by creating and defending alternatives and allocating guilt to the perpetrators instead of the negative image. Blocking endosocial authority.

Revolution: A change of the top of an oligarchical system, usually replacing an old oligarch with a representative of the largest or most powerful other group. The paradigm remains unchanged.

Sandbox villages: Societies (do not have to be geographically defined) for trying out new ideas for governance and collaboration.

Scientific superstition: Fear by scientists to look at topics outside of their endoreality which is largely the perspective of very endosocial people, primarily endo-ideals and endoselves. Superstition causes a refusal to study, or even acknowledge, anything associated with their negative image, primarily women and indigenous people. Scientists often misrepresent this superstition as *skepticism,* which is withholding judgment, the opposite of superstition.

Sealed well: Databases which have access controlled by web pages.

Second age of nations: Hierarchical trade empires which included a powerful extranational merchant class which stood between artisans and the upper stratas who owned property and those buying their products. These merchants had access to foreign knowledge and access to those who controlled power and wealth in more than one empire. The widespread adoption of currency provided them with dissociated membership in multiple societies and access to all the privileges of membership. They also had their own networks within the merchant strata of many nations and even frequently their own international language.

Secondary euphoria: Euphoria, or a substitute for it, obtained through fear or other stress responses of another, or filth and destruction. Possibly related to adrenalin or dopamine since the same people seem attracted to these as well. This is not the same as primary euphoria as it does not result in the experience of joy.

Secrecy: 1. Ownership of the intimate knowledge of another. 2. Ownership and control over the information belonging to and affecting a group, including information obtained through violation of the privacy of others.

Seductive coercion: Coercion which persuades rather than forces but can be much more powerful than force, particularly if unnoticed or acknowledged. Manipulation and control of information and authoritative endoreality. Based on shunning and inclusion.

Self: The unique positioning of an individual relative to society created through a network of empathic and euphoric conduits.

Self-governance: Governance by user group.

Sex: There are three powers of sex. The exosocial power creates strong euphoric and empathic bonds with another person. The endosocial power creates an endosocial membrane, with the subjects joined within the membrane or divided by it. The endogroup power can be used to sublate one self to another within an endogroup membrane.

Shame: Shame is the experience of being shunned and the internalization of the perception of the self as the negative image. Shame inhibits the establishment of euphoric conduits.

Share: Division of goods or services to benefit all participants. Sharing is considered fair if all participants have an equal amount or as much as they want or need. Sharing is typically practised among members of a physical community such as a tribe or family or an endogroup such as a corporation or state. It is distinct from giving, which is the allocation of goods or services the recipient is not socially entitled to.

Singularity: Common definition is of a technological singularity, a time when artificial intelligence will have progressed to the point of a greater-than-human intelligence. I refer to social or societal singularities to describe society that is already far too complex and requiring far too much information processing for individual comprehension to be attainable. We now require mass collaboration to understand any aspect of society or to be able to rationally govern ourselves.

Social singularity: A singularity between all living things, near and distant, collaborative or hostile.

Societal singularity: A singularity achieved between the members of a specific society.

Society: A network of interdependent relationships between people.

Solidarity: The (usually revolutionary) demand that reflectors (the Commoners) unquestioningly uphold endoreality. This is necessary as revolution needs a large hammer with which to remove the old oligarchy and replace it with themselves and also because a revolution which calls itself The [endo-identity] People loses credibility if those people disagree. Primarily, this is a demand for sublation of the mind as it always eventually requires reflection of reality that is at extreme odds with universal reality.

Sorrow: Sorrow is a result of euphoric depletion due to the blockage of euphoric conduits, the unavailability of euphoric sources, the need for an increase in euphoric sources prior to exosocial expansion or the assignment of debt through guilt. There are three primary types of sorrow: *loss sorrow,* when euphoric sources are no longer available, *expansion sorrow,* when exosocial expansion is forced, restricted or diverted, and *shame sorrow,* when exosocial freedom is lost due to the destruction of self by shame.

State: Highly militarized partitioning of societies into economic markets imposed for segregating, competing, allocating and establishing property ownership. Endogroup.

Stigmergy: Action based method of collaboration which follows an idea. If people understand and agree on a goal, everyone has autonomy as to how or whether they work to further that goal. Communication is through transparency. Secrecy and ownership of ideas are in opposition to stigmergy.

Strata slumming: Fulfillment of a humiliation or degradation fantasy by associating or identifying with those one perceives as the negative image. Often a precursor to an ownership claim by a migratory endo-ideal.

Stratification: The creation of different classes of society and formation of hierarchy based on roles.

Sublation: The process by which an individual self or an endogroup is merged into a larger endogroup and identifies more strongly with the larger group's endo-ideal than with their earlier self.

Supranational: Above the power of states or nations.

Sympathy: Pity for another as a result of cognitive imagination and moral judgment.

Systems: Interacting people, ideas, infrastructure and labour which work in a common area, similar to ministries in today's governance. Health, transportation and housing are examples of three different systems. Systems can overlap and cooperate with each other and they have local and global levels. The global level usually acts as an epistemic community of ideas and the local level controls acceptance and rejection of ideas and implementation of them.

Systems of dissociation: Systems constructed to isolate and divide people from their basic needs or each other and their ability to collaborate.

The Taxpayer: The obedient reflector of industrial endo-idealism, closely related to The Working Class and The Honest Hardworking Man. Someone willing to exploit their communities and the unpaid labour of lifegivers and caregivers and employ reversed accounting to accuse others of parasiting off of them. Serves an abstracted endo-ideal anthropomorphized as The Economy.

Third age of nations: A supranational empire where trade has fully abstracted the relationship between oligarchs and the people they exploit. The merchants are so powerful and their extranational society so networked, they control the states with a higher supranational form of governance and law in the form of trade agreements and treaties. Unlike power under the elite of the second age, the supranational class at the top of today's global empire does not need to govern or be involved in any way with the divided state-societies below them. Power has become completely dissociated from governance or the well being of the people of the world under a global mono-empire.

Thought bubble: A group which is closed to outside thought by forum or propaganda. An endogroup with a strong endoreality.

Torture: An external force instigating a struggle for control over the most intimate circle of self, that containing the body, mind, self and life. An attempt to fully sublate another.

Trade: An endosocial transaction which does not involve the establishment of empathic bonds and so is not subject to guilt in the case of imbalance. Trade is conducted between those with no social ties or desire for social ties that would come with sharing or gifting.

Trade relationship: An endosocial relationship allowing transactions of unequal force and the accumulation of power.

Transcendence: The sublation of smaller endogroups into a higher authoritative endogroup.

Transcendental endogroup: An endogroup formed through the sublation of smaller endogroups.

Tribe: A first age nation barely removed from a family structure where all relationships are direct and there is little to no hierarchy or stratification.

Trade economy: An economy which values only goods and services traded to the wealthy for currency. This creates a form of approval dissociated from society and placed in the hands of the powerful as an abstracted force for coercing unbalanced transactions.

Trade empire: One which includes an extranational merchant class and is wealthy in large part due to trade.

Transaction: Exchanges which do not establish empathic or euphoric conduits.

Trust networks: A network of people who rely on each other's knowledge and judgment to filter information and sources.

Truth dictatorships: Online platforms or endogroups which present one view of reality as a complete 'truth' or 'fact'.

User group: The entire population which will be affected by an action, including no one not affected. User groups range from one person to the entire world.

Universal reality: Reality which is outside the subjective viewpoint of the endo-ideal and is not based on the laws of endoreality.

USian: Resident of the United States.

Vapour capital: Equity, options, intellectual property and rights, or social capital as a product of class such as position, education, citizenship and connections.

Vapour wealth: Conceptual wealth, not tied to any physical property.

Violence: Forceful violation of bodily autonomy. Violence can be used for the same social purposes as laughter: experience of euphoria, self affirmation, self destruction, social affirmation, social exclusion, endogroup domination and endogroup submission. It also has the same powers as sex: the exosocial power creates strong euphoric and empathic bonds with another person, the endosocial power creates an endosocial membrane, with the subjects joined within the membrane or divided by it, and the endogroup power can be used to sublate one self to another within an endogroup membrane.

Wealth: An accumulation of social approval, abstracted or otherwise.

Witches: Sources of knowledge or innovation where authoritative power does not want knowledge and innovation.

Wretches: Those hidden from endogroup perspective by the one-way mirror of reflectors and made to absorb all of society's guilt and punishment. The negative image.

Citations

1) Boddy, A. M., Fortunato, A., Sayres, M. W., & Aktipis, A. (2015, August 28). Fetal microchimerism and maternal health: A review and evolutionary analysis of cooperation and conflict beyond the womb. WILEY Periodicals, Inc. Retrieved from https://onlinelibrary.wiley.com/doi/full/10.1002/bies.201500059

2) Crean, A. J., Kopps, A. M., & Bonduriansky, R. (2014, September 30). Revisiting telegony: offspring inherit an acquired characteristic of their mother's previous mate. John Wiley & Sons Ltd and CNRS. Retrieved from https://onlinelibrary.wiley.com/doi/full/10.1111/ele.12373.

3) Yehuda, R., & Lehrner, A. (2018, September 7). Intergenerational transmission of trauma effects: putative role of epigenetic mechanisms. World Psychiatric Association. Retrieved from https://onlinelibrary.wiley.com/doi/full/10.1002/wps.20568.

4) Spencer, N. J., Hibberd, T. J., Travis, L., Wiklendt, L.,

Costa, M., Hu, H., … Sorensen, J. (2018, June 13). Identification of a Rhythmic Firing Pattern in the Enteric Nervous System That Generates Rhythmic Electrical Activity in Smooth Muscle. Journal of Neuroscience. Retrieved from https://www.jneurosci.org/content/38/24/5507.

5) Stern, D.B. (2012, January). Witnessing across time: Accessing the present from the past and the past from the present. The Psychoanalytic Quarterly. Retrieved from https://www.tandfonline.com/doi/abs/10.1002/j.2167-4086.2012.tb00485.x.

6) Horney, K. (1991). Neurosis and human growth: the struggle toward self-realization. New York: Norton.

7) Durkheim, E. (2002). Suicide. London: Routledge.

8) Galinsky, A. D., Magee, J. C., Inesi, M. E., & Gruenfeld, D. H. (2006). Power and Perspectives Not Taken. Psychological Science. Retrieved from https://journals.sagepub.com/doi/10.1111/j.1467-9280.2006.01824.x

9) Yang, W., Li, Q., Guo, M., Fan, Q., & He, Y. (2017). The effects of power on human behavior: The perspective of regulatory focus. Acta

Psychologica Sinica. Retrieved from http://journal.psych.ac.cn/xlxb/EN/10.3724/SP.J.1041.2017.00404

10) Henderson, M.M. (2013). Taming Power: The Effects of Perspective Taking on Behavioral and Verbal Power Tactics. The University of Michigan. Retrieved from https://www.semanticscholar.org/paper/Taming-Power%3A-The-Effects-of-Perspective-Taking-on-Henderson/242e0eb1122a8d801f3a10fc0a12b216666d054b.

11) Russell, B. (1996). Principles of Mathematics. W.W. Norton & Company.

12) Weber, M., Roth, G., & Wittich, C. (1978). Economy and Society (p. 672). University of California.

13) (2014, July 12) Teen's rape ordered by Indian village council, police say. CBS News. Retrieved from https://www.cbc.ca/news/world/india-village-council-accused-of-ordering-retaliation-rape-of-teen-girl-1.2705038.

14) Weber, M., Roth, G., & Wittich, C. (1978). Economy and Society (p. 676). University of California.

15) Weber, M., Roth, G., & Wittich, C. (1978). Economy and Society (p. 692). University of California.

16) Noman Cohn. (1970). The pursuit of the millenium: revolutionary millenarians and mystical anarchists of the middle ages. Oxford University Press.

17) Riggs, M. (2013, February 19). Is Your Local Police Department Using Pictures of Pregnant Women and Children for Target Practice?. Reason.com. Retrieved from https://reason.com/2013/02/19/is-your-local-police-department-using-pi/.

18) Fee, E. Nineteenth-Century Craniology: The Study of the Female Skull.

19) P.-J. Proudhon. (1875). La pornocratie ou les femmes dans les temps modernes A. Lacroix in Paris.

20) Silvia Federici. (1975). Wages Against Housework. Power of Women Collective and Falling Wall Press.

21) Arendt, H. (1951). The Origins of Totalitarianism. Schocken Books.

22) Hegel, G. W. F., & Butler, C. (1984). Hagel: the letters. Bloomington: Indiana Univ. Pr.

23) H.R. Knickerbooker. (1945, February). Is Tomorrow Hitler's? Omnibook Magazine. Retrieved from http://www.oldmagazinearti

cles.com/carl_jung_studied_hitler.

24) Blader, S. L., Shirako, A., & Chen, Y.-R. (2016). Looking Out From the Top: Differential Effects of Status and Power on Perspective Taking. Personality and Social Psychology Bulletin.

25) Eleftheriou-Smith, L.-M. (2015, January 12). Watch out radical feminists - this Cardinal is blaming you for paedophile priests. The Independent. Retrieved from https://www.independent.co.uk/news/world/americas/american-cardinal-raymond-leo-burke-blames-paedophile-priests-on-radical-feminists-9973240.html.

26) Tønnessen, L. (2016). Women's Activism in Saudi Arabia: Male Guardianship and Sexual Violence. CMI. Retrieved from https://www.cmi.no/publications/5696-womens-activism-in-saudi-arabia.

27) Samuel, S. (2019, August 5). Facebook is building tech to read your mind. The ethical implications are staggering. Vox Retrieved from https://www.vox.com/future-perfect/2019/8/5/20750259/facebook-ai-mind-reading-brain-computer-interface.

28) Wexler, B. E. (2019, December 3). Mind Control in China's Classrooms. Yale Online Retrieved from https://yaleglobal.yale.edu/co

ntent/mind-control-chinas-classrooms.

29) Albert, E (2018, October 11). The State of Religion in China. CFR Retrieved from https://www.cfr.org/backgrounder/religion-china.

30) Kirby, J. (2018, November 7). China's brutal crackdown on the Uighur Muslim minority, explained. Vox Retrieved from https://www.vox.com/2018/8/15/17684226/uighur-china-camps-united-nations.

31) Lee, Y. (2016, August 11). 2 words keep sick Samsung workers from data: trade secrets. AP Retrieved from https://apnews.com/ea1b8280b50b4ad3a9bdcd9def798914/2-words-keep-sick-Samsung-workers-from-data:-trade-secrets.

32) Cameron, D. (2014, September 25). PM speech at the UN General Assembly 2014. UK Gov Retrieved from https://www.gov.uk/government/speeches/pm-speech-at-the-un-general-assembly-2014.

33) Woolf, V. (1989). A Room of One's Own. Harcourt Brace Jovanovich.

34) Woolf, V. (1967). Collected essays "Professions for Women" Harcourt, Brace & World.

35) Rauer, C. (2016, June 13). Mann and Gender in Old English Prose: A Pilot Study. Springer

36) Flood, A. (2013, April 25). Wikipedia bumps women from 'American novelists' category. Guardian Retrieved from https://www.theguardian.com/books/2013/apr/25/wikipedia-women-american-novelists.

37) Fell, C. E., Clark, C., & Williams, E. (1987). Women in Anglo-Saxon England. Blackwell Pub.

38) (2019, January 21). 26 individuals are as wealthy as half of all humanity combined. Oxfam. Retrieved from https://www.ctvnews.ca/world/26-individuals-are-as-wealthy-as-half-of-all-humanity-combined-oxfam-report-1.4262012.

39) Bendix, R. (1977). Max Weber: an intellectual portrait. Berkeley: Univ. Of California Press.

40) Machiavelli, N (1532). The Prince

41) Doyle, R. (1996). The Woman Who Walked Into Doors Penguin Books

42) Lispector, C. (1988). The Passion According to G.H. University of Minnesota Press

43) Hegel, G. W. F. (1977). Phenomenology of spirit. (p.152). Oxoford: Clarendon Press.

44) Gruenfeld, D.,Inesi, M.E. (2008). Power and the objectification of social targets.(p.111–127). Journal of Personality and Social Psychology.

43) Hegel, G. W. F. (1977). Phenomenology of spirit. (p.152) Oxoford: Clarendon Press.

45) Foucault, M., & Ewald François. (2008). Society must be defended.(p. 37). Penguin.

46) Lacan, J., Sheridan, A., & Miller, J. A. The four fundamental concepts of psychoanalysis: The seminar of Jaques Lacan Book XI.(p. 258) W.W Norton & Company.

47) Foucault, M., & Ewald François. (2008). Society must be defended.(p. 157). Penguin.

48) Sartre, J.-P. (1969). Being and nothingness: an essay in phenomenological ontology. Washington Square Press.

49) Beddington, J. (2013). Future Identities Changing Identities in the UK: the next 10 years. Foresight Government Office for Science.

50) Hegel, G. W. F. (1977). The difference between

Fichtes and Schellings system of philosophy. tate University of New York Press.

51) LaFrance, A. (2019, March 31). Fox Got It Wrong With '3 Mexican Countries,' but It Also Got It Right. The Atlantic. Retrieved from https://www.theatlantic.com/ideas/archive/2019/03/foxs-3-mexican-countries-chyron-message/586195/.

52) Fishman, C. (2015, July 31). Who Are Those Sassy Sisters In The Volkswagen Campaign? Adage. Retrieved from https://adage.com/article/cmo-strategy/hilarious-elderly-women-make-campaign-viral/299762.

53) Bakunin, M. (1870). Letters to a Frenchman on the Present Crisis.

54) Abusch, T. (2015). The Witchcraft Series Maqlû. SBL Press.

55) Horton, S., Merchant, B., Jackson, G., Trenchard, T., Gordon, D., & Choi, S. (2013, May 1). The Guantánamo "Suicides". Harpers. Retrieved from https://harpers.org/archive/2010/03/the-guantanamo-suicides/.

56) Harsey, S. J., Zurbriggen, E. L., & Freyd, J. J. (2017). Perpetrator Responses to Victim Confrontation: DARVO and Victim Self-Blame. Journal of

Aggression, Maltreatment & Trauma.

57) McCauley, C. Moskalenko, S. (2008). Mechanisms of Political Radicalization: Pathways Loring. Toward Terrorism. Routledge Taylor & Francis Group.

58) McGuire, P. (2015, January 15). Behind Anonymous's Operation to Reveal Britain's Elite Child-Rape Syndicate. Vice. Retrieved from https://www.vice.com/en_ca/article/8gdj74/behind-anonymouss-operation-to-reveal-britains-elite-child-rape-syndicate-273.

59) Salter, M (2017). Crime, justice and social media. Routledge.

60) Benedicts, R. (1989). The chrysanthemum and the sword: patterns of Japanese culture. Mariner Books.

61) Stanton, G. (2016). 10 Stages of Genocide. Genocide Watch Retrieved from http://genocidewatch.net/genocide-2/8-stages-of-genocide/.

62) Hitler, A. (1938). Mein Kampf Zentralverlag der NSDAP.

63) Lerner, J., Keltner, D. (2001). Fear, Anger, and Risk.

Journal of Personality and Social Psychology.

64) (2013, September 24). Neurological basis for lack of empathy in psychopaths. Frontiers.

65) Mackie, D., Devos, T., Smith, E. (2000). Intergroup Emotions: Explaining Offensive Action Tendencies in an Intergroup Context. Journal of Personality and Social Psychology.

66) Potegal, M., Stemmler, G., & Spielberger, C. D. (2010). International handbook of anger: biological, psychological, and social processes. Springer-Verlag.

67) Tiedens, E., Tiedens, M. (2000). Sentimental Stereotypes: Emotional Expectations for High-and Low-Status Group Members. Personality and Social Psychology Bulletin.

68) Mohr P., Howells K., Gerace A., Day A., Wharton M. (2007). The role of perspective taking in anger arousal. Personality and Individual Differences.

69) Day A.,Mohr P., Howells K., Gerace A., Lim L. (2012). The role of empathy in anger arousal in violent offenders and university students. International Journal of Offender Therapy and Comparative Criminology.

70) DeSteno, D., Dasgupta., Bartlett, M., Cajdric, A. (2004). Prejudice From Thin Air: The Effect of Emotion on Automatic Intergroup Attitudes. Psychological Science.

71) Zilber, A. (2018, May 6). NXIVM cult doctor is charged with conducting 'fright study' experiments. Dailymail Retrieved from https://www.dailymail.co.uk/news/article-5695523/NXIVM-cult-.

68) P, Mohr., Howells, K., Gerace, A., Day, A., Wharton, P. (2007). The role of perspective taking in anger arousal. Personality and Individual Differences.

72) Aarts, H. (2010, November 1). Anger makes people want things more. Psychological Science.

73) Maitlis, E. (2019). Prince Andrew Newsnight interview: Transcript in full. BBC. Retrieved from https://www.bbc.com/news/uk-50449339.

74) Bergson, H. (2014) Laughter: An Essay on the Meaning of the Comic. Martino Fine Books

75) (2017, December 7). John Belushi Was A Misogynist, SNL Star Alleges. HuffPost. Retrieved from https://www.huffpost.com/entry/john-belushi-sexist-jane-curtain_n_848646.

76) Hewitt, L. (1958). Student perceptions of traits desired in themselves as dating and marriage partners. Marriage and Family Living.

77) Hobbes, T (2009). The treatise on human nature and that on liberty and necessity. Kessinger Publishing.

78) Moser, D. (2004, November 16). Stifled Laughter: How the Communist Party Killed Chinese Humor Danwei.

79) Nasiri, F.; Mafakheri, F. (2015). Higher Education Lecturing and Humor: From Perspectives to Strategies. Canadian Center of Science and Education.

80) Bressler, E., Balshine, S. (2006). The influence of humour on desirability: Evolution and Human Behavior. Elsevier.

81) Kuiper, N., Martin, R. (1993). Humor and self-concept. International Journal of Humor Research.

82) Aristotle, & Rackham, H. (2003). The Nicomachean ethics. Harvard University Press.

83) Aristotle., Noorden, S. (2003). A translation of Aristotle's Rhetoric. The Classical Review.

84) Wirth, M.M., Welsh, K.M. (2006). Salivary cortisol changes in humans after winning or losing a dominance contest depend on implicit power motivation. Hormones and Behavior.

85) Takahashi, H., Kato, M., Matsuura, M., Mobbs, D., Suhara, T., & Okubo, Y. (2009). When Your Gain Is My Pain and Your Pain Is My Gain: Neural Correlates of Envy and Schadenfreude. Science.

82) Aristotle.,Rackham, H. (2003). The Nicomachean ethics. Harvard University Press.

86) Kant, I. (1996). Metaphysics of Morals. Cambridge University Press.

87) Billan, R (2019) Tall Poppy Syndrome: The office trend killing morale. HCmag

88) Sartre, J.-P. (1972). Being and nothingness: a phenomenological ontology. (p.395-407) Washington Square Press.

89) Bartlett M. Y.; Desteno D. (2006). Gratitude and Prosocial Behavior: Helping When It Costs You. Psychological Science.

90) Singer, T., Seymour, B., O'Doherty, J.P., Stephan, K.E., Dolan, RJ., Frith C.D. (2006, January) Empathic

neural responses are modulated by the perceived fairness of others. Nature.

91) Fan, Y., Duncan, N. W., Greck, M. D., & Northoff, G. (2011). Is there a core neural network in empathy? An fMRI based quantitative meta-analysis. Neuroscience & Biobehavioral Reviews.

92) Cox, C. L., Uddin, L. Q., Martino, A. D., Castellanos, F. X., Milham, M. P., & Kelly, C. (2011). The balance between feeling and knowing: affective and cognitive empathy are reflected in the brains intrinsic functional dynamics. Social Cognitive and Affective Neuroscience.

93) Meffert, H., Gazzola, V., Boer, J. A. D., Bartels, A. A. J., & Keysers, C. (2013). Reduced spontaneous but relatively normal deliberate vicarious representations in psychopathy. Brain.

94) Smith, D. G. (2018, November 9). Neuroscientists Make a Case against Solitary Confinement. Scientific American.

95) Wilson, T. D., Reinhard, D. A., Westgate, E. C., Gilbert, D. T., Ellerbeck, N., Hahn, C., … Shaked, A. (2014). Just think: The challenges of the disengaged mind. Science.

96) Briere, J., Runtz, M. (1988). Symptomatology associated with childhood sexual victimization in a nonclinical adult sample. Child Abuse and Neglect.

97) Freud, S. (1896). the aetiology of hysteria. Standard Edition.

98) Freud, S. (1986). An Autobiographical Study W.W. Norton & Company, Inc.

99) Freud, S. (1930). Civilization and its discontents. Cape & Smith.

100) Freud, S. (1960). The Ego and the Id. W.W. Norton & Company, Inc.

101) Freud, S. (1923). Two Encyclopedia Articles. Standard Edition.

102) Freud, S. (1922). Beyond the pleasure principle. The International Psycho-Analytical Press.

103) Freud, S. (1923). Two Encyclopedia Articles. Standard Edition.

105) Arendt, H. (1994). Some Questions of Moral Philosophy. The Johns Hopkins University Press.

106) Frontiers. (2013, September 24). Neurological basis for lack of empathy in psychopaths. ScienceDaily.

107) Stern, D.B. (2012). Witnessing across time: Accessing the present from the past and the past from the present. The Psychoanalytic Quarterly.

108) Freud, S. (1922). Sigmund Freud: group psychology and the analysis of the ego. Liveright Pub. Co.

109) Kohut, H. (2013). The Analysis of the Self A Systematic Approach to the Psychoanalytic Treatment of Narcissistic Personality Disorders. University of Chicago Press.

110) Shapiro, L.J, Stewart, E.S. (2011). Pathological guilt: a persistent yet overlooked treatment factor in obsessive-compulsive disorder.

111) Buckner, J. D., Schmidt, N. B., Lang, A. R., Small, J. W., Schlauch, R. C., Lewinsohn, P. M. (2008). "Specificity of social anxiety disorder as a risk factor for alcohol and cannabis dependence. Journal of Psychiatric.

112) (2016). ICD-10 The Classification of Mental and Behavioural Disorders. WHO

113) Haridy, R. (2017). Inside the brains of psychopaths. New Atlas

114) Arnett, J. J. (2008). The neglected 95%: Why

American psychology needs to become less American. American Psychologist.

115) Henrich, J, Heine, S. J., Norenzayan, A. (2010). The weirdest people in the world? Behavioral and Brain Sciences.

116) Aretaeus. (1 CE). The Causes, Symptoms and Cure of Acute and Chronic Diseases.

117) Myers, B. (2014). "Drapetomania": Rebellion, Defiance and Free Black Insanity in the Antebellum United States. UCLA.

118) Strous, R. (2010). Psychiatric Genocide: Reflections and Responsibilities. Schizophrenia Bulletin.

119) Bonnie, R. (2002). Political Abuse of Psychiatry in the Soviet Union and in China: Complexities and Controversies. Journal of the American Academy of Psychiatry and the Law.

120) Angelides, S. (2005). The Emergence of the Paedophile in the Late Twentieth Century. University of Melbourne.

Index

D

E

T

Heather Marsh

This book is part of a series which begins by examining the nature of self, life, will, reality and power. The rest of the series examines the societal institutions which have grown up around nations, economy, law, governance, architecture and technology. These books are all a further examination of the problems identified in *Binding Chaos* in 2013.

Self – *The Creation of Me, Them and Us*
Life - *Abstracting Divinity*
Reality – *Shaping Reality*
Will – *Free Will and Seductive Coercion*
Power - *Great Men, Commoners, Witches and Wretches*
Nation – *The Fourth Age of Nations*
Economy – *The Approval Economy*
Law – *Law and Chaos*
Governance - *Autonomy Diversity Society*
Architecture – *Rethinking the Moats and Mountains*
Technology - *Code Will Rule*

Printed in Great Britain
by Amazon

41692647R00260